Continuous-Time Models in Corporate Finance, Banking, and Insurance

Continuous-Time Models in Corporate Finance, Banking, and Insurance

Santiago Moreno-Bromberg
&
Jean-Charles Rochet

PRINCETON UNIVERSITY PRESS
PRINCETON AND OXFORD

Published by Princeton University Press
41 William Street, Princeton, New Jersey 08540

In the United Kingdom: Princeton University Press
6 Oxford Street, Woodstock, Oxfordshire, OX20 1TR

Library of Congress Cataloging-in-Publication Data

Names: Moreno-Bromberg, Santiago, author. | Rochet, Jean-Charles,
    author.
Title: Continuous-Time Models in Corporate Finance, Banking, and
    Insurance / Santiago Moreno-Bromberg, Jean-Charles Rochet.
Description: Princeton : Princeton University Press, 2018. | Includes
    bibliographical references and index.
Identifiers: LCCN 2017029691 | ISBN 9780691176529 (hardback)
Subjects: LCSH: Corporations–Finance. | Options (Finance) | Banks and
    banking. | BISAC: BUSINESS & ECONOMICS / Corporate Finance.
    BUSINESS & ECONOMICS / Economics / General. | BUSINESS &
    ECONOMICS / Economics / Theory.
Classification: LCC HG4026 .M6647 2018 — DDC 658.1501/515222–dc23
LC record available at https://lccn.loc.gov/2017029691

British Library Cataloging-in-Publication Data is available

This book has been composed in LATEX

The publisher would like to acknowledge the authors of this volume for
providing the print-ready files from which this book was printed

Printed on acid-free paper. ∞

press.princeton.edu

Printed in the United States of America

10 9 8 7 6 5 4 3 2 1

To Ivar Ekeland, our mentor...

...to the B....mi inspiración
(S M-B)

and to N., my soulmate.
(J-C R)

Contents

Contents

Contents

Preface

The objective of this book is to bridge the gap between option pricing and corporate finance. Modern research in theoretical corporate finance uses complex mathematical methods that are very similar to those developed with option pricing in mind. However, finance PhD students are often unaware of these similarities. To our knowledge, this book is the first to cover these methods in a unified framework and to make them accessible to a wide audience. The only prerequisites for reading the book are to be well acquainted with option-pricing models and to have some elementary knowledge of corporate finance. Our target audience includes PhD students not only in finance, but also in economics and applied mathematics. We hope our book also proves to be useful for academic researchers and finance professionals who wish to have access to recent research in corporate finance, banking and insurance.

This monograph derives from a course that we taught repeatedly in the SFI PhD Program in Finance at the University of Zürich. It draws heavily on important work written in the past fifty years by many influential researchers such as Fisher S. Black, John C. Cox, Jaksa Cvitanic, Peter M. DeMarzo, Bernard Dumas, Michael Harrison, Bjarne Hoegaard, Julien Hugonnier, Monique Jeanblanc, Ioannis Karatzas, Hayne E. Leland, Semyon Malamud, Robert C. Merton, Alistair Milne, Erwan Morellec, Roy Radner, Yuliy Sannikov, Myron S. Scholes, Lawrence A. Shepp, Albert Shiryaev, Suresh Sundaresan and Michael Taksar. We have also learned a great deal from our own research on the topic, which has been a joint venture with our coauthors Andrea Barth, Bruno Biais, Jean-Paul Décamps, Nataliya Klimenko, Thomas Mariotti, Sebastian Pfeil, Oleg Reichmann, Guillaume Roger and Stéphane Villeneuve. We must also thank our students and colleagues who have provided useful comments on preliminary drafts.

Santiago Moreno-Bromberg
Jean-Charles Rochet

Zurich and Geneva, May 1, 2017

Continuous-Time Models in Corporate Finance, Banking, and Insurance

Introduction

CONTINUOUS-TIME STOCHASTIC models have become a necessary ingredient of the finance student's curriculum, due to their widespread applications to derivatives pricing. These methods, which were made famous by the seminal papers of Black and Scholes (1973) and Merton (1973, 1974), have proved so powerful that most (if not all) advanced programs in market finance include at least one course on continuous-time stochastic models that covers such technical tools as Itô calculus, parabolic partial differential equations, and the Feyman-Kac formula, which were initially developed for applications in other fields, such as physics.

This book is an introduction to another, equally important, field of application of the same methods (plus some additional tools), namely, corporate finance. It applies the rigor of the mathematical techniques mentioned above to concrete financial problems faced by corporations, for instance, how to finance their investments, when to distribute dividends or issue new securities and, possibly, when to default on their debt. As a result, the book combines the mathematical tools of stochastic calculus and the accounting measures that corporate managers follow actively, namely their profit and loss (P&L) accounts and balance sheets.

The target audience of the book includes PhD students in finance, economics and mathematics, as well as financial-industry professionals and academic researchers who want to get acquainted with recent research developments in continuous-time corporate finance, banking and insurance. The mathematical methodology is presented in a very practical manner: we do not prove any new theorems, but we give access to these powerful methods to the largest possible audience while preserving mathematical rigor.

The book's prerequisites are limited to two ingredients: the standard, continuous-time, stochastic methods that are used in derivatives-pricing courses and a basic knowledge of accounting. After reading this book, everyone should be able to follow current frontier research in corporate finance, banking and insurance and, possibly, to develop original models on his or her own. Although highly technical, the mathematical methods presented in the book can be made accessible to a wide audience and used in a very intuitive way. This is the main objective of this book.

Before the 1970s, the mathematical methods of finance were reduced to the cross-multiplication formula and the computation of discounted sums. The fantastic development of arbitrage-pricing methods has made Itô calculus and the Feyman-Kac formula part of the necessary toolbox in asset pricing. It would be a pity to be unable to also use them to solve corporate-finance, banking and insurance problems, only because their axiomatic foundations remain too technical for the majority of finance and economics students. Thus, we have striven to make these methods widely accessible.

Contents of the book

Chapter 1   starts by explaining the basic reason why the mathematical methods of option pricing are also powerful in corporate finance, banking and insurance. It is a simple consequence of a brilliant intuition of Black and Scholes (1973) and Merton (1974): given that the shareholders of a company are protected by limited liability, they have an **option** to default. Thus, the value of their shares is formally equivalent to the value of a call option on the assets of the company, with strike price equal to the nominal debt of the company. Shareholders have the option to repay the company's debt, in which case they keep control of the assets of the company. Alternatively they may default on this debt, and lose everything.

Chapter 1 uses this far-reaching insight to derive formulas for pricing debt and equity contracts of corporations and to evaluate the risk premium that markets attach to their probability of default. The computation of the total value (equity plus debt) of a corporation gives rise to the celebrated Modigliani-Miller theorem: in the absence of frictions, such as tax exemptions on debt and liquidation costs, the total value of a company is independent of the way it is financed, i.e., the proportions of debt and equity in its liabilities, which is called the capital structure of the company. In the same vein, a world without frictions is a world where all financial decisions (when to distribute dividends and when to retain earnings, how to manage cash, when to issue new securities, etc.) would have no impact on the total value of the company. In that hypothetical world, corporate-finance decisions would be irrelevant.

Corporate finance becomes interesting only when frictions are introduced. This is the first departure from the standard option-pricing models, which typically rule out frictions. Several types of financial frictions are considered in the book: tax subsidies on debt and liquidation costs (Section 1.4), costs of issuing new securities (Chapters 2 to 6) and, finally, agency costs (Chapter 7). In the academic literature, all these costs were initially considered in one-period or discrete-time models, which provided valuable intuition on how these frictions impacted the financial decisions of corporations. However, discrete-time models are often inelegant and cannot be properly calibrated to real data. By contrast, the continuous-time setup that we use throughout this book allows us to get the best of two worlds: formal elegance as well as applicability to real-life problems. Derivative traders and risk managers use the same kind of models (with some simple twists) in their pricing and hedging decisions.

The fourth section of Chapter 1 presents the first attempt to overcome the Modigliani-Miller irrelevance result: when debt payments are tax deductible and asset liquidation involves deadweight losses, there is a trade-off between tax deductions and liquidation costs that leads to an optimal debt-to-equity ratio. This section presents one famous version of this "trade-off" theory in a continuous-time setting, namely, the Leland (1994) model.

Unfortunately, the predictions of the trade-off theory are not really consistent with what we observe in the real world. For reasonable calibrations of its parameters, the trade-off model predicts levels of corporate debt that are often too high.[1] A vast academic literature has endeavored to enrich the trade-off model to bring its predictions closer to the observed behavior of firms. This literature is surveyed, among others, in the excellent works by Sundaresan (2013), Grasselli and Hurd (2010) and Bielecki and Rutkowski (2004).

We have decided to place most of our emphasis on a different type of frictions, namely issuance costs. We maintain the convenient (and not too unrealistic) assumption of perfect secondary markets, where existing stocks and bonds are traded with negligible transaction costs, but we explicitly take into account the frictions that exist in **primary markets**, where **new** stocks and bonds are issued. With issuance costs, which are sometimes sizable, it is important for companies to keep liquid reserves, and **liquidity management** becomes an important issue. Liquidity management is, therefore, a central topic of this book.

Chapter 2 presents the base liquidity-management model, where issuing costs are so high that companies never issue new securities and

---

[1] As a matter of fact, the only sector in which firms borrow as much as predicted by the trade-off model is the financial sector, studied in Chapters 4 (banks) and 5 (insurance companies).

are liquidated when they run out of cash. Hence, the management of cash reserves becomes crucial, because it determines the company's survival. This model was first studied (independently) by Jeanblanc-Picqué and Shiryaev (1995) and Radner and Shepp (1996). It will be our workhorse for Chapters 3 to 6.

Chapter 3 introduces the possibility of new equity issues into the base model. In the Leland model presented in Section 1.4, these new issues were considered costless, so firms could always use them to compensate their losses. In that case, cash reserves were useless. However, in practice, firms are reluctant to issue new equity because these issues are quite costly. In that context cash reserves are useful to absorb possible losses and limit the frequency of new equity issues. In this chapter we determine the optimal timing and size of new equity issues and study the implications of issuing costs on equity prices. Even with a stationary profitability (independent and identically distributed, or i.i.d., earnings), stock returns exhibit stochastic volatility. The assumption of constant volatility of stock returns (used by Black-Scholes and Merton) is only compatible with zero issuance costs.

Chapter 4 applies the base model of liquidity management to banks. Section 4.1 presents a simple model, due to Milne and Whalley (2001), that allows the study of the impact of regulatory capital requirements on the liquidity-management decisions of banks. Section 4.2 looks at portfolio-management decisions: the bank has a fixed amount of deposits and starts with some equity. As in the base model, it is too costly to issue new securities, which makes the management of cash reserves crucial. The bank's manager decides how much to invest in some risky asset (loans or securities) with i.i.d. returns, and also how much to keep as cash reserves. This is reminiscent of the portfolio-management problem in Merton (1969), where the investor is characterized by some concave utility function and is, therefore, risk averse. Here the bank's risk aversion is endogenous and stems from the financial frictions: even though shareholders are risk neutral or fully diversified, the bank behaves in a risk-averse way because unexpected losses may force it to liquidate assets or even stop operating. In Section 4.3, we present a model that deals with a richer liability side (short-term and unsecured long-term debt), in which we address issues of optimal bank funding through equity, and short- and long-term debts.

Chapter 5 presents several applications of the base model to the insurance sector. Section 5.1 studies the impact of large losses on financial strategies of insurance companies. This is an extension of the base model where the firm's net-earnings process also includes a Poisson component. Sections 5.2 and 5.3 deal with reinsurance strategies, which are crucial for insurance firms. In the former we study the reinsurance of small (Brownian) losses, whereas in the latter the (potential) losses to be reinsured are large (Poisson) ones.

Chapter 6 is dedicated to the determinants of corporate investment. Section 6.1 discusses the case without frictions: the q-theory of Tobin, as formalized in Hayashi (1982). Section 6.2 introduces external frictions and liquidity management into this model. Section 6.3 looks at the impact of external frictions on the decision to invest in a new technology.

Chapter 7 introduces agency frictions in a continuous-time framework. Although these frictions are very different from the external frictions studied so far, much of the methodology developed in Chapters 1–6 can be used. Section 7.1 presents an extension of the trade-off model of Section 1.4.1 where agency issues are present in the form of asset substitution problems. This means that shareholders may increase the firm's exposure to risk after debt has been issued, thereby extracting additional value from debtholders. Section 7.2 solves the optimal-contracting problem between an entrepreneur and a group of financiers. There, the agency problem is due to the fact that the entrepreneur may divert part of the firm's cashflows for private consumption. The optimal contract can be implemented through a combination of cash reserves, debt and equity. This allows us to discuss the firm's optimal capital structure. Finally, we explore a similar setting where the agent may reduce his risk-prevention efforts, which exposes the firm to potentially large (Poisson) losses. The optimal contract uses downsizing of the firm after a large loss as a punishment device (the proverbial stick), whereas good performances lead to bonus payments to the manager (the proverbial carrot). There is now a large body of literature on agency models in continuous time, e.g. Cvitanić and Zhang (2013), Cadenillas et al. (2007) and the references therein.

Chapter 8 puts the base model into a general-equilibrium framework, where returns and prices are endogenized. Section 8.1 present the influential paper of Brunnermeier and Sannikov (2014) and showcases the complexities associated with the introduction of financial frictions into a macroeconomic context. Section 8.2 presents a simpler model in the same spirit, which is very stylized, so as to keep it tractable and transparent. Section 8.3 presents a similar model that is specifically targeted at the insurance industry.

The last section of each chapter is devoted to suggesting further reading material. There are four appendixes. The first contains the mathematical proofs of the core results and other technical material; the second is devoted to the celebrated Modigliani-Miller "theorem." The last appendix recalls useful mathematical results.

1 Why Is Option Pricing Useful in Corporate Finance?

THIS CHAPTER PROVIDES a transition from option pricing to corporate finance. Option pricing methods seek to find the "right" price of an option as a function of the value of its underlying security and several parameters. Similarly, one of the main questions examined in corporate finance is how to find the "right" price of a corporate security, typically debt or equity, as a function of the value of the assets of the company that has issued this security. The brilliant intuition of Black and Scholes (1973) and Merton (1973) was that the equity of a company was similar to a call option on the assets of the company, with a strike price equal to the company's nominal debt. Shareholders are indeed protected by limited liability. This means that they have the option to repay the debt and keep control of the assets of the company, or default on the debt and lose the assets. This idea was thoroughly explored by Merton (1974) and Black and Cox (1976), on which Sections 1.2 and 1.3 are based. We then present in Section 1.4 a version of the trade-off theory, where taxes and bankruptcy costs are incorporated so as to determine the optimal capital structure of a firm.

1.1 Modeling assumptions

Throughout the book, we use the same modeling setup, where time t is a continuous variable that, unless otherwise indicated, has an infinite horizon, i.e. $t \in [0, \infty)$. The riskless rate $r > 0$ is taken to be constant. We assume that financial (secondary)[1] markets are perfect, i.e. competitive,[2] frictionless[3] and complete. Therefore, the prices of

---

[1] Financial securities are issued on primary markets (in which there may be frictions) and later retraded on secondary ones (which we assume to be perfect).

[2] This means that participants take security prices as given. We also assume that there are no quantitative restrictions on portfolios: all short and long positions are possible.

[3] Of course, we will consider other kinds of frictions: issuance costs on primary markets, tax deductions on debt, liquidation costs and agency costs. However, secondary markets will always be assumed to be perfect.

all financial securities will be equal to the expected discounted sums of their future payments under the risk-adjusted probability measure.[4]

Contrary to option-pricing textbooks, which are at times very abstract and do not say much about the securities underlying the options, this book is about corporations and needs to be somewhat more concrete. In particular we have to start with some analysis of the fundamentals of these corporations. This is done via two ingredients: the net-earnings process (see below) and the BALANCE SHEET of each company, which is basically a snapshot of what the company owes (liabilities) and what the company owns (assets) at a given point in time. It has typically the following (simplified) structure:

assets	liabilities
M_t	D_t
S_t	E_t

On the ASSET SIDE (left), M_t represents the LIQUID RESERVES of the company at time t, S_t represents the (market) value of the company's productive assets, i.e. the risk-adjusted expectation of future discounted cashflows generated by these assets until liquidation. On the LIABILITY SIDE (right), D_t represents the market value of the company's debt. The remaining term $E_t = M_t + S_t - D_t$, i.e. total assets minus debt liabilities, determines the market value of equity, which incorporates the limited-liability option. Note that we use MARKET-VALUE ACCOUNTING. The BOOK VALUES of the company's debt and equity differ in general from their market values.

In order to model the evolution of the firm's balance sheet, we consider a probability space $(\Omega, \mathcal{A}, \mathbb{Q})$ on which a standard Brownian motion $Z = \{Z_t, t \geq 0\}$, which generates the filtration $\mathcal{F} = (\mathcal{F}_t, t \geq 0)$, is defined. Unless otherwise indicated, this probabilistic setup is used throughout this book. To avoid unnecessary notation, we adopt the convention that $\mathbb{Q}$ is already the risk-adjusted probability measure and $\mathbb{E}[\cdot]$ the corresponding expectation operator. The value of the firm's assets (which are supposed to be tradable at no cost)[5] evolves according to the following stochastic differential equation:

$$dS_t = S_t\big[(r - \beta)dt + \sigma dZ_t\big], \quad S_0 = S, \qquad (1.1.1)$$

---

[4]This is a consequence of the absence of arbitrage opportunities. For a precise definition of risk-adjusted probability measures see, for instance, Björk (2009), Duffie (2002) and Föllmer and Schied (2004).
[5]We relax this assumption in the next chapters.

where β is the payout rate of the assets (assumed to be constant): this means that the OPERATING INCOME βS_t is proportional to the asset value, whose volatility is $\sigma > 0$. By absence of arbitrage opportunities, the total expected return on the firm's assets under the risk-adjusted measure $\mathbb{Q}$ equals the risk-free rate:

$$\mathbb{E}\left[\frac{dS_t}{S_t} + \beta dt\right] = rdt.$$

The company's net earnings equal its operating income $\beta S_t dt$ plus its financial income $rM_t dt$ (we assume that liquid reserves are remunerated at rate r) minus the total payment $C_t dt$ to the firm's creditors. The level of liquid reserves $M = \{M_t, t \geq 0\}$ evolves according to

$$dM_t = (\beta S_t + rM_t - C_t)dt - dL_t, \quad M_0 = m, \quad (1.1.2)$$

where dL_t represents the transfer from the company to shareholders. If positive, it represents share buy-backs or dividends. If negative, it represents new equity issues or recapitalizations. For the moment, we assume that recapitalizations can be made at no cost. In this section, taxes are neglected. They are introduced in Section 1.4.

1.2 Pricing corporate debt

We are in a position to use option-pricing methods to find the market value of the firm's equity and debt. Following Merton (1974), we take for the time being the simplest possible framework, where debt has a zero coupon ($C_t \equiv 0$) with a single promised repayment B at some future date T. This implies that default can occur only at date T. Merton also assumes that the payout rate of the assets is zero ($\beta = 0$) and that the firm keeps no cash reserves, i.e., $M_t \equiv 0$. In this setting this is without loss of generality, as new equity can be issued at no cost whenever required. Later, we will study more general frameworks where all of these assumptions are relaxed.

Given that $\beta = 0$, the firm asset value evolves according to

$$dS_t = S_t(r\,dt + \sigma\,dZ_t), \quad S_0 = S.$$

Therefore, the discounted value of assets is a martingale. In particular,

$$\mathbb{E}\left[e^{-rT}S_T\right] = S.$$

The only financial decision to be made by the shareholders of the firm in this very simple setup is whether or not they default on their debt (i.e. whether or not they exercise their limited-liability option) at date T. Therefore, the market value of the company's equity, which we denote by E_t, is the value of a European call option written on the assets of the company with an exercise price equal to the nominal debt B. As a consequence, the value of equity at date $t = 0$ is

$$E_0 = \mathbb{E}\big[e^{-rT}\max(0, S_T - B)\big]. \tag{1.2.1}$$

Similarly, the market value of debt at date $t = 0$ is

$$D_0 = \mathbb{E}\big[e^{-rT}\min(B, S_T)\big],$$

where $\min\{B, S_T\} = S_T - \max\{0, S_T - B\}$ is the creditors' payoff at maturity. Note that

$$E_0 + D_0 = \mathbb{E}\big[e^{-rT}S_T\big] = S.$$

At date 0, the firm has to decide on the nominal value B of its debt, which determines the market value D_0 of this debt. The rest of the investment, $I - D_0$, is self-financed by shareholders (I is the total investment required to start the firm). The net shareholder value SV_0 generated by the investment at $t = 0$ is equal to the difference between E_0, the equity value after the investment, and the amount $I - D_0$ that shareholders have invested in the firm:

$$SV_0 = E_0 - (I - D_0).$$

Note that this equals $S - I$, the economic value added by the firm. It is independent of nominal debt B. This is a simple form of the Modigliani-Miller theorem.

In order to get explicit formulas for D_0 and E_0, we can directly apply the option-pricing formulas derived by Black and Scholes (1973) and Merton (1973). To this end, let $\boldsymbol{N}$ denote the standard normal cumulative distribution function and define

$$x_1 := \frac{1}{\sigma\sqrt{T}}\left[\log\left(\frac{S}{B}\right) + \left(r + \frac{\sigma^2}{2}\right)T\right] \quad \text{and} \quad x_2 := x_1 - \sigma\sqrt{T}.$$

Then

$$D_0 = \boldsymbol{N}(-x_1)S + Be^{-rT}\boldsymbol{N}(x_2). \tag{1.2.2}$$

Note that $\boldsymbol{N}(x_2)$ may be interpreted as the risk-adjusted probability of **not** exercising the option to default. Expression (1.2.2) shows the decomposition of the value of debt at date 0. The first term corresponds to the expected present value of what creditors receive in case of default. The second one is the present value of the nominal debt, times the risk-adjusted probability that the firm does **not** default.

If we denote by R the YIELD TO MATURITY of the debt, then by definition $D_0 = B e^{-RT}$. Therefore, the ratio between the market value of debt D_0 and its nominal value d_0 is

$$\frac{D_0}{B e^{-rT}} = e^{-(R-r)T} = N(-x_1)\frac{S}{B e^{-rT}} + N(x_2).$$

The DEFAULT SPREAD $R - r$ is given by the following expression:

$$R - r = -\frac{1}{T} \log \left(N(-x_1)\frac{S}{B e^{-rT}} + N(x_2) \right).$$

This formula is commonly used by financial analysts and fixed-income traders. However, it has a crucial drawback when $T \to 0$ (short maturities). Indeed, due to the continuity of diffusion processes, the probability of a default tends to zero as T approaches 0. This implies that the spread converges to 0 independently of the fundamentals of the company, a property that is rejected by the data. To overcome this problem, modern credit risk analysis uses more complex models with jump processes and imperfect accounting information (see, e.g. Duffie and Lando (2001)).

1.3 Endogenous default date

This section is based on Black and Cox (1976). A key departure from the model studied in Section 1.2 is the possibility of the firm defaulting on its debt **before** maturity. This is because shareholders may decide to stop paying coupons when the value of the firm's assets falls below a certain threshold. In mathematical terms, this leads to the concept of the FIRST PASSAGE TIME of a stochastic process (in this case the value of the firm) below a pre-specified boundary. We revisit this concept several times in the ensuing chapters when studying different forms of bankruptcy.

1.3.1 The general form of the valuation equation

The simplest method is to specify an exogenous DEFAULT BOUNDARY $\{K_t, t \in [0, T]\}$, such that liquidation occurs the first time that $S_t \le K_t$. Below we present a general VALUATION EQUATION, valid for any generalized "bond" whose coupon flow $C(t, S)$ may depend on time and the firm asset value S and has a final payoff $F(S)$ at maturity. We denote by B_t the liquidation value of the firm should the boundary K_t be hit at date t. For example, if the creditors can liquidate the firm at no cost when $B_t = S_t = K_t$, the boundary payoff is zero for the shareholders and K_t for the bondholders. We relax the condition $\beta = 0$: the dynamics of S_t are given again by Expression (1.1.1).

Proposition 1.3.1. *The price $P(t,S)$ of the bond described above satisfies the following partial differential equation:*

$$rP(t,S) = \frac{\partial P}{\partial t}(t,S) + (r-\beta)S\frac{\partial P}{\partial S}(t,S) + \frac{\sigma^2}{2}S^2\frac{\partial^2 P}{\partial S^2}(t,S) + C(t,S) \quad (1.3.1)$$

for $0 \le t \le T$, $0 \le S \le K_t$, together with the boundary conditions

$$P(t, K_t) = B_t \quad and \quad P(T, S) = F(S).$$

Proof. See Appendix A.1.

The right-hand side of Equation (1.3.1) represents the flow of expected gains of holding the security (the first three terms are the expected capital gains, given by the Itô formula).[6] Due to the no-arbitrage condition, it must equal the flow of income obtained by investing $P(t,S)$ at the riskless rate. Figure 1.1 presents the two regimes in the (t,S) plane: the continuation region, where Equation (1.3.1) is satisfied, is in white. The shaded area corresponds to the liquidation region.

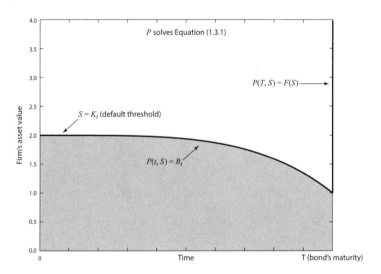

Figure 1.1: The price $P(t,S)$ and the default threshold B_t

---

[6]See Appendix C for a reminder of the Itô formula.

1.3.2 The price of a consol bond

When the maturity is infinite ($T = \infty$) and the coupon is constant ($C(t, S) \equiv C$), the security is called a CONSOL BOND. This section determines the price $D(S)$ of a consol bond that pays the coupon C continuously until S_t falls below a bankruptcy threshold S_B, which we assume is chosen by the shareholders. Let us denote by $\mu :=r - \beta$ the expected growth rate of the asset value. The valuation equation (1.3.1) takes the form

$$rD(S) = \mu SD'(S) + \frac{\sigma^2}{2}S^2 D''(S) + C. \qquad (1.3.2)$$

Observe that there is no parameter t in Equation (1.3.2) and, consequently, no partial derivative with respect to it. This is because the infinite maturity and the constant coupon rate render the problem STATIONARY. In other words, the only determinant of the bond price D is the firm's current asset value S and the date is irrelevant. The homogeneous differential equation associated to Equation (1.3.2) is

$$rD(S) = \mu SD'(S) + \frac{\sigma^2 S^2}{2}D''(S).$$

It is commonly referred to as EULER'S DIFFERENTIAL EQUATION and has the general solution

$$f(S) = \kappa_1 S^{\gamma_1} + \kappa_2 S^{\gamma_2}, \qquad (1.3.3)$$

where κ_1 and κ_2 are arbitrary and $\gamma_1 < 0 < \gamma_2$ are the roots of the CHARACTERISTIC EQUATION

$$r = \mu\gamma + \frac{\sigma^2}{2}\gamma(\gamma - 1). \qquad (1.3.4)$$

Clearly, C/r is a particular solution to Equation (1.3.2); hence, its general solution is[7]

$$D(S) = \kappa_1 S^{\gamma_1} + \kappa_2 S^{\gamma_2} + C/r.$$

In order to determine κ_1 and κ_2, observe that, when the value of the firm approaches infinity, the probability of default goes to zero and the bond's value must approach its nominal value

$$\frac{C}{r} = \int_0^\infty C e^{-rt} dt.$$

---

[7]Recall that the general solution to a nonhomogeneous differential equation like (1.3.2) is obtained by adding a particular solution of this equation to the general solution of the homogeneous equation.

Therefore,

$$D(S) \to \frac{C}{r} \text{ as } S \to \infty.$$

Given that $\gamma_1 < 0 < \gamma_2$, this implies that $\kappa_2 = 0$. Finally, κ_1 is determined by the other boundary condition. If there are no liquidation costs, $D(S_B) = S_B$; thus, we have that

$$\kappa_1 S_B^{\gamma_1} + \frac{C}{r} = S_B.$$

This in turn yields

$$\kappa_1 = S_B^{1-\gamma_1} - (C/r)S_B^{-\gamma_1};$$

hence, the value of the bond is

$$D(S) = \frac{C}{r} - S_B^{-\gamma_1}\left(\frac{C}{r} - S_B\right)S^{\gamma_1}. \tag{1.3.5}$$

We can also make use of the valuation equation to find the value $E(S)$ of the firm's equity. In this case we have

$$rE(S) = \beta S - C - \mu S E'(S) + \frac{\sigma^2 S^2}{2} E''(S),$$

subject to $E(S_B) = 0$ and $E(S) \approx S - C/r$ as $S \to \infty$. Operating as before we obtain:

$$E(S) = S - \frac{C}{r} + \left(\frac{C}{r} - S_B\right)S_B^{-\gamma_1} S^{\gamma_1} = S - D(S).$$

Observe that the Modigliani-Miller theorem also holds here: $E(S) + D(S) \equiv S$. This is because there are neither liquidation costs nor taxes, both of which are introduced in the next section. The shareholders choose S_B so as to maximize $S_B^{-\gamma_1}(C/r - S_B)$ (note that this is independent of S), which is a strictly concave function of S_B on $(0, C/r)$, and zero at the interval's endpoints (recall that $\gamma_1 < 0$). Therefore, the first-order condition is sufficient to characterize the value S_B^* that maximizes $E(S)$. This first-order condition is

$$\frac{d}{dS_B} S_B^{-\gamma_1}\left(S_B - \frac{C}{r}\right) = S_B^{-1-\gamma_1}\left(S_B(1 - \gamma_1) + \gamma_1 \frac{C}{r}\right) = 0,$$

which yields

$$S_B^* := \frac{\gamma_1}{\gamma_1 - 1}\frac{C}{r}. \tag{1.3.6}$$

We show in Figure 1.2 the graph of the equity value as a function of S for parameter values $C = 0.5$ $r = 15\%$ and $\gamma_1 = -1$. The fact that the value of equity is a convex function of S implies that the shareholders have no incentives to engage in risk-management activities: they are risk lovers! This is because they have the option to default, but they are never obliged to exercise it. In Chapters 2 to 8 we examine models in which firms may instead be **forced** to default. In that case shareholder value becomes a **concave** function, implying that risk management is useful for them. Before introducing these involuntary defaults, the next section examines the dynamic version of the trade-off theory and summarizes the important work of Leland (1994), who also assumes that shareholders can recapitalize at no cost; hence, cash reserves are also useless. However, Modigliani-Miller does not hold anymore, due to the presence of taxes and bankruptcy costs.

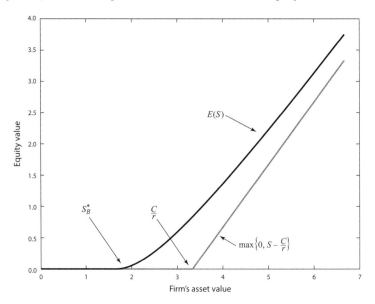

Figure 1.2: Equity value as a function of the asset's value

1.4 Dynamic trade-off theory

In practice, firms find that debt is an attractive way to finance their operations because debt coupons are tax deductible. This tendency, however, is limited by the risk of costly liquidation of the firm's assets if debt is not repaid and the firm defaults. Kraus and Litzenberger (1973) introduced these two elements (taxes and costly liquidation) to the analysis of capital structure and showed that doing so resulted in a trade-off: more debt increases tax subsidies, yet less debt reduces

expected bankruptcy costs. The OPTIMAL CAPITAL STRUCTURE min-
imizes the sum of these costs. This section is based on Leland (1994),
who developed a dynamic trade-off model in continuous time. We
will use the same notation as in the Black-Cox model of Section 1.3.

1.4.1 Taxes and liquidation costs

The firm's debt is a consol bond, i.e. a bond that pays a constant
total coupon C until bankruptcy, which occurs the first time that
the asset value S_t falls below a threshold S_B that is chosen by the
shareholders. Accordingly, we define the BANKRUPTCY TIME[8] as

$$\tau := \inf \{ t > 0 \,|\, S_t \leq S_B \}.$$

Taxes equal a fraction $\theta \in [0,1]$ of the operating income βS_t, net of
coupon payments C. The flow of taxes paid by the firm is, thus,

$$\theta[\beta S_t - C]. \qquad (1.4.1)$$

Leland assumes that shareholders can always inject cash into the
firm at no cost. This implies that liquid reserves are useless; thus,
$M_t \equiv 0$. At date τ, the firm is liquidated and debtholders collect
$(1 - \alpha)S_B$, where $\alpha \in [0,1]$ parametrizes the after-tax LIQUIDATION
COSTS. The flow payoff to the shareholders is equal to net earnings
after taxes:

$$(1 - \theta)[\beta S_t - C].$$

Optimal leverage trades off the tax benefits of debt and the expected
liquidation costs.

1.4.2 Asset pricing

The value of the firm's assets follows Equation (1.1.1):

$$\frac{dS_t}{S_t} = \mu dt + \sigma dZ_t.$$

Given that debt pays a constant coupon C, the model is stationary
and the values of debt and equity,

$$D_t = D(S_t) \quad \text{and} \quad E_t = E(S_t),$$

respectively, are only functions of the current level of the firm's value
$S_t = S$. The value of debt corresponds to the discounted stream of

---

[8]In technical terms, τ is a STOPPING TIME. A precise definition is provided in
Appendix C.4.

coupon payments until bankruptcy, plus the payout to creditors when
the said event takes place:

$$D(S) = \mathbb{E}\left[\int_0^\tau e^{-rt}C\,dt + e^{-r\tau}(1-\alpha)S_B\,\middle|\,S_0 = S\right] \tag{1.4.2}$$

$$= \frac{C}{r} - \mathbb{E}\left[e^{-r\tau}\,\middle|\,S_0 = S\right]\left[\frac{C}{r} - (1-\alpha)S_B\right]. \tag{1.4.3}$$

Observe that $\mathbb{E}[e^{-r\tau}|S_0 = S]$ is the present value of one unit of cash
paid at the bankruptcy date τ. Hence, the value of debt is that of a
nondefaultable consol bond, C/r, minus the present value of what is
lost, i.e. C/r, plus what is recovered, i.e. $(1-\alpha)S_B$ when bankruptcy
takes place. Using the general valuation equation (1.3.1) we see that
the function $D(\cdot)$ satisfies the following boundary-value problem:

$$\begin{cases} rD(S) = \mu SD'(S) + \frac{\sigma^2 S^2}{2}D''(S) + C, & S > S_B; \\ D(S_B) = (1-\alpha)S_B, & D(S) \to \frac{C}{r} \text{ as } S \to \infty. \end{cases} \tag{1.4.4}$$

Given that the firm holds no cash reserves and there are no corporate expenditures, the operating income is used to pay coupons
and taxes, and the remainder is paid out to the shareholders. As a
consequence, equity value equals the expected, discounted value of
after-tax profits:

$$E(S) = \mathbb{E}\left[(1-\theta)\int_0^\tau e^{-rt}(\beta S_t - C)\,dt\,\middle|\,S_0 = S\right]. \tag{1.4.5}$$

In this case the valuation equation yields the following boundary-value
problem:

$$\begin{cases} rE(S) = \mu SE'(S) + \frac{\sigma^2 S^2}{2}E''(S) + (1-\theta)(\beta S - C), & S > S_B; \\ E(S_B) = 0, & E(S) \sim (1-\theta)\left(S - \frac{C}{r}\right) \text{ as } S \to \infty. \end{cases}$$
$$\tag{1.4.6}$$

We know from Section 1.3.2 that the differential equation

$$rF(S) = \mu SF'(S) + \frac{\sigma^2 S^2}{2}F''(S)$$

has the general solution

$$F(S) = \kappa_1 S^{\gamma_1} + \kappa_2 S^{\gamma_2},$$

where $\gamma_1 < 0 < \gamma_2$ are the roots of the characteristic equation

$$r = \mu\gamma + \frac{\sigma^2}{2}\gamma(\gamma - 1).$$

In order to obtain expressions for the values of debt and equity we must find particular solutions to the corresponding nonhomogeneous equations, and then use the boundary conditions to determine κ_1 and κ_2. Particular solutions to the nonhomogeneous equations are easy to find by considering the no-default case ($\tau = \infty$). One obtains $D(S) = C/r$ and $E(S) = (1-\theta)(S - C/r)$. The conditions at infinity in Problems (1.4.4) and (1.4.6) are

$$\lim_{S \to \infty} D(S) = \frac{C}{r} \quad \text{and} \quad E(S) \sim (1-\theta)\left(S - \frac{C}{r}\right) \quad \text{as } S \to \infty. \quad (1.4.7)$$

Therefore $D(S) = C/r + \kappa_1 S^{\gamma_1}$, as the coefficient in front of the term S^{γ_2} must be zero, given that $S^{\gamma_2} \to \infty$ when $S \to \infty$. From the boundary condition at $S = S_B$ we conclude that

$$D(S) = \frac{C}{r} - \underbrace{\left[\frac{C}{r} - (1-\alpha)S_B\right]\left(\frac{S}{S_B}\right)^{\gamma_1}}_{\text{default premium}}. \quad (1.4.8)$$

In particular, we deduce that

$$\mathbb{E}\left[e^{-r\tau} | S_0 = S\right] = \left(\frac{S}{S_B}\right)^{\gamma_1}.$$

Similarly, the coefficient of S^{γ_2} in $E(S)$ is also zero, so that

$$E(S) = (1-\theta)\left(S - \frac{C}{r}\right) + \kappa_1 S^{\gamma_1}.$$

The condition $E(S_B) = 0$ yields

$$\kappa_1 = (1-\theta)\left(\frac{C}{r} - S_B\right)S_B^{-\gamma_1},$$

which in turn gives us the following expression for the value of equity:

$$E(S) = (1-\theta)\left[S - \frac{C}{r} + \underbrace{\left(\frac{C}{r} - S_B\right)\left(\frac{S}{S_B}\right)^{\gamma_1}}_{\text{limited-liability option}}\right]. \quad (1.4.9)$$

Using the same method, we can also compute the expected present value of taxes

$$T(S) = \mathbb{E}\left[\int_0^\tau \theta(\beta S_t - C)d | S_0 = St\right] = \frac{\theta}{1-\theta}E(S)$$

$$= \theta\left[S\frac{C}{r} + \left(\frac{C}{r} - S_B\right)\left(\frac{S}{S_B}\right)^{\gamma_1}\right]$$

and liquidation costs

$$L(S) = \mathbb{E}\big[e^{-r\tau}\alpha S_B | S_0 = S\big] = \alpha S_B \Big(\frac{S}{S_B}\Big)^{\gamma_1}.$$

Observe that $E(S) + D(S) + T(S) + L(S) = S$. Therefore, given that $T(S)$ and $L(S)$ are positive, we have that $E(S) + D(S) < S$, as a consequence of taxes and bankruptcy costs.

1.4.3 Financial decisions

With the asset-pricing formulas at hand, we are now in a position to study how financial decisions are made. We assume the following timing:

1. The firm chooses the total coupon payment C promised to debtholders;

2. Debt is issued to investors for the market value D_0.

3. Shareholders choose the bankruptcy threshold S_B.

We assume shareholders cannot commit ex-ante to the bankruptcy threshold and they will choose it to maximize ex-post shareholder value, which creditors anticipate. From Equation (1.4.9) this implies that shareholders choose S_B to maximize the value of their limited-liability option; thus, they solve

$$\max_{S_B} \Big\{ \Big(\frac{C}{r} - S_B\Big) S_B^{-\gamma_1} \Big\}.$$

The solution is again independent of S. Notice that this is the same optimization problem that we solved in Section 1.3.2 to obtain Expression (1.3.6); hence, as before

$$S_B^* = \frac{\gamma_1}{\gamma_1 - 1} \frac{C}{r} < \frac{C}{r}. \qquad (1.4.10)$$

Therefore, in the trade-off model **default is always strategic**, since shareholders are not cash constrained and can always pay the coupons. Default represents the exercise of the shareholders' limited-liability option. This is why equity prices are convex functions of S and, as a consequence, shareholders have no incentives to manage risk, but quite the contrary.

The market value of debt at $t = 0$, namely D_0, can be found directly from Equation (1.4.8): for a bankruptcy threshold S_B and an initial firm value S, we have

$$D_0 = \frac{C}{r} - \left[\frac{C}{r} - (1-\alpha)S_B\right]\left(\frac{S}{S_B}\right)^{\gamma_1}.$$

Shareholder value at date $t = 0$ is equal to

$$SV_0 = E_0 - (I - D_0),$$

where E_0 is the value of equity at $t = 0$, i.e., $E(S)$, and $I - D_0$ is the money initially injected by shareholders. We have from Equations (1.4.8) and (1.4.9) that

$$SV_0 = (1-\theta)\left[S - \frac{C}{r} + \left(\frac{C}{r} - S_B\right)\left(\frac{S}{S_B}\right)^{\gamma_1}\right] + \frac{C}{r}$$
$$- \left[\frac{C}{r} - (1-\alpha)S_B\right]\left(\frac{S}{S_B}\right)^{\gamma_1} - I.$$

Reordering terms we obtain

$$SV_0 = \underbrace{\left(1-\theta\right)S - I}_{\substack{\text{NPV of after-tax} \\ \text{earnings}}} + \underbrace{\theta\frac{C}{r}\left[1 - \left(\frac{S}{S_B}\right)^{\gamma_1}\right]}_{\text{expected tax rebate}} - \underbrace{(\alpha-\theta)S_B\left(\frac{S}{S_B}\right)^{\gamma_1}}_{\text{expected net liq. costs}}.$$

If shareholders could commit on the bankruptcy threshold S_B, they would choose not to default ($S_B = 0$). However, given that they cannot commit, SV_0 has to be maximized under Constraint (1.4.10): the default threshold is determined by the choice of coupon C. Alternatively, shareholders may choose S_B^* freely under the constraint that

$$C = r\frac{\gamma_1 - 1}{\gamma_1}S_B^*.$$

Replacing C by this value in the expression of SV_0 yields a new formula for shareholder value as a function of S_B^* only:

$$SV_0(S_B^*) = \left(1-\theta\right)S - I + \frac{\gamma_1 - 1}{\gamma_1}S_B^*\left[\theta + \frac{\theta - \alpha\gamma_1}{\gamma_1 - 1}\left(\frac{S}{S_B^*}\right)^{\gamma_1}\right]. \quad (1.4.11)$$

SV_0 is a strictly concave function of S_B^*; therefore, shareholder value is maximized for the value S_B^* that satisfies

$$SV_0'(S_B^*) = 0 \Leftrightarrow \theta = (\theta - \alpha\gamma_1)\left(\frac{S}{S_B^*}\right)^{\gamma_1}.$$

In other words, the choice of S_B^* that maximizes shareholder value is

$$S_B^* = S\left(\frac{\theta}{\theta - \alpha\gamma_1}\right)^{-\frac{1}{\gamma_1}}. \tag{1.4.12}$$

The optimal coupon is, thus,

$$C^* = r\frac{\gamma_1 - 1}{\gamma_1} S\left(\frac{\theta}{\theta - \alpha\gamma_1}\right)^{-\frac{1}{\gamma_1}}.$$

Substituting Expression (1.4.12) in Equation (1.4.11) we get

$$\begin{aligned} SV_0^* &= (1 - \theta)S - I + \frac{\gamma_1 - 1}{\gamma_1} S\left(\frac{\theta}{\theta - \alpha\gamma_1}\right)^{-\frac{1}{\gamma_1}}\left[\frac{\theta\gamma_1}{\gamma_1 - 1}\right] \\ &= (1 - \theta)S - I + \theta S\left(\frac{\theta}{\theta - \alpha\gamma_1}\right)^{-\frac{1}{\gamma_1}}. \end{aligned} \tag{1.4.13}$$

The last term in this expression corresponds to the firm's gain from leverage. Given that $\gamma_1 < 0$ and $\alpha > 0$, the term $\left(\theta/(\theta - \alpha\gamma_1)\right)^{-1/\gamma_1}$ is smaller than one. This implies that the gains from leverage are lower than θS, the expected present value of the taxes paid by the unlevered (that is, not indebted) firm. Shareholders could have entirely financed the investment I, in which case they would have obtained $(1-\theta)S - I$. By optimally trading off tax benefits of debt and liquidation costs, they are able to get more.

1.4.4 Testable predictions

A standing criticism to trade-off theory is that it predicts a too-high leverage. In fact, many extensions to this theory have focused on addressing this issue. A crucial step is a proper calibration of the model parameters, something that has been addressed by many authors. For example, Leland (1998) uses the following parameters: default costs $\alpha = 25\%$, tax rate $\theta = 20\%$ and payout ratio $\beta = 0.05$. In the example below we use the riskless rate $r = 6\%$ and a volatility of earnings $\sigma = 0.25$.

We have from the previous section that the optimal default threshold is

$$S_B^* = S\left(\frac{\theta}{\theta - \alpha\gamma_1}\right)^{-\frac{1}{\gamma_1}} \tag{1.4.14}$$

and the optimal coupon is

$$C = \frac{r(\gamma_1 - 1)}{\gamma_1} S_B^*. \tag{1.4.15}$$

The debt-to-assets ratio equals the nominal value of debt over that of the assets. Making use of Equations (1.4.14) and (1.4.15) it can be measured as

$$\frac{C/r}{S} = \frac{\gamma_1 - 1}{\gamma_1} \left(\frac{\theta}{\theta - \alpha\gamma_1} \right)^{-\frac{1}{\gamma_1}}. \qquad (1.4.16)$$

Let us now apply the parameter values given above to this formula. We have that γ_1 is the negative root of the equation

$$0.06 = -0.02\gamma + 0.03\gamma^2,$$

which yields $\gamma_1 \approx -1.08$. If we substitute this value, together with $\alpha = 0.25$ and $\theta = 0.20$, in Equation (1.4.16) we get

$$\frac{\text{debt}}{\text{assets}} \approx 1.92 \left(\frac{0.20}{0.20 + 0.27} \right)^{0.92} \approx 86\%.$$

This is much higher than observed debt-to-assets ratios of nonfinancial firms. As an illustration, Table 1.1 presents the debt-to-assets ratio on March 23, 2017, of ten large firms in different sectors.[9]

Company	Sector	Debt/Assets
American Airlines Group Inc.	Aviation	47.47%
BHP Billiton Ltd. ARD	Mining	30.62%
Boeing Co.	Aerospace	11.06%
General Electric Co.	Tech./financial	37.30%
Exxon Mobil Corp.	Oil/gas	12.95%
FedEx Corp.	Logistics	30.10%
Fiat Chrysler Aut. N.V.	Automotive	32.05%
Fluor Corp.	Construction	16.86%
Microsoft Corp.	Technological	27.72%
Vodafone Group PLC	Telecommunications	33.91%

Table 1.1: Debt-to-assets ratios

1.5 Further reading

The topic "pricing corporate debt" that we addressed briefly in Section 1.2 is part of a wide-ranging literature on credit risk. Among

---

[9]Source: Marketwatch

many others, Bielecki and Rutkowski (2004) and Duffie and Singleton (2003) are two comprehensive references. Moreover, understanding and modeling the evolution of interest rates goes hand-in-hand
with the study of credit risk. This is a field in itself, where mathematical finance has played an important role (see, e.g. Brigo and
Mercurio (2006), Carmona and Tehranchi (2006) and Ekeland and
Taflin (2005)).

Static (as opposed to dynamic) models on optimal capital structure predated the (continuous-time) trade-off theory presented in Section 1.4. For instance, Kraus and Litzenberger (1973) introduce
bankruptcy costs and corporate taxes in a one-period model where
firms issue debt and equity. The authors use a finite state-space formulation and then determine the optimal equity-debt mix (via the
division of solvency and insolvency states) that maximize firm value
and conclude the latter is not, in general, a concave function of financial leverage.

One of the first dynamic models to address optimal capital structure
in the presence of taxes is Brennan and Schwartz (1978). The authors
assume that the value of a levered firm is a function of the value of an
otherwise identical, yet unlevered firm (where the assets' value follow
a Geometric Brownian Motion) and the face value of debt, its coupon
and its time to maturity. So far, this setup is very similar to the one
studied in this chapter. Taxes come into play through the payment
of debt coupons. There is a wedge between the increase in value to
debtholders that comes from the payment of coupons and the (taxed)
proceeds from selling assets to make these payments, which is similar
to what we observed in Section 1.4. The value of the levered firm
is then computed numerically as a function of its leverage (in this
case the resulting function is concave) for different parameter values,
which allows for an estimation of the optimal capital structure.

Sundaresan (2013) presents a synthesis of the literature on credit
risk that uses option-pricing methodology. The author starts with Merton (1974) and also summarizes the results of Black and Cox (1976)
and Leland (1994). The exposition is chronologically ordered and
provides the reader with a clear picture of the path followed, until
very recently, by the academic research on optimal capital structure
that uses structural models in continuous time.

Leland and Toft (1996) extend the results presented in this chapter
and allow the firm to choose the amount of debt that it issues as well
as its maturity. The authors consider debt that pays a continuous
coupon until the principal is paid out at maturity. In the case of
premature default, the creditors do not recover the full value of the

principal. For a given bankruptcy threshold, it is then possible to use arbitrage-pricing techniques to determine the price of debt. If there were a single issuance date, the model would lose its stationarity and the assumption of a single, time-independent, default threshold (to be chosen endogenously) would be inconsistent. In order to avoid the additional difficulty that having time-dependent thresholds would entail, the authors assume that a constant proportion of debt is renewed at each date. This allows for the computation of a time-invariant optimal default threshold.

Goldstein et al. (2001) also use an extension of the classical trade-off model to analyze the optimal capital structure of a firm in a dynamic setting. The firm may issue new debt in the future, as opposed to the one-shot nature of debt issuance studied in this chapter. Having such an option results in initial levels of debt that are well below what an identical stationary firm would chose.

Hennessy and Whited (2005) use a dynamic trade-off model in discrete time to study optimal capital structure. In their model, issuing new equity is possible but it implies transaction costs. Importantly, borrowing and lending at the risk-free rate is possible but debt, which is short term (they do not tackle the question of optimal debt maturity), is subject to collateral constraints. The latter are determined by the fire-sale price of the assets. The authors also contemplate a differentiated tax structure, with interest income and dividends being taxed at different rates. They find that the optimal leverage ratio is time dependent. Hennessy and Whited carefully calibrate their model on real data and provide extensive comparative statics.

Cheng and Milbradt (2012) modify the classical trade-off model in three significant ways. First, the manager may choose at any time to switch between "good" and "bad" projects, i.e. one with high drift and low volatility and another one with a low drift and high volatility. This is what is called "risk shifting." Second, instead of an infinite time horizon, now there is a random time horizon modeled by an exponentially distributed random variable. The manager's objective is to maximize the firm's final value. Finally, the maturity of debt is staggered, as each debt contract matures with the arrival of an independent Poisson process. Creditors whose debt matures may either withdraw at its face value or roll it over. This introduces incentives against risk shifting, as the manager may want to be prudent when the firm is in poor shape, so as to avoid a rollover freeze. The optimal maturity is associated to a rollover threshold that avoids excessive rollover risk while still providing sufficient incentives for the manager to avoid risk shifting when the firm is in good health.

He and Milbradt (2016) study the dynamic evolution of debt maturity and default decisions. The firm issues both long- and short-term debt and shareholders are unable to commit ex-ante to a particular debt-maturity structure. Instead, as firm fundamentals and bond prices evolve dynamically, shareholders adjust the proportions of the types of debt in the firm's liabilities. This affects the shareholders' endogenous default decision, since they must finance the shortfall between the face value of maturing bonds and the market value of newly issued ones.

2 The Base Liquidity-Management Model

THIS CHAPTER IS based on the independent works of Jeanblanc-Picqué and Shiryaev (1995) and Radner and Shepp (1996). It will serve as the foundation for the models studied in Chapters 3–6, which rely on "external" frictions (as opposed to "internal" frictions studied in Chapter 7), such as the lack of access to bank credit and to financial markets, or the fact that issuing new securities is costly. Our objective is to explain LIQUIDITY-MANAGEMENT decisions of corporations on top of the other corporate decisions regarding financing and default that we investigated previously.

The base model considers a firm, held by risk-neutral shareholders, that operates under the following conditions: i) it must keep positive liquid reserves at all times, otherwise it is liquidated and ii) it has no access to external funds. The firm's operations generate random net earnings that may be negative. Therefore, managing the firm's liquid reserves is essential. In order to do so, shareholders (or the manager, acting on behalf of the latter) must choose when to retain earnings and when to distribute dividends. Intuitively, the firm must fund its day-to-day operations by tapping into its liquid reserves. Given that the value of the shareholders' equity corresponds to the discounted stream of dividends distributed over the firm's lifespan, they face the trade-off between retaining earnings as a precautionary measure against the risk of liquidation and distributing dividends.

2.1 The dynamics of net earnings

Consider a firm that has i.i.d. earnings and that holds no debt.[1] Cumulative earnings from 0 to t are denoted by Y_t and follow an ARITHMETIC BROWNIAN MOTION:

$$dY_t = \mu dt + \sigma dZ_t, \quad Y_0 = 0, \qquad (2.1.1)$$

where μ and σ are positive and $Z = \{Z_t, t \geq 0\}$ is a standard Brownian motion. Given that μ is greater than zero, the firm is (on average)

---

[1] Debt financing is sub-optimal in this model, as there are neither taxes nor agency frictions. In this context, 100% equity financing is optimal.

profitable. It may, however, incur operating losses, because σ is not zero. An Arithmetic Brownian Motion captures the idea of a fixed-size firm, which allows us to focus on liquidity issues.[2] More specifically, we assume for the moment that retained earnings cannot be invested into growing the firm. This assumption is relaxed in Chapter 6, which is entirely dedicated to the determinants of corporate investments, with and without financial frictions.[3]

At this point, the earnings process $Y = \{Y_t, t \geq 0\}$ is exogenous. In the upcoming chapters we endogenize it in several applications to different industries and adapt the base model accordingly. In this chapter, the firm has no access to financial markets or bank credit. In particular, no overdraft on the firm's current account (i.e. negative cash reserves) is allowed.[4] Under this extreme form of financial frictions, the only instrument at the manager's disposal is the dividend policy, which we study below.

2.2 Risk-averse shareholders

In this section we assume shareholders are risk-averse. They have no other source of income than the flow of dividends distributed by the firm. The DIVIDEND FLOW is denoted $l = \{l_t, t \geq 0\}$, with $l_t \geq 0$, and the instantaneous utility derived by shareholders at date t is $u(l_t)$, where $u : \mathbb{R} \to \mathbb{R}$ is a nondecreasing and concave utility function. Shareholders choose the timing and size of dividend payouts. Decisions concerning the distribution of dividends take place continuously and, due to limited liability, dividends must be nonnegative. The set of all $\mathcal{F}$-adapted dividend flows is denoted by $\overline{\mathscr{A}}$. For any choice of $l \in \overline{\mathscr{A}}$, the dynamics of the firm's cash reserves are described by the

---

[2]Processes such as Geometric Brownian Motions introduce other issues: the firm may also be liquidated because it is not profitable anymore (see, e.g. Paulsen (2008)).

[3]Notice that this case is not consistent with assuming that Y is a Geometric Brownian Motion, as we did in Chapter 1. There, the firm asset value S_t can also be interpreted as the firm's size.

[4]In general, we assume that injecting new cash can only be done by issuing new securities (equity, since debt brings here no benefit), which is costly. This makes cash reserves relevant. Indeed, in the presence of issuance costs, the fact that the firm may suffer operational losses implies that the latter must be offset by cash reserves. This is a crucial difference with Leland-type models, where shareholders bear no costs when raising new equity and, as a result, there is no need for liquid reserves: all profits are distributed as dividends and all losses are offset via new equity issuances, as long as it is optimal to maintain the firm afloat.

stochastic differential equation

$$dM_t^l = \mu dt + \sigma dZ_t - l_t dt, \quad M_0 = m.$$

For simplicity, we have assumed that reserves are not remunerated. This is an extreme case of DEADWEIGHT COSTS of hoarding cash in the company (for an example of less extreme deadweight costs see Section 4.2). Observe that the firm's cash reserves increase (or decrease) via its net earnings and decrease whenever dividend distribution takes place. We stress that, due to financial frictions, reserves may only be increased via retained earnings and not by infusions of outside capital.

The firm is liquidated at zero value[5] as soon as $M_t^l < 0$, as it is unable to finance its operations; hence, any dividend distribution carries an implicit cost: it increases the risk that cash reserves become negative. The LIQUIDATION TIME τ_l associated to a dividend flow $l \in \overline{\mathscr{A}}$ is defined as

$$\tau_l := \inf \left\{ t > 0 \big| M_t^l < 0 \right\}.$$

As a consequence of the structure of the net cashflows, even if the manager were to choose $l \equiv 0$, there would always be a positive probability that the firm would eventually go bankrupt. This stems from the fact that the volatility of earnings does not scale down to zero as M becomes very small. This issue is obviously exacerbated when any positive l is chosen.

Proposition 2.2.1. *For any $l \in \overline{\mathscr{A}}$ and $m, t > 0$ there is a positive probability that the firm is liquidated before date t.*

Proof. See Appendix A.2.

The manager must balance the trade-off between accumulating reserves, which entails an opportunity cost because they are not remunerated, and paying out dividends, which increases the risk of liquidation.

2.2.1 Shareholder value

Shareholders discount the future at the strictly positive rate ρ. The manager's objective is to maximize shareholder value.[6] For an initial level of liquid reserves m, the value of the shareholders' claim is defined as the present value of the expected utility of dividend payouts

---

[5]The assumption of a zero liquidation value is made to simplify the exposition. It can be easily relaxed.

[6]We are assuming for the time being that there are no conflicts of interest between management and owners.

during the firm's lifetime. For a given choice of $l \in \overline{\mathscr{A}}$ and an initial level of liquidity m, shareholder value[7] is

$$V^l(m) = \mathbb{E}\left[\int_0^{T_l} e^{-\rho t} u(l_t) dt \,\middle|\, M_0^l = m\right].$$

An important observation is that the model is stationary because the cash reserves have a Markovian structure and there is no finite time horizon. Thus, at any date, the manager's choices and the value of the firm depend exclusively on the current level of cash reserves: decisions at date t are made as if $t = 0$, paying attention only to the current level m of liquid reserves. In the dynamic-programming terminology, m is called the STATE VARIABLE. We analyze the problem through the properties of the VALUE FUNCTION

$$V(m) := \sup_{l \in \overline{\mathscr{A}}} V^l(m), \quad m \geq 0, \tag{2.2.1}$$

where l is the CONTROL VARIABLE. Similar to the valuation equation (1.3.1) in Chapter 1, on $(0, \infty)$ the value function V satisfies the equation

$$\max_{l \geq 0} \left\{ \frac{\sigma^2}{2} V''(m) + (\mu - l)V'(m) - \rho V(m) + u(l) \right\} = 0. \tag{2.2.2}$$

What kind of properties should we expect V to have? First, $V(m) = 0$ when $m < 0$, as the firm is liquidated at zero value. It can be shown that V is continuous at zero.[8] In other words $V(0) = 0$. The risk of liquidation implies that the marginal value of cash in the firm is high when m is small. This risk diminishes as m grows and, given that the firm retains earnings only to avoid liquidation, it is natural to expect $m \mapsto V'(m)$ to be a decreasing mapping, i.e. V to be a concave function, which we verify ex-post.[9] Finally, V is an increasing

---

[7] Given that there is no debt, this is also the value of the firm

[8] Intuitively, one can approximate the net-earnings process by a Bernoulli one:

$$\Delta Y_t = \mu \Delta t + \sigma \sqrt{\Delta t} \epsilon_t,$$

where Δt is small and $\epsilon_t = \pm 1$ with probability $1/2$. When $m = 0$, the Bellman equation gives:

$$(1 + \rho t)V(0) = \frac{1}{2}V(\mu \Delta t + \sigma \sqrt{\Delta t}) + \frac{1}{2}V(\mu \Delta t - \sigma \sqrt{\Delta t}).$$

The last term equals zero when $\mu \Delta t - \sigma \sqrt{\Delta t} < 0$, which is true for Δt small enough. A Taylor expansion of order zero (when $\Delta t \to 0$) yields $V(0) = (1/2)V(0)$, implying $V(0) = 0$.

[9] The concavity of the value function can be interpreted as a sort of "corporate" risk aversion arising from the risk of liquidation (see e.g. Milne and Robertson (1996) for a discussion on this feature). In other words, the shareholders are reluctant to lose the FRANCHISE VALUE of the firm, i.e. the future payouts that they would be entitled to in the future if the firm continued in operation.

function: all other things equal, the value of a firm grows with its reserves.

2.2.2 The optimal dividend flow

In the sequel we concentrate on the particular case where u has the following form:[10]

$$u(l) = \min\{l, \bar{l}\}, \qquad (2.2.3)$$

for some $\bar{l} > 0$ given. This piecewise-linear utility function exhibits SATIATION, i.e. shareholders do not want to consume more than $\bar{l}$ per unit of time. The Bellman equation (2.2.2) becomes

$$\max_{l \geq 0} \left\{ \frac{\sigma^2}{2} V''(m) + (\mu - l)V'(m) - \rho V(m) + \min\{l, \bar{l}\} \right\} = 0. \quad (2.2.4)$$

Let us isolate the terms in l in this equation. A useful definition is

$$\mathcal{V}(l, V'(m)) := \min\{l, \bar{l}\} - lV'(m) = \begin{cases} l(1 - V'(m)), & l < \bar{l}; \\ \bar{l} - lV'(m), & l \geq \bar{l}. \end{cases}$$

This convex function is maximized either for $l = 0$ or $l = \bar{l}$. More specifically:

$$\operatorname*{argmax}_{l \geq 0} \mathcal{V}(l, V'(m)) = \begin{cases} 0, & \text{if } V'(m) > 1; \\ \bar{l}, & \text{if } V'(m) \leq 1. \end{cases} \qquad (2.2.5)$$

Remark. *Expression (2.2.5) implies that the Bellman equation (2.2.4) can be rewritten as*

$$\max_{l \in \{0, \bar{l}\}} \left\{ \frac{\sigma^2}{2} V''(m) + (\mu - l)V'(m) - \rho V(m) + l \right\} = 0.$$

In other words, assuming that the shareholders' preferences are as in Expression (2.2.3) is, in technical terms, equivalent to imposing an upper bound on the dividend rate.

---

[10]We have chosen this particular form of u as it provides a simple transition to the setting with risk-neutral shareholders that is present in most of this book.

2.2.3 The value function

Observe that dividends are only distributed when the marginal value of cash in the firm does not exceed 1. By the concavity of V, there is a DIVIDEND-DISTRIBUTION THRESHOLD m^* (that depends on $\bar{l}$), such that dividends are only distributed once liquid reserves exceed m^*. We say that dividend distribution follows a THRESHOLD STRATEGY. In order to find m^*, we solve the differential equation

$$\rho V(m) = \begin{cases} \frac{\sigma^2}{2} V''(m) + \mu V'(m), & m \in (0, m^*]; \\ \frac{\sigma^2}{2} V''(m) + (\mu - \bar{l})V'(m) + \bar{l}, & m \in (m^*, \infty). \end{cases} \quad (2.2.6)$$

subject to $V(0) = 0$ and the smooth-pasting condition at $m = m^*$:

$$V(m^*_-) = V(m^*_+) \quad \text{and} \quad V'(m^*_-) = V'(m^*_+) = 1.$$

Observation. *Determining m^* is equivalent to finding the optimal dividend flow l^* :*

$$l^*(m) = \begin{cases} 0, & m \le m^*; \\ \bar{l}, & m > m^*. \end{cases}$$

The general solution to the differential equation $\rho V = (\sigma^2/2)V'' + \mu V'$ is

$$V(m) = b_1 e^{r_1 m} + b_2 e^{r_2 m}, \quad (2.2.7)$$

where $r_1 < 0 < r_2$ solve the characteristic equation $\rho = (\sigma^2/2)r^2 + \mu r$ (note that $|r_1| > |r_2|$). From the boundary conditions $V(0) = 0$ and $V'(m^*) = 1$ we have that on $[0, m^*)$

$$V(m) = \frac{e^{r_2 m} - e^{r_1 m}}{r_2 e^{r_2 m^*} - r_1 e^{r_1 m^*}}.$$

We now analyze the second differential equation. Clearly, a particular solution V_p to

$$\rho V = \frac{\sigma^2}{2} V'' + (\mu - \bar{l})V' + \bar{l} \quad \text{is} \quad V_p \equiv \frac{\bar{l}}{\rho}.$$

The general solution V_h to the homogeneous equation

$$\rho V = \frac{\sigma^2}{2} V'' + (\mu - \bar{l})V' \quad \text{is} \quad V_h(m) = C_1 e^{\gamma_1 m} + C_2 e^{\gamma_2 m},$$

where C_1 and C_2 are constants and $\gamma_1 < 0 < \gamma_2$ are the roots of a different characteristic equation: $\rho = (\sigma^2/2)\gamma^2 + (\mu - \bar{l})\gamma$. We then have that for $m \in [m^*, \infty)$

$$V(m) = V_p(m) + V_h(m) = \frac{\bar{l}}{\rho} + C_1 e^{\gamma_1 m} + C_2 e^{\gamma_2 m}.$$

In order to determine C_1 and C_2, observe that if reserves remained above m^* for all $t \geq 0$, there would be a constant dividend flow $\bar{l}$ and $\tau = \infty$. Then, the NPV of dividend payouts to shareholders would be

$$\int_0^\infty e^{-\rho t} \bar{l} \, dt = \frac{\bar{l}}{\rho}.$$

This means that $\bar{l}/\rho$ is an upper bound for V. Given that $\gamma_2 > 0$, it must hold that $C_2 \leq 0$. However, a negative C_2 implies that the mapping $m \mapsto V(m)$ is decreasing for m large enough; thus, we conclude that $C_2 = 0$. So to find C_1 we make use of the boundary condition $V'(m^*) = 1$:

$$1 = V'(m_+^*) = C_1 \gamma_1 e^{\gamma_1 m^*} \Rightarrow C_1 = \frac{1}{\gamma_1 e^{\gamma_1 m^*}}.$$

The target cash level m^* is then found by solving

$$\frac{e^{r_2 m^*} - e^{r_1 m^*}}{r_2 e^{r_2 m^*} - r_1 e^{r_1 m^*}} = \frac{\bar{l}}{\rho} + \frac{1}{\gamma_1 e^{\gamma_1 m^*}} e^{\gamma_1 m^*} = \frac{\bar{l}}{\rho} + \frac{1}{\gamma_1} =: A(\bar{l}).$$

Given that γ_1 depends on $\bar{l}$, the sign of $A(\bar{l})$ is not obvious. However, it can be shown that the equation $A(\bar{l}) = 0$ has a unique solution l_0 and that $A(\bar{l}) \leq 0$ if $\bar{l} \leq l_0$ and $A(\bar{l}) > 0$ if $\bar{l} > l_0$. In the former case $m^* = 0$, i.e. the firm pays out a constant dividend flow $\bar{l} dt$ until it is liquidated. Summarizing, we have the following result:

Proposition 2.2.2. *The optimal strategy of the firm is to distribute dividends at rate $\bar{l}$ when cash reserves m exceed m^* and to retain all earnings when $m < m^*$. Furthermore, there exists $l_0 > 0$ such that $m^* = 0$ if $\bar{l} \leq l_0$.*

We present in Figure 2.1 the value of m^* for different levels of $\bar{l}$. We have set $\mu = 0.3, \sigma = 0.5$ and $\rho = 0.15$, in which case $l_0 \approx 0.06$. The more interesting case is $\bar{l} > l_0$. We present in Figure 2.2 the plot of the value function V with the same parameters as before and $\bar{l} = 0.5$, as well as the plot of the marginal value of cash V'. Observe that $V'(m) < 1$ for $m > m^* > 0$.

What happens when $\bar{l} \to \infty$? In other words, what is the limit situation when shareholders become risk neutral? We answer this question in the following section, in which we present the model that serves as the basis for most of the remainder of this book.

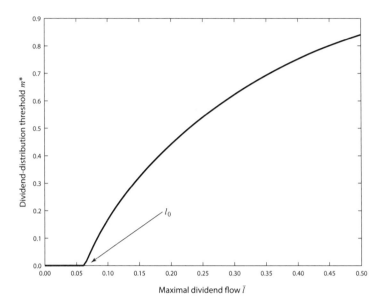

Figure 2.1: The dividend-distribution threshold for different $\bar{l}$'s.

2.3 Risk-neutral shareholders

As we saw previously, when preferences are given by the utility function

$$u(l) = \begin{cases} l, & l < \bar{l}; \\ \bar{l}, & l \geq \bar{l}, \end{cases}$$

the shareholders' optimal decisions regarding dividend distribution result in bang-bang dividend-distribution rates $l \in \{0, \bar{l}\}$. If shareholders became risk neutral in the sense that $\bar{l} \to \infty$ (or if the restriction $l \leq \bar{l}$ were lifted), we would have the optimal dividend-distribution rate also tending to infinity. Intuitively, this would result in dividends being distributed at an infinite rate over infinitesimally short periods of time. In order to formalize this, we have to enlarge the set of admissible dividend strategies. Instead of writing $l_t dt$ for the dividends paid out over $[t, t + dt]$, we write dL_t, with $L = \{L_t, t \geq 0\}$ being a nondecreasing, càdlàg,[11] $\mathcal{F}$-adapted process that we call a

---

[11] The French acronym càdlàg stands for right continuous with left limits (rcll in English) and is important in the study of stochastic processes. The reason for requiring this property is the following: the cumulative dividend policy may have jumps, which correspond to lump-sum payments. For example, imagine that no dividends have been paid out over $[0, t)$, i.e. $L_s = 0$ for $s < t$, then a

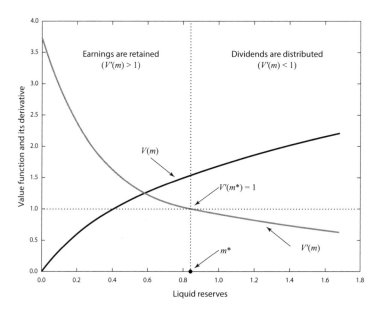

Figure 2.2: A typical value function and its derivative when $m^* > 0$.

CUMULATIVE DIVIDEND PROCESS: L_t represents the cumulative dividends paid out over $[0, t]$. This enlarges the set of admissible dividend strategies to $\mathscr{A}$.

2.3.1 The dynamics of liquid reserves and the value function

The dynamics of the firm's cash reserves are

$$dM_t^L = dY_t - dL_t, \quad M_0^L = m, \qquad (2.3.1)$$

for $L \in \mathscr{A}$ and an initial level of liquidity m. The corresponding shareholder value is given by

$$V^L(m) := \mathbb{E}\left[\int_0^{\tau_L} e^{-\rho t} dL_t \,\middle|\, M_0^L = m\right],$$

---

dividend of size 1 is paid out at date t, i.e. $L_t = 1$, and no dividends are ever paid out again. If we plot $\{L_s, s \geq 0\}$, it is a horizontal line at level zero until t_- (i.e. the left limit of L at t is $L_{t-} = 0$ and then a horizontal line at level 1 for $s \geq t$ (L is right continuous at t).

where τ_L is again the first time that M^L becomes negative. The value function $\mathbf{V}$ is defined as

$$\mathbf{V}(m) := \sup_{L \in \mathscr{A}} V^L(m), \quad m \geq 0. \tag{2.3.2}$$

Observation. *The value function defined in Expression (2.3.2) is used as a benchmark in the upcoming chapters. For this reason it is denoted by the reserved symbol $\mathbf{V}$; otherwise value functions are denoted by V.*

Remark. *Let us revisit the question of how the model would change if Y were a Geometric Brownian Motion. With the current setup, if $dM_t^L = M_t^L(\mu dt + \sigma dZ_t) - dL_t$, then either $\mathbf{V}(m) = \infty$ (if $\rho < \mu$) or $\mathbf{V}(m) = m$ (if $\rho \geq \mu$). The intuition is simple: when $\rho < \mu$ one can distribute a sufficiently large fraction of earnings as dividends to offset the discounting by ρ. A Geometric Brownian Motion starting at $m > 0$ never hits zero; thus, the firm is never liquidated and the net present value (NPV) of the expected dividend stream is infinite. When $\rho > \mu$ the opposite happens and shareholders view the firm as a decreasing-value enterprise; therefore, the optimal strategy is immediate liquidation. We leave the formal proof as an exercise.*

Once again we use dynamic programming techniques to find $\mathbf{V}$. In this case, however, the description of the problem does not readily provide us with the structure of the optimal dividend-distribution strategy, as in Section 2.3. Instead, once $\mathbf{V}$ has been found, we use it to derive the optimal $L^* = \{L_t^*, t \geq 0\}$. What does remain unchanged is that $\mathbf{V}(0) = 0$ and that the marginal value of cash in the firm decreases as the level of liquid reserves increases:

Proposition 2.3.1. *The mapping $m \mapsto \mathbf{V}(m)$ is nonnegative, increasing and concave.*

Proof. See Appendix A.2.

As before, the risk neutrality of the firm's owners implies that dividends are paid out if and only if $V' \leq 1$. As a result, whenever $V' > 1$, all earnings are retained. In this RETENTION REGION, a differential equation describes the value function and changes in value obey exclusively the variations of the level of liquid reserves through the net earnings. On the other hand, $\mathbf{V}'$ cannot be smaller than 1, otherwise shareholders would collect dividends at an "infinite rate". We obtain what is referred to as a COMPLEMENTARITY CONDITION. The value function satisfies a Hamilton-Jacobi-Bellman VARIATIONAL INEQUALITY and the manager's problem is embedded in a SINGULAR CONTROL framework.

Proposition 2.3.2. *The mapping $m \mapsto \mathbf{V}(m)$ is twice continuously differentiable and satisfies the following Hamilton-Jacobi-Bellman variational inequality for all $m \geq 0$:*

$$\max \left\{ \frac{\sigma^2}{2} \mathbf{V}''(m) + \mu \mathbf{V}'(m) - \rho \mathbf{V}(m), \, 1 - \mathbf{V}'(m) \right\} = 0, \quad (2.3.3)$$

together with the boundary condition $\mathbf{V}(0) = 0$.

Proof. See Appendix A.2.

The left-hand term inside the maximization in Expression (2.3.3) is a standard Hamilton-Jacobi-Bellman equation. It is precisely Expression (2.2.2), with $l = 0$, when the manager's optimal decision is to retain earnings. Intuitively, the complementarity condition $\mathbf{V}'(m) \geq 1$ works as follows: We have that $\mathbf{V}'(0_+) > 1$, otherwise for small levels of m, retained earnings would be worth, from the risk-neutral shareholders' perspective, the same or less than they would if distributed as dividends, which would imply that $\mathbf{V}(m) \equiv m$: the shareholders would distribute all the cash reserves as dividends and liquidate the firm immediately. By concavity, the mapping $m \mapsto \mathbf{V}'(m)$ is decreasing and whenever $\mathbf{V}'(m) = 1$, shareholders earn dividends. There is threshold m^* for the liquid reserves, which in the sequel is referred to as the DIVIDEND BOUNDARY or the TARGET LEVEL of liquid reserves, such that no distribution of dividends takes place as long as $M^L < m^*$, and whenever $M^L \geq m^*$ dividends are distributed.

It should be noted that Proposition 2.3.2 only provides necessary conditions for optimality. Below we construct a candidate for the value function that satisfies these conditions. We then verify that our candidate is indeed the sought-after value function. This is the standard way to proceed when using a dynamic-programming approach. To this end, consider an arbitrary dividend boundary m^* and the corresponding value function $V(\cdot; m^*)$ (m^* is a parameter). For $m \in (0, m^*)$, the value function has exactly the same structure as in the restricted-dividends case:

$$V(m; m^*) = \frac{e^{r_2 m} - e^{r_1 m}}{r_2 e^{r_2 m^*} - r_1 e^{r_1 m^*}}.$$

Given that the factor $e^{r_2 m} - e^{r_1 m}$ is non-negative, finding a candidate for the value function among the family reduces to minimizing the mapping

$$m^* \mapsto r_2 e^{r_2 m^*} - r_1 e^{r_1 m^*},$$

which is positive and convex. Using the first-order condition for optimality we find

$$m^* = \frac{2}{r_1 - r_2} \log\left(-\frac{r_2}{r_1}\right) > 0. \qquad (2.3.4)$$

This choice of m^* implies that

$$V''(m^*; m^*) = 0 \quad \text{and} \quad V(m^*; m^*) = \frac{\mu}{\rho}.$$

Verifying that $\mathbf{V}' > 1$ on $(0, m^*)$ is equivalent to showing that the mapping $m \mapsto r_2 e^{r_2 m} - r_1 e^{r_1 m}$ is decreasing. This holds whenever

$$\left(\frac{r_2}{r_1}\right)^2 e^{(r_2 - r_1)m} < 1 \Leftrightarrow m < m^*.$$

On $[m^*, \infty)$ the value function is affine and has derivative equal to 1. As $\mathbf{V}$ must be continuous we have

$$\mathbf{V}(m) = (m - m^*) + \frac{\mu}{\rho} \quad m \geq m^*.$$

Notice that this means that, for $m > m^*$, the project's value is the sum of an immediate dividend of size $m - m^*$ plus the discounted value of a consol bond paying forever a continuous dividend μdt per unit of time.

The fact that the second derivative of $\mathbf{V}$ at m^* exists (and in this case equals zero) is commonly referred to as a SUPERCONTACT CONDITION. It appears repeatedly in the stochastic control literature, where it is often a necessary condition for optimality (see, e.g. Dumas (1991) and Hoejgaard and Taksar (1998)). We make use of supercontact conditions repeatedly in the upcoming chapters.

Summarizing, our candidate for the value function is

$$\mathbf{V}(m) = \begin{cases} V(m; m^*), & m \in [0, m^*); \\ (m - m^*) + \frac{\mu}{\rho}, & m \in [m^*, \infty). \end{cases} \qquad (2.3.5)$$

We plot $\mathbf{V}$ and $\mathbf{V}'$ in Figure 2.3, with $\mu = 0.3$, $\rho = 0.15$ and $\sigma = 0.5$ as in Section 2.1. An observation that will prove handy in Section 3.1 is that

$$m^* < \frac{\mu}{\rho}. \qquad (2.3.6)$$

This obeys the fact that $\mathbf{V}'(m) > 1$ for $m < m^*$ and, therefore, $\mathbf{V}(m^*) > m^*$. Then, the fact that $\mathbf{V}(m^*) = \mu/\rho$ implies Inequality (2.3.6).

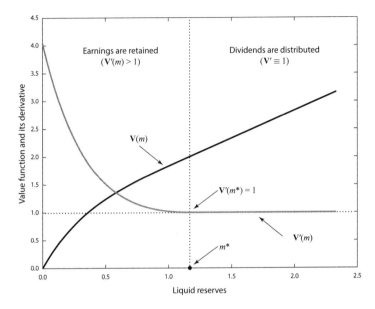

Figure 2.3: Candidate value function and the payout barrier

2.3.2 The optimal dividend-distribution strategy

With the target cash level m^* at hand, we may now describe the optimal dividend-distribution strategy $L^* = \{L_t^*, t \geq 0\}$. We know that whenever the level of cash reserves m grows over m^*, the difference $m - m^*$ must be paid out to shareholders. However, on $(0, m^*)$ the firm's reserves evolve continuously, since their dynamics are given by a diffusion process. This implies that, for any time $t > 0$, the optimal dividend-distribution strategy **reflects** the cash-reserves process M^* (to simplify notation, in the sequel we write M^* for any optimally controlled cash-reserves process) downward at the level $m = m^*$.[12] The reflection must be of an infinitesimal magnitude, given that for $m < m^*$ we have $\mathbf{V}'(m) > 1$, and then shareholders prefer to keep the cash in the firm. In this case we say that the optimal dividend-distribution strategy is of BARRIER TYPE. We can formalize this by defining

$$X_t^* := \max_{0 \leq s \leq t} \{Y_s - m^*\} \quad \text{and} \quad L_t^* := \max\{0, X_t^*\}.$$

---

[12]Before M^* could reach $m^* + \epsilon$, it would have to reach $m^* + \epsilon/2$, $m^* + \epsilon/4$ and so on. However, at each of these levels $\epsilon/2, \epsilon/4$, etc. would be paid out. Hence, M_t^* can never exceed m^* for $t > 0$.

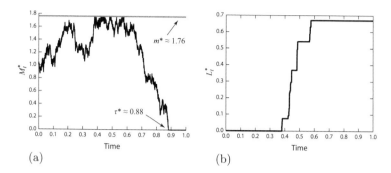

Figure 2.4: The cumulative-dividend process and the cash-reserves dynamics. (a) A path of the cash-reserves process. (b) The corresponding cumulative dividends.

Observe that before the net-earnings process reaches m^*, no dividend distribution takes place, as expected. However, as soon as the RUNNING MAXIMUM X^* exceeds zero, dividends are paid out. In Figures 2.4(a) and 2.4(b) we present a path of the processes M^* and L^*, respectively, for the following parameters (again chosen for illustration purposes): $\mu = 0.3$, $\rho = 0.15$ and $\sigma = 1.2$. The target cash level is $m^* \approx 1.76$. For the initial level of liquid reserves $m_0 = 1$ and the particular path depicted in Figure 2.4, the liquidation time is $t \approx 0.88$.

The problem of governing an Itô diffusion so as to keep it constrained to the interval $[0, \infty)$ by means of an instantaneous reflection was first studied in Skorokhod (1961).[13] In our case we want to constrain M^{L^*} to $(-\infty, m^*]$ and kill it at time τ_{L^*}, when it reaches 0. To formalize this, we consider the so-called Skorokhod problem on $(-\infty, m^*]$, which consists of finding two processes $\{M_t^*, t \geq 0\}$ and $\{L_t^*, t \geq 0\}$ that are adapted and solve

$$\mathcal{P} = \begin{cases} M_t^* = m + \int_0^t \mu ds + \int_0^t \sigma dW_s - L_t^*, \ 0 < t \leq \tau_L, & (2.3.7a) \\ M_t^* \leq m^*, \ 0 < t \leq \tau_{L^*}, & (2.3.7b) \\ \int_0^{\tau_L} \mathbb{1}_{\{M_t^* < m^*\}} dL_t^* = 0, & (2.3.7c) \end{cases}$$

where $\mathbb{1}_{\{.\}}$ is the zero-one indicator function. Equation (2.3.7a) describes the firm's cash reserves as we specify in Expression (2.3.1). Expression (2.3.7b) yields the constraining effect of the reflective barrier. The solution to the Problem $\mathcal{P}$ can be found, for instance, in Karatzas and Shreve (1991). The process L^* is the LOCAL TIME of M^* at level

---

[13]Comprehensive treatises on reflection problems can be found in Harrison (1985), Bass and Hsu (1990) and Kruk et al. (2007).

m^*. The impact of L^* on the dynamics of M^* is to reflect it at m^*, so that $M^* \leq m^*$. From Equation (2.3.7c) we see that the mass of the measure dL^* is carried by the sets $\{M^* = m^*\}$; thus, L^* is inactive whenever $M^* < m^*$. This just means that no dividend distribution takes place before the target level m^* is reached.[14] In this case we say that dividend distribution follows a BARRIER STRATEGY.[15] Summarizing, we have the following result:

Proposition 2.3.3. *The optimal strategy of the firm is to retain earnings as long as reserves are strictly lower than m^*. Dividends are distributed whenever $M_t^* = m^*$ so as to reflect the cash-reserves process, which satisfies $M_t^* \in [0, m^*]$ for all $t > 0$.*

To finalize our characterization of the solution to the manager's problem we must verify that $\mathbf{V}$ is indeed the value function, which is done in the following VERIFICATION THEOREM:

Theorem 1. *Let $\mu, \sigma, \rho > 0$ and let m^* be the corresponding target cash level. If $\mathbf{V}$ is the candidate value function defined in Equation (2.3.5) and $\{L_t^*, t \geq 0\}$ and is the local time of $\{M_t^*, t \geq 0\}$ at level m^*, then for all $m \geq 0$*

$$\mathbf{V}(m) = V^{L^*}(m) = \sup_{L \in \mathscr{A}} V^L(m).$$

Proof. See Appendix A.2.

Remark. *The dynamic-programming approach requires three steps:*
  1. *obtain a Hamilton-Jacobi-Bellman variational inequality by means of the dynamic-programming principle and the Itô formula;*
  2. *compute a candidate value function and the corresponding strategies;*
  3. *verify that the candidate is indeed the value function (verification theorem).*

To avoid proving too many similar verification theorems, in the upcoming sections we stick to steps (1) and (2) and write "max" instead of "sup" in the value-maximization problems. However, the reader should keep in mind that a complete proof of optimality requires a verification result.

---

[14] If $M_0^* > m^*$, an exceptional dividend $M_0^* - m^*$ is paid out at $t = 0$ and dL^* remains unchanged for $t > 0$.

[15] We differentiate between threshold strategies, which do not induce a reflection of the state variable, and barrier strategies, which do.

2.3.3 Economic implications

Let us further analyze the target cash level

$$m^* = \frac{2}{r_1 - r_2} \log\left(-\frac{r_2}{r_1}\right) > 0,$$

and how it depends on the expected cashflows and the variance of the firm's net earnings. Substituting the values for r_1 and r_2, it is not complicated to show that m^* is increasing in σ. This is not surprising, and it may be interpreted as the manager being more conservative when facing a riskier project. What may come across as unexpected is that m^* is not monotonic in μ. The target ratio decreases to zero as μ becomes large, as a highly profitable project requires less precautionary reserves. When μ is small, however, the target ratio must be adjusted downward to increase the probability that the cash reserves hit it, even if this implies a higher risk of default. Figure 2.5(a) depicts m^* as a function of μ for $\mu \in [0, 10]$, $\rho = 1.5$ and $\sigma = 1$, whereas in Figure 2.5(b) we see m^* as a function of σ for $\sigma \in [0, 10]$, $\rho = 1.5$ and $\mu = 3$ (as before, the choice of parameters is only for illustration purposes).

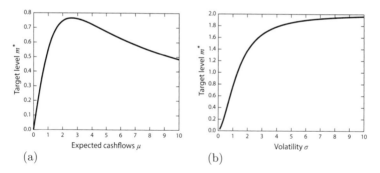

(a) (b)

Figure 2.5: Comparative statics for the dividend barrier m^*.
(a) m^* as a function of μ. (b) m^* as a function of σ.

An important benchmark is the FIRST-BEST case, where there are no financial frictions: the firm can issue equity at no cost so as to compensate losses. In this case the firm is never liquidated and its value is simply the sum of its cash reserves and the expected present value of the future cashflows:

$$V_{\text{fb}}(m) := m + \frac{\mu}{\rho}.$$

Comparing $\mathbf{V}(m) = (m - m^*) + \mu/\rho$ to V_{fb}, we see that when $m \geq m^*$ the financial frictions have become irrelevant. The cost of financial frictions may then be proxied by the difference $V_{\text{fb}}(m^*) - \mathbf{V}(m^*) = m^*$. This allows us to readily assess the gains from risk management. Namely, suppose we could reduce σ to $\sigma - \Delta\sigma$. In the absence of frictions this would have no impact on the value of the firm, as V_{fb} is independent of σ. In our context, however, reducing σ reduces the cost of financial frictions,[16] as $m^*(\sigma - \Delta\sigma) < m^*(\sigma)$.

2.4 Further reading

The choice of the dividend-distribution barrier m^* plays a central role in liquidity-management strategies and is closely related to the cumulative dividend-distribution process, since the latter is "localized" around m^*. This localized nature of the optimal dividend-distribution strategy is present throughout the different liquidity-management models that we study in the sequel. Regardless of the context, we find value functions as solutions of some Hamilton-Jacobi-Bellman equation on an interval $(0, m^*)$. The boundary condition $V(0)$ depends on the recapitalization options of the firm. However, the complementarity condition $V'(m^*) = 1$ is ubiquitous. In many cases the supercontact condition $V''(m^*) = 0$ is required so as to pin down the optimal dividend-distribution barrier.

The theory of instantaneously controlled Brownian motion was initially developed for other applications than corporate finance. For instance, Harrison and Taksar (1983) analyze the problem of a controller who continuously monitors a storage system. The inventory evolves, absent any control, as an Arithmetic Brownian Motion. Thus far, we are still in the same setting as that of the base liquidity-management model. Next, holding costs are introduced via a continuous function h (in the base liquidity-management model $h \equiv 0$). At any time, the controller may instantaneously increase or decrease the inventory, with different proportional costs in each case (in the base liquidity-management model the costs of increasing are infinite, whereas they are zero in case of decreasing) incurring a proportional cost of r times the size of the increase, or incurring a cost of l times the size of the decrease. The authors minimize the expected discounted sum of holding costs and control costs over an infinite planning horizon. They show that the optimal policy results, again, in a reflection at an upper threshold (like our target level), as well as at a lower one where the inventory is increased (see Section 3.2). The greater complexity of this model (compared to the base liquidity-management one) prevents the

---

[16]The implications of this observation in terms of risk management are explored in Rochet and Villeneuve (2011).

authors from obtaining closed-form expressions.

As mentioned at the beginning of this chapter, Radner and Shepp (1996) were among the first to the use liquidity-management (or inventory) models in corporate finance. This work is similar in spirit to Jeanblanc-Picqué and Shiryaev (1995), but it has some interesting additional features. For instance, instead of having access to only one production technology, the manager may switch between n different ones. Those whose corresponding net earnings have larger drifts also have higher volatilities, thus presenting the manager with a trade-off. Moreover, they also look into maximizing the time until bankruptcy, which somehow closes the loop that started with De Finetti (1957), who, wanting to move away from the minimization of the ruin probability as the objective of the manager of an insurance firm, first introduced the dividend-distribution problem (in discrete time).

Paulsen and Gjessing (1997) extend the base liquidity-management model in two ways: they allow for investment of the retained earnings and, besides the Brownian setting used in this chapter, they also consider net earnings where the random driver is a compound Poisson process with exponentially distributed claims. The latter case results in a free-boundary problem for an integro-differential equation. In this setting it is no longer a result, but rather an assumption, that the optimal dividend-distribution strategy is of barrier type. In such a setting they find the optimal solutions in the following cases: i) constant return on investments with Poisson-driven net earnings; ii) both the returns on investments and the net earnings (before investment) follow Arithmetic Brownian Motions. Finally, they include a discussion of the case of a time-dependent barrier.

Jiang and Pistorius (2012) investigate an extension of the base liquidity-management model in the spirit of the multitechnology setting of Radner and Shepp (1996). The twist here is that instead of the manager deciding on the technology used, there are random "regime switches." More specifically, the firm's net earnings are locally governed by an Arithmetic Brownian Motion, but the drift and the discount rate are modulated by a finite-state Markov chain. They show that if the drift is always positive, there exist optimal, regime-dependent barrier strategies. The authors also look at the case where the drift is small and negative in one state, which leads to optimal strategies that are not of barrier type. They conduct numerical experiments so as to illustrate the sensitivities of the optimal barriers and the influence of regime switching.

As liquidity-management models become more complex, the use of numerical analysis comes to the forefront (see, e.g. Section 4.3). For

example, Barth et al. (2016) extend the base liquidity-management
model to allow for finite time horizons (thus ruling out stationarity) and stochastic interest rates. In contrast to Jiang and Pistorius (2012), the latter follows a diffusion process (a mean-reverting
Cox-Ingersoll-Ross process, to be specific). This results in a family
of Hamilton-Jacobi-Bellman variational inequalities whose solutions
must be approximated numerically. To do so, the authors use a finite-
element approximation in two dimensions (reserves+interest rates)
and a time-marching scheme for the time dimension. They show that
the level and speed of mean reversion of the short rate are the driving
forces behind the structure of the optimal strategies. The latter are
still of barrier-type, but given the higher dimensionality of the model,
they are surfaces at each date.

3 Equity Issuance

IN THIS CHAPTER we relax the assumption of the base liquidity-management model concerning the impossibility of new equity issuance.[1] We introduce imperfect refinancing possibilities, where injecting fresh equity into the firm is either costly or uncertain. In the former case there are costs (either fixed or proportional) that shareholders have to incur when refinancing the firm. In the latter case, the issuance process is per se costless, but finding new investors is uncertain. As a consequence, new equity may be issued preemptively: depending on how likely it is to find investors, the manager may decide to issue equity at levels of reserves at which the firm is still relatively well capitalized.

3.1 Fixed issuance cost and stock-price dynamics

In the base liquidity-management model, the only instrument that the manager has at his disposal to control the firm's level of cash reserves is the distribution of dividends. In this section, which is based on Décamps et al. (2011), we enlarge the set of controls and introduce the possibility of new equity issuance. In practice this is a costly process, specially when the firm is in financial distress. For example, Franks and Sanzhar (2006) found, when studying a UK sample of distressed equity issues from 1989 to 1998, that the direct costs of underwriting new equity were 12.74% of the market value of existing equity.[2] In practice, publicly traded companies typically issue new shares by organizing seasoned equity offerings (SEOs), which are quite costly operations. Costs include the fees paid to the investment banks managing the issuance, as well as other direct expenses, such as legal and auditing costs. Ross et al. (2008) estimate the total direct costs of SEOs by U.S. corporations from 1990 to 2003 to be, on average, 6.72% of gross proceeds, rising to 12.88% for issuances of less than

---

[1] As already noted, debt financing is suboptimal in this model.

[2] There are also wealth transfers from existing shareholders to creditors and new shareholders. Franks and Sanzhar (2006) estimate that, in their data set, the average total costs to existing shareholders of an equity issue were 19.68% of the pre-issue market value of equity.

$10 million. As a consequence, new issuances of equity are relatively infrequent and typically involve substantial amounts. For simplicity, we start by studying the case where equity issuance only involves a fixed cost. We then look at the case of a proportional cost of issuance.[3] Regarding mathematical methods, many of the proofs of the results in Chapter 2 can be easily adapted for use in the current chapter.

3.1.1 Optimal equity issuance with a fixed issuance cost

We consider a firm with fixed assets in place generating net earnings as in Expression (2.1.1) of the base model, but we now assume that the manager has the possibility of issuing new equity. We model the issuance cost in the following way: if the manager wants to inject x units of cash into the firm, then $(x + \kappa)$ units of cash must be raised, where $\kappa \geq 0$ captures the FIXED COST of issuance.[4]

Given that the firm's size is fixed, the sole purpose of equity issuance in this model is to bolster liquid reserves. Put differently, we analyze how equity issuance is used to avoid liquidation. The possibility of using the proceeds of an equity issue to expand the firm is studied in Chapter 6. An optimal policy must determine when issuance should take place (if at all), as well as the issuance amount. A CUMULATIVE ISSUANCE PROCESS is any nondecreasing and $\mathcal{F}$-adapted process $J = \{J_t, t \geq 0\}$. Associated with any J, a cost κ is incurred whenever $dJ_t > 0$. Observe that the (fixed) cost structure readily implies that on any finite interval $[t_0, t_1]$ only a finite number of issues may take place; issuance times are denoted $\tau_1, \tau_2, \ldots$.

Let L be a cumulative dividend process and Z a standard Brownian motion as in Chapter 2. For an initial level of cash reserves m, the dynamics of the firm's cash reserves given a strategy $\pi = (L, J)$ are

$$dM_t^\pi = \mu dt + \sigma dZ_t - dL_t + dJ_t, \quad M_0^\pi = m.$$

Whenever $M_t^\pi = 0$, either some new equity is issued (so that $M_{t+}^\pi > 0$) or the firm is liquidated. The liquidation time corresponding to a strategy π is

$$\tau_\pi = \inf \{t > 0 | M_{t+}^\pi < 0\}.$$

Observe that any nontrivial cumulative issuance process J induces jumps in M^π. Stochastic control problems where the control may gen-

---

[3]Décamps et al. (2011) consider the case where equity issuance incurs both a fixed and a variable cost.

[4]An excellent reference for applications of stochastic-control theory to economic models with fixed costs is Stokey (2003).

erate jumps in the state variable are referred to as IMPULSE CONTROL PROBLEMS.

We denote by $\mathscr{A}_i$ (the subindex "i" stands for "issuance") the set of all admissible strategies $\pi = (L, J)$. An important observation is that for large values of κ, relative to the firm's "frictionless value" μ/ρ, equity issuance may very well be too costly and thus never takes place. In such situations the firm is liquidated whenever its cash reserves hit zero, and we revert to the base liquidity-management model. We determine in Section 3.1.3 the critical value of κ above which there are no new equity issuances. For the time being, we assume that κ is small and that new equity issuances may take place.

The following result characterizes the optimal issuance times. It formalizes the intuition that, given that new equity is not used to expand the firm but simply to ward off liquidation, the manager should delay issuance for as long as possible.

Proposition 3.1.1. *Assume that an admissible strategy π dictates an issuance time τ_i such that $M^\pi_{\tau_i} > 0$. Then there exist $\tilde{\pi} \in \mathscr{A}_i$ such that $V^\pi(m) < V^{\tilde{\pi}}(m)$ for all $m > 0$.*

Proof. See Appendix A.3.

Proposition 3.1.1 tells us that for any optimal dividend-issuance strategy, equity issuance occurs, if ever, exclusively when the firm's reserves hit zero. Furthermore, the fact that the model is stationary implies that, whenever an equity issuance takes place, it involves the same amount $\hat{m} > 0$. Therefore, given a cumulative dividend process L and an issuance amount $\hat{m}$, cash reserves M^π evolve in the following way:

1. New equity $\hat{m} + \kappa$ is issued every time $M^\pi_t = 0$, in which case $M^\pi_{t+} = \hat{m}$.
2. The issuance times $\tau^\pi_1, \tau^\pi_2 \ldots$ correspond to the dates when M^π_t hits zero.
3. Between issuance dates, M^π evolves according to

$$dM^\pi_t = \mu dt + \sigma dZ_t - dL_t.$$

The shareholder value corresponding to a strategy π is

$$V^\pi(m) = \mathbb{E}\left[\int_0^\infty e^{-\rho t} dL_t - \sum_{i=1}^\infty e^{-\rho \tau^\pi_i}(\hat{m} + \kappa)\Big| M^\pi_0 = m\right]. \quad (3.1.1)$$

Observe that the upper limit of the integral in the expression above is now ∞. This showcases the main drawback of this model: if κ is small enough to allow distressed equity issuance, the firm is never liquidated. On the other hand, if κ is too large, new equity is never issued and we are back in the base liquidity-management model of Chapter 2. In practice, however, firms sometimes issue new equity and other times they are liquidated.[5]

As before, the manager's objective is to find a strategy π^* that implements the value function

$$V(m) := \max_{\pi \in \mathscr{A}_i} V^\pi(m) = V^{\pi^*}(m), \quad m \in \mathbb{R}_+. \qquad (3.1.2)$$

3.1.2 The impact of equity-issuance on the value function

Given that the difference between the base liquidity-management model and the current one is the manager's option to inject fresh equity into the firm, and that this may only happen at $m = 0$, it should come as no surprise that V is twice continuously differentiable and satisfies the Hamilton-Jacobi-Bellman variational inequality (2.3.3). The target cash level at which dividends are distributed is denoted by m_κ^*. The only difference with the base liquidity-management model is in the boundary condition at 0:[6]

$$V(0) = \max_{\hat{m} \geq 0} \left\{ V(\hat{m}) - \hat{m} - \kappa \right\}.$$

The first-order condition gives

$$V'(\hat{m}) = 1.$$

As $V'(m) = 1$ if $m \geq m_\kappa^*$, this implies that $\hat{m} \geq m_\kappa^*$. Without loss of generality, we can choose $\hat{m} = m_\kappa^*$: optimal refinancing equals the target cash level.[7] This yields the following result.

Proposition 3.1.2. *Let μ, ρ, σ and κ all be greater than zero. There exists a unique $m_\kappa^* \geq 0$ such that boundary-value below has a unique solution:*
  i) $\rho V(m) = \frac{\sigma^2}{2} V''(m) + \mu V'(m)$ and $V'(m) > 1$ for $m \in (0, m_\kappa^*)$;
  ii) $V(m) = V(m_\kappa^*) + (m - m_\kappa^*)$ for $m \geq m_\kappa^*$;
  iii) $V'(m_\kappa^*) = 1$ and $V''(m_\kappa^*) = 0$;

---

[5] The model in Section 3.3 allows for both types of scenarios.
[6] Recall that we have assumed that κ is small enough so that equity issuance takes place.
[7] We have ruled out variable costs of new equity issuance; therefore, any $\hat{m} \geq m_\kappa^*$ is optimal. However, issuing more than m_κ^* does not make economic sense, as the difference $\hat{m} - m_\kappa^*$ would be immediately distributed as a dividend.

iv) $V(0) = V(m_\kappa^*) - m_\kappa^* - \kappa$.
The resulting V is the shareholder value function.

Combining the supercontact condition $V''(m_\kappa^*) = 0$ and the smooth-pasting condition $V'(m_\kappa^*) = 1$ yields the following solution to $\rho V = (\sigma^2/2)V'' + \mu V'$ on $(0, m_\kappa^*)$:

$$V(m) = \frac{1}{r_1 r_2}\left(\frac{r_2^2}{r_2 - r_1}e^{r_1(m-m_\kappa^*)} - \frac{r_1^2}{r_2 - r_1}e^{r_2(m-m_\kappa^*)}\right), \quad (3.1.3)$$

where $r_1 < 0 < r_2$ solve the characteristic equation $\rho = (\sigma^2/2)r^2 + \mu r$ and are given in Equation (2.2.7). This implies that, as in the base liquidity-management model, $V(m_\kappa^*) = \mu/\rho$. The value of m_κ^* is obtained by using the boundary condition at 0. On the one hand, we have

$$V(0) = V(m_\kappa^*) - m_\kappa^* - \kappa = \frac{\mu}{\rho} - m_\kappa^* - \kappa.$$

On the other hand, from Equation (3.1.3)

$$V(0) = \frac{r_2}{r_1(r_2 - r_1)}e^{-r_1 m_\kappa^*} + \frac{r_1}{r_2(r_2 - r_1)}e^{-r_2 m_\kappa^*}.$$

Therefore, the target cash level is found by solving

$$\phi(m) := \frac{r_2}{r_1(r_2 - r_1)}e^{-r_1 m} + \frac{r_1}{r_2(r_2 - r_1)}e^{-r_2 m} = \frac{\mu}{\rho} - m - \kappa. \quad (3.1.4)$$

To see that the solution m_κ^* always exists, observe that, from Equation (3.1.3), we have

$$\phi(0) = \frac{r_2^2 - r_1^2}{r_1 r_2(r_2 - r_1)} = V(m_\kappa^*) = \frac{\mu}{\rho};$$

hence, $\phi(0) > \mu/\rho - \kappa$. Notice also that

$$\frac{r_2}{r_1(r_2 - r_1)}e^{-r_1 m} \to -\infty \quad \text{and} \quad \frac{r_1}{r_1(r_2 - r_1)}e^{-r_2 m} \to 0 \quad \text{as } m \to \infty.$$

Moreover, $r_2 e^{-r_1 m}/(r_1(r_2 - r_1))$ decreases exponentially in m, but $\mu/\rho - m - \kappa$ does it linearly. This implies that there exists a unique $m_\kappa^* > 0$ that satisfies Equation (3.1.4). Given that $\mu/\rho - m - \kappa$ is decreasing in κ we have the following result:

Lemma 3.1.3. *The target cash level m_κ^* is a nondecreasing function of κ. In particular $m_\kappa^* \le m_\infty^* = m^*$ (the target level of the base model), with equality for κ large enough.*

In other words, whenever κ is such that fresh equity is issued, dividend distribution occurs sooner than in the base liquidity-management model. This is because dividend distribution is only postponed in order to decrease the probability of liquidation. Having a second instrument to do this, namely the possibility to issue new equity, reduces the marginal value of cash in the firm, which in turn implies that the manager may lower the target cash level. In Figure 3.1 we plot the value functions corresponding to issuance costs $\kappa = 0.5$ and $\kappa = 1$, together with the corresponding dividend-distribution barriers, for $\mu = 0.7$, $\sigma = 0.5$ and $\rho = 0.2$. The value function $\mathbf{V}$ and the dividend-payoff boundary m^* of the base liquidity-management model, with the same parameters, are also plotted.

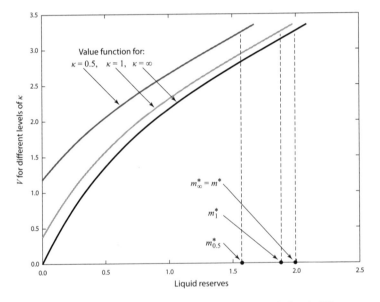

Figure 3.1: The value function and the target cash level different levels of κ

3.1.3 When is equity issuance too costly?

When κ is small enough, the firm issues equity for an amount $m_\kappa^* + \kappa$ every time it runs out of cash reserves. At that point, the value of the firm is

$$V(0) = V(m_\kappa^*) - m_\kappa^* - \kappa$$
$$= \frac{\mu}{\rho} - m_\kappa^* - \kappa.$$

Given that the mapping $\kappa \mapsto m_\kappa^* + \kappa$ is increasing and unbounded, there exists a unique value $\bar{\kappa}$ for which

$$\frac{\mu}{\rho} = m_{\bar{\kappa}}^* + \bar{\kappa}.$$

For all $\kappa \geq \bar{\kappa}$, new equity issues are too expensive and we revert to the base liquidity-management model, where $m_\kappa^* = m^*$ and $V(0) = 0$. These observations, together with arguments analogous to those found in the proof of Theorem 1, yield the following result.

Proposition 3.1.4. *Let μ, ρ and σ all be greater than zero, then there exists a unique $\bar{\kappa} \geq 0$ such that*

  i) if $\kappa \in [0, \bar{\kappa})$ then equity is issued at date t whenever cash reserves are depleted ($M_t^\pi = 0$). In this case the optimal strategy is $\pi^* = (m_\kappa^*, L^*)$, where m_κ^* solves Equation (3.1.4) and $L^* = \{L_t^*, t \geq 0\}$ is the local time of $M^* = \{M_t^*, t \geq 0\}$ at level m_κ^*;

  ii) if $\kappa > \bar{\kappa}$ then $\frac{\mu}{r} - \kappa < m^*$, new equity is never issued, and we revert to the base liquidity-management model where $V(0) = 0$ and $m_\kappa^* = m^*$.

In the absence of frictions, i.e. when $\kappa = 0$, the first-best is attainable. In this case $m^* = 0$; thus, the firm does not keep any cash reserves and the dividend policy becomes irrelevant. Namely, cashflows, whether positive or negative, are absorbed by shareholders (dividends or new equity issuance). In this case

$$V(m) = V_{\text{fb}}(m) = m + \frac{\mu}{\rho}.$$

3.1.4 Stock-price dynamics

Let the process $n = \{n_t, t \geq 0\}$ represent the number of shares outstanding at date $t \geq 0$. By convention $n_0 = 1$. Observe that n_t remains constant between any two consecutive issuance times $\tau_i < \tau_{i+1}$. In the sequel, the process $S = \{S_t, t \geq 0\}$ represents the price per share of the firm's stock, so the firm's market capitalization at each date $t \geq 0$ is $n_t S_t$. This quantity is nothing else than the market value of equity; hence, it satisfies

$$n_t S_t = V(M_t^*), \quad t \geq 0. \tag{3.1.5}$$

Dividends are only distributed when $M_t^* \geq m_\kappa^*$ and new equity is only issued when $M_t^* = 0$; thus, as long as $0 < M_t^* < m_\kappa^*$, we have $dn_t = 0$ and the dynamics of the stock price may be derived from Equation (3.1.5) and the Itô formula:

$$d(n_t S_t) = n_t dS_t + S_t dn_t = n_t dS_t \tag{3.1.6}$$

and

$$dV(M_t^*) = V'(M_t^*)dM_t^* + \frac{\sigma^2}{2}V''(M_t^*)dt. \qquad (3.1.7)$$

Equating the right-hand terms of Expressions (3.1.6) and (3.1.7) and using again Equation (3.1.5) we obtain:

$$\frac{dS_t}{S_t} = \frac{[\mu V'(M_t^*) + (\sigma^2/2)V''(M_t^*)]dt + \sigma V'(M_t^*)dZ_t}{V(M_t^*)}.$$

On $(0, m_\kappa^*)$ it holds that $\rho V = (\sigma^2/2)V'' + \mu V'$; hence

$$\frac{dS_t}{S_t} = \rho dt + \sigma(t, S_t)dZ_t, \qquad (3.1.8)$$

where

$$\sigma(t, S_t) := \sigma \frac{V'(V^{-1}(n_t S_t))}{n_t S_t} = \sigma \frac{V'(M_t^*)}{V(M_t^*)}.$$

Given that V is a concave, increasing function, the mappings $m \mapsto 1/V(m)$ and $m \mapsto V'(m)$ are decreasing; hence, $m \mapsto V'(m)/V(m)$ is also a decreasing mapping. Moreover, Equation (3.1.5) implies that, between two equity issuances, S_t and M_t^* always move in the same direction. Therefore, $s \mapsto \sigma(t, s)$ is a decreasing mapping for all $t \geq 0$. Put differently, the model predicts that the volatility of a stock increases after negative shocks (when S_t decreases), which is a well documented fact since Black (1975). It is also important to point out that, as dividend distribution keeps $M^* \leq m_\kappa^*$, the stochastic volatility $\sigma(t, S_t)$ is bounded below by $\sigma \rho/\mu$. This value coincides with the (constant) volatility of the firm's stock price when financial frictions disappear; thus, financial frictions increase stock-price volatility. Equation (3.1.5) also allows us to compute the ratio $k(\tau_j)$ of new shares to outstanding shares when equity issuance takes place. Indeed, let us consider the j-th issuance time τ_j, then

$$k(\tau_j) = \frac{n_{\tau_j} - n_{\tau_j-}}{n_{\tau_j}} = \frac{V(m_\kappa^*) - V(0)}{V'(m_\kappa^*)} \equiv k.$$

This shows that a constant dilution factor k affects individual share prices each time issuance occurs. Finally, we observe that, because n_t is an increasing process (we assume there are no share buybacks)[8] and dividend distribution keeps $M^* \leq m_\kappa^*$, the stock price in this model is bounded above, a property that is not satisfied in the constant-volatility case.[9]

---

[8] In this simple setup, share buybacks are equivalent to dividend distributions. Thus, without loss of generality, we can assume them away.

[9] Popular wisdom asserts that stock prices, like trees, do not grow to the sky.

To wrap up, the implications of costly issuance of new securities on the stock price of a firm with a fixed size are:

1. Stock prices oscillate between a low value (at which new equity is issued) and a high value (where dividends are distributed).
2. Between the two aforementioned values, volatility decreases with the stock price.

This contrasts with the Black-Scholes model, where the stock price follows a Geometric Brownian Motion: it is not bounded above and has a constant volatility. This corresponds to the limit case of our model when the issuance cost κ goes to zero.

3.2 Proportional issuance cost

The model studied in this section, which is based on Lokka and Zervos (2008), considers a purely proportional equity-issuance cost: injecting \$$x$ of fresh equity requires raising \$$(1+\beta)x$, with $\beta > 0$. The dynamics of liquid reserves remain as in Section 3.1:

$$dM_t^\pi = \mu dt + \sigma dZ_t - dL_t + dJ_t, \quad M_0^\pi = m,$$

where a strategy is a pair $\pi = (L, J)$ and a cumulative issuance process $J = \{J_t, t \geq 0\}$ is any nondecreasing, càdlàg and $\mathcal{F}$-adapted process. Given $\pi \in \mathscr{A}_i$, shareholder value is

$$V^\pi(m) = \mathbb{E}\left[\int_0^{\tau_\pi} e^{-\rho t}\left(dL_t - (1+\beta)dJ_t\right)\Big| M_0^\pi = m\right], \qquad (3.2.1)$$

(compare to the corresponding Expression (3.1.1) in the fixed-cost case), where

$$\tau_\pi := \inf\left\{t \geq 0 | M_{t+}^\pi < 0\right\}.$$

For $m \geq 0$, the value function is then given by

$$V(m) := \max_{\pi \in \mathscr{A}_i} V^\pi(m). \qquad (3.2.2)$$

We conjecture (and prove ex-post) that equity issuance i) only takes place whenever $M_t = 0$; ii) occurs if and only if the cost of issuance is not too high. Specifically, there is a threshold $\overline{\beta} > 0$ such that if $\beta < \overline{\beta}$, then equity is issued. This conjecture follows the same logic we used in Section 3.1. However, the techniques required to prove it differ enough that we provide a dedicated proof (Proposition 3.2.2 below).

3.2.1 The value function with a proportional issuance cost

For the time being we assume $\beta < \overline{\beta}$, which implies $\tau = \infty$. Then, equity is always issued whenever $M_t = 0$ and the value function must satisfy

$$V'(0) = 1 + \beta. \qquad (3.2.3)$$

As the marginal cost of equity issuance is $1 + \beta$, Expression (3.2.3) is simply equating the marginal benefit $(V'(0))$ to the marginal cost of recapitalization. Given that the mapping $m \mapsto V(m)$ is concave, this results in $V'(m) \leq 1 + \beta$ for $m \geq 0$. We have the following result:

Proposition 3.2.1. *The value function defined in Equation (3.2.2) is concave, twice continuously differentiable and it satisfies the following equation for all $m \geq 0$:*

$$\max \left\{ \frac{\sigma^2}{2} V''(m) + \mu V'(m) - \rho V(m),\ 1 - V'(m),\ V'(m) - (1 + \beta) \right\} = 0.$$
$$(3.2.4)$$

As before, there is a target liquidity level m_β^* such that earnings are retained whenever $m \in (0, m_\beta^*)$. Furthermore, in this region no new equity is issued; hence, for $m \in (0, m_\beta^*)$ the value function is given by

$$\rho V(m) = \frac{1}{2} \sigma^2 V''(m) + \mu V'(m). \qquad (3.2.5)$$

3.2.2 Characterizing the optimal dividend-distribution barrier

Just as in the base liquidity-management model, the solution to Equation (3.2.5) that satisfies $V'(m_\beta^*) = 1$ and $V''(m_\beta^*) = 0$ is

$$V(m) = \frac{1}{r_1 r_2} \left(\frac{r_2^2}{r_2 - r_1} e^{r_1 (m - m_\beta^*)} - \frac{r_1^2}{r_2 - r_1} e^{r_2 (m - m_\beta^*)} \right). \qquad (3.2.6)$$

Recall $r_1 < 0 < r_2$ solve the characteristic equation $\rho = (\sigma^2/2) r^2 + \mu r$. Unlike the base liquidity-management model, though, determining m_β^* is done by using the condition $V'(0) = 1 + \beta$:

$$V'(0) = \frac{r_2}{r_2 - r_1} e^{-r_1 m_\beta^*} - \frac{r_1}{r_2 - r_1} e^{-r_2 m_\beta^*} = 1 + \beta. \qquad (3.2.7)$$

In order to see that this equation always has a positive solution for any $\beta > 0$, we define

$$\psi(m) := \frac{r_2}{r_2 - r_1} e^{-r_1 m} - \frac{r_1}{r_2 - r_1} e^{-r_2 m}.$$

Clearly, $\psi(0) = 1$. Moreover, ψ is an increasing function. To see this, we compute

$$\psi'(m) = \frac{r_1 r_2}{r_2 - r_1}\left[e^{-r_2 m} - e^{-r_1 m}\right] > 0, \quad m > 0.$$

The strict inequality is due to the facts that $(r_1 r_2)/(r_2 - r_1) < 0$ and, given that $-r_2 < 0 < -r_1$, then $e^{-r_2 m} - e^{-r_1 m} < 0$ for $m > 0$. Finally, the relation $-r_2 < 0 < -r_1$ also implies that

$$e^{-r_2 m} \to 0 \quad \text{and} \quad e^{-r_1 m} \to \infty \quad \text{as} \quad m \to \infty.$$

This allows us to conclude that $\psi(m) \to \infty$ as $m \to \infty$, which, together with the fact that $\psi(0) = 1$ and the Intermediate Value Theorem, yields the existence of a unique $m_\beta^* > 0$ that solves Equation (3.2.7).

Recall that the analysis of the base liquidity-management model used the assumption that new equity issuance was either impossible or prohibitively costly. Therefore, in order to find the maximal cost $\overline{\beta}$ for which issuance takes place, we must find the solution to

$$\psi(m^*) = 1 + \overline{\beta},$$

where m^* is the target cash level of the base liquidity-management model given in Expression (2.3.4). When this happens, $m^* = m_{\overline{\beta}}^*$, which implies that issuing new equity is no longer optimal. We formalize below the results that we have obtained so far:

Proposition 3.2.2. *For $\mu, \sigma, \rho > 0$ given, there exists $\overline{\beta} > 0$ such that*

    i) new equity is never issued if $\beta > \overline{\beta}$;
    ii) if $\beta \le \overline{\beta}$, equity issuance takes place if and only if $M_t = 0$.

We present in Figure 3.2 the values of m_β^* for $\mu = 0.3, \sigma = 0.5$ and $\rho = 0.15$. We observe that, as expected, $m_0^* = 0$ (the first-best target cash level), and $\overline{\beta} \approx 3.042$.

Remark. *In this setting, it is very simple to see that when β decreases to 0, the value function converges to the first-best function $V_{\mathrm{fb}}(m) = m + \mu/\rho$. Indeed, the boundary condition at zero becomes $V'(0) = 1$, which implies $m_0^* = 0$. Inserting this into Equation (3.2.6) yields $V(0) = \mu/\rho$.*

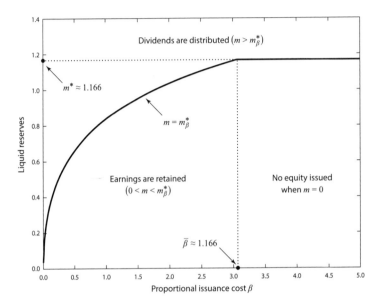

Figure 3.2: The target cash level for different values of β

3.2.3 The optimal equity-issuance strategy when the issuance cost is proportional

We saw in Section 3.1 that the optimal way to issue new equity in the presence of a fixed cost κ was to issue $\$m^*_\kappa$ whenever $M_t = 0$. (see footnote 7). When there is only a proportional cost of equity issuance, the optimal equity-issuance strategy is no longer an impulse control. Instead, it is quite similar to the dividend-distribution strategy. To be more precise, J^* is the local time at level zero of the process M^* determined by the equation

$$dM^*_t = \mu dt + \sigma dZ_t - dL^*_t + dJ^*_t, \quad M^*_0 = m,$$

where $L^* = \{L^*_t, t \geq 0\}$ is, as before, the local time of M^* at level m^*_β. This means that when equity issuance is only subject to proportional costs, the optimal cumulative-distribution strategy induces a reflection at level zero of the liquid-reserves process: infinitesimal amounts of new equity are issued every time that $M_t = 0$.

It may be argued that the equity-issuance strategies, both in the fixed-cost and the proportional-cost settings, are not realistic: in the former, the distressed firm issues new equity and immediately afterward is very likely to distribute dividends; in the latter, the firm avoids liquidation by repeatedly issuing infinitesimally small amounts of equity. Décamps et al. (2011) obtain a more realistic setup by combining both costs, in which case equity is issued in a lumpy way when reserves hit zero, but only up to a level $m_i < m^*$, where $V'(m_i) = 1 + \beta$.

3.3 Uncertain refinancing opportunities

The previous models have the drawback that either equity is never issued (and the firm is liquidated the first time its cash reserves are exhausted) or equity is issued each time that the cash-reserves process hits zero (and the firm is never liquidated). In reality, firms sometimes issue new equity and sometimes they are liquidated. In this section, we present a model that allows for the coexistence of both scenarios. It is based on Hugonnier et al. (2015). We assume that the manager is never certain of finding investors willing to purchase new equity. Thus, for precautionary reasons, he will try to inject fresh equity into the firm before it runs out of cash. If this is not possible due to unavailability of investors, the firm could ultimately be liquidated even if the issuance cost is small.

3.3.1 The cash-reserves dynamics with uncertain refinancing

In order to formalize our notion of UNCERTAIN REFINANCING OPPOR-TUNITIES, let $N = \{N_t, t \geq 0\}$ be a Poisson process with intensity λ that is independent of the Brownian motion Z. We assume that each arrival of N corresponds to availability of investors; hence, the larger λ is, the likelier it is to fulfill the firm's refinancing needs (the probability of an arrival of N over an interval $[t, t + dt]$ equals λdt). Whenever investors become available, the manager chooses the amount $f(m)$ to issue as a function of the current level m of liquid reserves. We show below that $f(m)$ is zero for m large enough: firms only issue equity when their cash reserves are relatively low.[10] The set of admissible strategies consists of pairs of the form (L, f), where L is the cumulative-dividend process. The cash-reserves process corresponding to a strategy $\pi = (L, f)$ satisfies

$$dM_t^\pi = \mu dt + \sigma dZ_t - dL_t + f(M_t)dN_t, \quad M_0 = m.$$

Observe that, in contrast with the case of certain refinancing opportunities of Section 3.1, we have written $f(M_t)dN_t$ instead of dJ_t for

---

[10]Recall that we are not considering the case where the manager may invest some of the firm's reserves to expand the business; thus, equity is only issued to avoid liquidation. When investment in the firm is possible, the issuance strategies are substantially different (see, e.g. Section 2.2 in Hugonnier et al. (2015)).

the increment in liquid reserves brought along by equity issuance. This makes it explicit that the sequence of stopping times $\{\tau_i\}$ when equity is issued is a subset of the set of times when the process N jumps, which correspond to the presence of potential investors. In other words, issuance takes place at $\sigma(Z,N)-$ stopping times. Below we characterize the optimal issuance function f and study how its choice impacts shareholder value. Notice that if $\lambda = 0$, then refinancing is impossible and we revert to the base liquidity-management model.

3.3.2 The amount of uncertain refinancing

As in Section 3.1, we assume that, whenever investors are found and equity is issued, a fixed issuance cost κ must be incurred. If $\lambda = \infty$, then refinancing is always possible and we go back to the setting of Section 3.1. If instead $0 < \lambda < \infty$, the manager must decide, upon each arrival of prospective investors, whether or not to issue new equity. Intuitively, if such an arrival takes place when the level of liquid reserves is low, then the refinancing opportunity is taken. Otherwise, the firm would be exposed to a high risk of liquidation before the next chance to issue equity came around. In contrast, the presence of a fixed issuance cost implies that issuance never takes place at high levels of liquid reserves.

In order to determine whether it is desirable to issue equity when the cash reserves are m,[11] we define the surplus generated by an inflow of cash when the current level of liquid reserves is m as

$$SV(m) := \max_{f \geq 0} \Big\{ \underbrace{V(m+f) - V(m)}_{\text{increment in firm value}} - \underbrace{(f+\kappa)}_{\text{investment and cost}} \Big\}.$$

Let us denote by $\eta := (\kappa, \lambda)$ the vector of parameters that determines the firm's optimal financial policy. From the results in Section 3.1 we know that, due to the absence of proportional costs, optimal equity issues bring the firm's liquidity to the target cash level m_η^*.[12] Recall that if $\lambda = \infty$ and κ is small enough, then optimal equity issuance only happens when the firm's liquid reserves are depleted. Now, however, equity is only issued if i) investors are available and ii) $SV(m) \geq 0$.

---

[11]We write "desirable" to stress the fact that equity issuance may not occur: investors must be available for equity issues to indeed take place

[12]To see this, compute the first-order condition of the problem

$$\max_{f \geq 0} \Big\{ V(m+f) - V(m) - f - \kappa \Big\}.$$

The latter yields the following necessary condition for new equity issuance:

$$\mathcal{S}V(m) = V(m_\eta^*) - V(m) - (m_\eta^* - m) - \kappa \geq 0.$$

We show in Section 3.3.3 that $V(m_\eta^*) = \mu/\rho$. Moreover, as the processes Z and N are independent, there is a zero probability that a refinancing opportunity arises exactly when the liquid reserves run out (i.e. when $m = 0$). Therefore, we have that $V(0) = 0$ and equity issuance is desirable when $m = 0$ only if

$$\mu/\rho - m_\eta^* - \kappa > 0. \tag{3.3.1}$$

In the following we assume that κ is such that Expression (3.3.1) holds. Notice that

$$\mathcal{S}V(m_\eta^*) = -\kappa < 0.$$

In other words, equity issuance is never desirable when reserves are at the target cash level. Given that

$$\mathcal{S}V'(m) = -V'(m) + 1 \leq 0,$$

we have that the surplus $\mathcal{S}V$ is a decreasing function of m. Therefore, the Intermediate Value Theorem guarantees the existence of a unique $\overline{m}_\eta < m_\eta^*$, which we call the UPPER REFINANCING LIMIT, such that $\mathcal{S}V(\overline{m}_\eta) = 0$. Given that the mapping $m \mapsto \mathcal{S}V(m)$ is decreasing, we have that

$$\mathcal{S}V(m) \geq 0 \quad \text{if and only if} \quad m \in [0, \overline{m}_\eta].$$

Put differently, if equity issuance is desirable when reserves are zero, then there exists $\overline{m}_\eta > 0$ such that an arrival of investors is followed by equity issuance to the amount $m_\eta^* - m$ only if $m \leq \overline{m}_\eta$. This condition is also sufficient: issuing equity when $m = \overline{m}_\eta$ generates a nonnegative surplus but, given that equity issuance is uncertain, postponing an issuance may result in liquidation. Therefore, it is optimal to choose

$$f(m) = \begin{cases} m_\eta^* - m & \text{if } m \leq \overline{m}_\eta; \\ 0 & \text{otherwise.} \end{cases} \tag{3.3.2}$$

In this case we say that equity issuance follows a THRESHOLD STRATEGY and that equity is issued preemptively, in the sense that the firm may issue equity before it has run out of cash reserves. Interestingly, even when $\kappa = 0$ we do not recover the first-best solution. This is because the uncertainty of finding prospective investors is an indirect cost. In that case $\overline{m}_\eta = m_\eta^*$ (equity is always issued after an arrival of investors) and the solution to the manager's problem is equivalent to the solution of the base liquidity-management model, but with a larger discount rate $\rho + \lambda$ (see Equation (3.3.3a) below).

3.3.3 The refinancing region and the target cash level

The Hamilton-Jacobi-Bellman equation has some new components: first, we have to account for the issuance region; second, on the latter we must include the JUMP TERM λSV that takes into account the probability that investors arrive (λ) as well as the surplus earned if that happens (SV). We have that the value function solves the following boundary-value problem:

$$\rho V(m) = \begin{cases} \dfrac{\sigma^2}{2} V''(m) + \mu V'(m) + \lambda SV(m), & m \in (0, \overline{m}_\eta); \quad (3.3.3a) \\[2mm] \dfrac{\sigma^2}{2} V''(m) + \mu V'(m), & m \in (\overline{m}_\eta, m_\eta^*), \quad (3.3.3b) \end{cases}$$

together with

$$\underbrace{V(0) = 0, \ V'(m_\eta^*) = 1}_{\text{boundary conditions}} \quad \text{and} \quad \underbrace{V(\overline{m}_{\eta-}) = V(\overline{m}_{\eta+})}_{\text{VALUE-MATCHING CONDITION}}.$$

Observe that now we have to determine **two** free boundaries: $\overline{m}_\eta$ and m_η^*. As before, the optimal target cash level m_η^* has to satisfy the super-contact condition $V''(m_\eta^*) = 0$. However, now m_η^* has to be chosen together with the upper refinancing limit $\overline{m}_\eta$ so as to satisfy the SMOOTH-PASTING CONDITION

$$V'(\overline{m}_{\eta-}) = V'(\overline{m}_{\eta+}).$$

Recall that $SV(\overline{m}_\eta) = 0$, therefore the value-matching and smooth-pasting conditions at $\overline{m}_\eta$ guarantee that $V''(\overline{m}_{\eta-}) = V''(\overline{m}_{\eta+})$.

It is not possible to find a closed-form solution to the piecewise-defined ordinary differential equation (3.3.3a)–(3.3.3b). However, we can obtain a quasi-explicit solution that allows for numerical approximations. We provide a sketch of how this is done in Appendix A.3. We present in Figure 3.3(a) the value function with parameters: $\kappa = 0.5$, $\lambda = 1, \mu = 0.7, \rho = 0.5$ and $\sigma = 0.5$. The upper-refinancing limit is $\overline{m}_\eta \approx 0.24$, whereas the dividend-distribution barrier is $m_\eta^* \approx 0.99$. Figure 3.3(b) shows, using the same parameter values (except λ) how $\overline{m}_\eta$ decreases as λ grows. When investors are available more frequently, the need for preemptive equity issuance decreases.

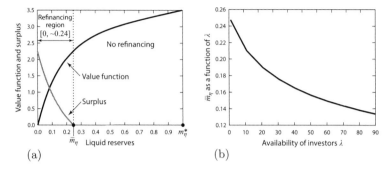

Figure 3.3: The refinancing region for $\lambda = 1$ and $\overline{m}_\eta$ for $\lambda \in (1, 90)$. (a) The value function and the refinancing surplus as a function of liquid reserves. (b) The upper refinancing limit $\underline{m}_\eta$ as a function of the availability of investors.

3.4 Further reading

Scheer and Schmidli (2011) study the equivalent to the fixed issuance-costs model presented in Section 3.1 when net earnings are modeled using the so-called CLASSICAL RISK MODEL. This means that instead of a Brownian motion, the stochastic driver is a compound Poisson process. Such modeling choice is common in the insurance literature. The authors go beyond the voluntary-recapitalization setting that we have used and instead assume that equity issuance must take place if the firm's reserves become negative. It is worth mentioning that with only Poisson risk, the visitation and crossing times of zero no longer coincide; thus, recapitalization only happens if liquidity is strictly negative. The authors consider both proportional and fixed reinvestment costs. They show that the Hamilton-Jacobi-Bellman equation has an integro-differential form. In contrast with our Brownian setting, the optimal dividend strategy is of BAND TYPE. That is, as long as the cash reserves stay within a certain interval, dividends are paid out at a continuous rate. By virtue of the fixed-costs component, reinjections of cash are lumpy and exceed the shortfall under zero.

Anderson and Carverhill (2012) use a generalized Arithmetic Brownian Motion, where the drift follows a mean-reverting process, to study the dividend and equity issuance policies (with proportional cost) of a firm that is financed using short- and long-term debt and equity. The structure of the drift is a proxy for the business cycle. The firm is allowed to have negative cash reserves, which means that its bank provides a credit line up to a maximal amount called the default level. The latter corresponds to the value of the firm's collateral, i.e. the liquidation value of its assets; thus, the default level depends on the current level of the drift. Besides the default level, expected profitability impacts the target level of cash reserves (they move in opposite directions). The authors show that high levels of long-term debt result in firms that hold more liquid reserves and use less short-term debt funding.

Akyildirim et al. (2014) add a significant twist to the model presented in Section 3.1. Namely they assume that interest rates and (fixed) issuance costs are governed by an exogenous Markov chain, which in their model corresponds to macroeconomic shocks. They show that these two aggregate factors have opposing effects: all things being equal, firms distribute more dividends when interest rates are high and less when issuing costs are high. Anticipating higher issuance costs in the future, the manager may decide to recapitalize the firm at strictly positive levels of liquid reserves when issuance costs are low.

4 Applications to Banking

THIS CHAPTER USES our base model in order to develop a theory of liquidity and risk management in the banking sector. Given that banks essentially finance themselves by short-term deposits from the public and grant loans that are typically long term, liquidity and risk management are crucial for them. The first section showcases one of the first applications of the base model of Chapter 2 to banking. It is drawn from Milne and Whalley (2001) and studies the impact of capital regulation on banks' decisions to retain earnings or distribute dividends. The second section is based on Rochet and Villeneuve (2005). It looks at a portfolio-management problem à la Merton (1969), where the bank's manager decides on how much the bank invests in risky loans and securities, as well as on the dividend payouts to shareholders. In this model, the volume of bank deposits is fixed. In the third section, we present a model, based on Klimenko and Moreno-Bromberg (2016), that takes assets as given and focuses on the liability side, in which the question of optimal bank funding is addressed.

4.1 A simple continuous-time model of a bank

This section is based on Milne and Whalley (2001), who were among the first to adapt the base liquidity-management model to study the liquidity decisions of a bank. We present a simple model of a bank that operates under minimum capital requirements imposed by a regulator.

4.1.1 The model

Consider a bank that has a fixed volume D of (insured) retail deposits and a fixed volume A of risky assets (say, loans) that generate i.i.d. cashflows

$$\mu dt + \sigma dZ_t,$$

where $\mu, \sigma > 0$ and, as before, $Z = \{Z_t, t \geq 0\}$ is a standard Brownian motion. The balance sheet of the bank at date t is

assets	liabilities
M_t	D
A	E_t

The structure of this balance sheet implies that $E_t = M_t + A - D$. The BOOK VALUE E_t of the bank equity then varies one-to-one with the volume of cash reserves M_t. We assume, for simplicity, that neither cash reserves nor deposits are remunerated; thus, the dynamics of cash reserves are

$$dM_t^L = \mu dt + \sigma dZ_t - dL_t, \quad M_0 = m, \qquad (4.1.1)$$

where, as before, $L = \{L_t, t \geq 0\}$ is the non-decreasing process of cumulative dividends paid out to shareholders.

There is a DEPOSIT INSURANCE SYSTEM that reimburses depositors in full in case the bank is liquidated and collects the liquidation proceeds. A typical situation is when $A > D$, in which case the bank is still solvent ($E_t > 0$) when it runs out of cash ($M_t = 0$). We study this case but assume that if $M_t < 0$, the bank cannot issue new equity or deposits, which forces it to liquidate its assets hastily for a price lower than the fundamental value of these assets. This is commonly referred to as a FIRE SALE of assets. We model fire-sale losses via the parameter $\alpha \in [0, 1)$, where $\alpha A < D$ represents the proceeds of liquidating the bank's assets at a fire-sale price. In this case, the bank cannot pay back the retail deposits in full. The Deposit Insurance System that has to provide the shortfall $D - \alpha A$. In order to avoid this, the regulator may impose a MINIMUM-CAPITAL REQUIREMENT $\underline{e}$,[1] as we show below.

4.1.2 The impact of a minimum-capital requirement

We assume that the bank operates under minimum-capital regulation, i.e. the first time τ such that $E_\tau \leq \underline{e}$ the regulator forces liquidation.[2] The threshold $\underline{e}$ is designed in such a way that the liquidation of the bank results in no cost to the Deposit Insurance System:

$$\underline{e} = A(1 - \alpha).$$

---

[1] In practice, minimum-capital requirements are proportional to the size of the bank's assets A (possibly weighted according to risk). Here A is fixed, hence the minimum-capital requirement $\underline{e}$ is also fixed.

[2] In practice, however, there is often a long delay between the first time the regulation is violated and the liquidation time.

This means that the bank's equity is sufficient to cover losses due to liquidation. Observe that this condition is equivalent to imposing a minimum-liquidity threshold

$$\underline{m} := D - \alpha A.$$

The shareholder value function under regulation is

$$V(m) = \sup_{L \in \mathcal{A}} \mathbb{E}\left[\int_0^{\tau_L} e^{-\rho t} dL_t \Big| M_0 = m\right],$$

where $\mathcal{A}$ is the set of all $\mathcal{F}$-adapted, nondecreasing and nonnegative processes and

$$\tau_L := \inf\{t > 0 | M_t^L < \underline{m}\}.$$

The state variable M evolves according to Expression (4.1.1). It is simple to see that, as in the base model, the optimal strategy for the bank is to retain all earnings until its cash reserves reach some threshold m_r^* (where the subindex "r" refers to regulation), the target cash level under regulation. On the interval $(\underline{m}, m_r^*)$, the value function satisfies the Hamilton-Jacobi-Bellman equation

$$\rho V(m) = \frac{\sigma^2}{2} V''(m) + \mu V'(m),$$

just as in Chapter 2. The boundary conditions are

$$V(\underline{m}) = 0 \quad \text{and} \quad V'(m_r^*) = 1$$

and the supercontact condition $V''(m_r^*) = 0$ characterizes the optimal dividend-distribution threshold. Given that μ, σ and ρ are constant, it is not complicated to see (we leave it as an exercise) that V is obtained by a simple shift to the right of the value function $\mathbf{V}$ of the base liquidity-management model, where there is no regulation:

$$V(m) = \mathbf{V}(m - \underline{m}).$$

In particular,

$$m_r^* = m^* + \underline{m},$$

where m^* is the target cash level in the absence of regulation. This immediately implies that the franchise value of the bank (shareholder value at the target cash level) remains unchanged under a minimum-capital (or equivalently liquidity) requirement:

$$V(m_r^*) = \mathbf{V}(m^*) = \frac{\mu}{\rho}.$$

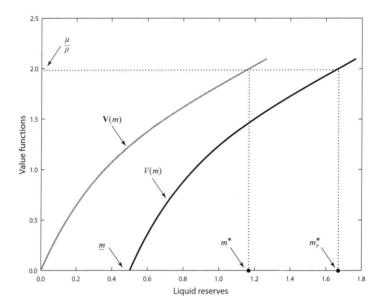

Figure 4.1: The value function and the first best

Figure 4.1 presents the plots for $\mathbf{V}$ and V, as well as the corresponding target cash levels, for $\mu = 0.3, \sigma = 0.5, \rho = 0.15$ and $\underline{m} = 0.5$.

In this section, we have assumed that the bank is liquidated as soon as it fails the minimum-liquidity requirement. In the following section we allow shareholders to recapitalize the bank in order to avoid liquidation.

4.1.3 A minimum-capital requirement with recapitalization

As in Section 3.1, we assume for simplicity that recapitalization entails only a fixed cost κ. Mimicking Section 3.1.2, we have that the amount ΔM of fresh equity injected by the new shareholders when $M_t = \underline{m}$ is chosen so as to maximize the net increase in shareholder value:

$$\max_{\Delta M} V(\underline{m} + \Delta M) - V(\underline{m}) - \Delta M - \kappa.$$

The first-order condition for this problem is

$$V'(\underline{m} + \Delta M) = 1,$$

which implies that

$$\Delta M = m_r^{**} - \underline{m},$$

where m_r^{**} denotes the (new) dividend threshold also characterized by $V'(m_r^{**}) = 1$. The Hamilton-Jacobi-Bellman equation that characterizes the value function remains unchanged

$$\rho V(m) = \frac{\sigma^2}{2} V''(m) + \mu V'(m),$$

but the boundary conditions are now

$$V(\underline{m}) = V(m_r^{**}) - (m_r^{**} - \underline{m}) - \kappa \quad \text{and} \quad V'(m_r^{**}) = 1.$$

From the super-contact condition $V''(m_r^{**}) = 0$ we have once more

$$V(m) = \frac{1}{r_1 r_2}\left(\frac{r_2^2}{r_2 - r_1} e^{r_1(m - m_r^{**})} - \frac{r_1^2}{r_2 - r_1} e^{r_2(m - m_r^{**})}\right), \quad (4.1.2)$$

where $r_1 < 0 < r_2$ solve the characteristic equation $\rho = (\sigma^2/2)r^2 + \mu r$. In contrast with Section 3.1.2, however, m_r^{**} is now found solving[3]

$$\phi_r(m_r^{**}) = \frac{\mu}{\rho} - (m_r^{**} - \underline{m}) - \kappa, \quad (4.1.3)$$

where

$$\phi_r(m) := \frac{r_2}{r_1(r_2 - r_1)} e^{r_1(\underline{m} - m)} + \frac{r_1}{r_2(r_2 - r_1)} e^{r_2(\underline{m} - m)}.$$

Notice that, in writing Equation (4.1.3), we have used the fact that, from Expression (4.1.2), $V(m_r^{**}) = \mu/\rho$. To see that the translation property of Section 4.1.2 still holds, set

$$m_r^{**} = m_\kappa^* + \underline{m},$$

where m_κ^* is the dividend threshold of the unregulated case with equity issuance, and insert this in Expression (4.1.3) to obtain $\phi(m_\kappa^*) = \mu/\rho - m_\kappa^* - \kappa$, which is true by definition of m_κ^*.

4.2 A bank's portfolio problem

The model presented in this section (drawn from Rochet and Villeneuve (2005)) shares many mathematical features with the models presented in Chapter 3. The focus, however, switches from liquidity

---

[3]Recall that in the unregulated case with equity issuance, m_κ^* was found solving

$$\phi(m) = \frac{r_2}{r_1(r_2 - r_1)} e^{-r_1 m} + \frac{r_1}{r_2(r_2 - r_1)} e^{-r_2 m} = \frac{\mu}{\rho} - m - \kappa.$$

management in a firm with fixed expected profitability to a portfolio-decision problem *à la Merton* (see Merton (1969)) from the point of view of a bank. More specifically, we study the optimal investment decisions of the manager of a bank whose balance sheet at date t is the following:

assets	liabilities
M_t	D
A_t	E_t

D represents the volume of retail deposits that the bank has collected, which are remunerated at the constant risk-free rate $r > 0$. M_t is the level of cash reserves in the bank, which also earn interest r. We show below that in this model the bank never defaults. This implies that deposits are riskless; thus, there is no default spread. E_t is the book value of equity that plays the role of the sole state variable (instead of the reserves level, as in the previous sections). In contrast to the model in Section 4.1, the bank's portfolio of risky assets (say, loans) does not have a fixed size. In the case at hand, A_t represents the amount invested in risky assets, which return

$$\mu dt + \sigma dZ_t$$

per unit of investment. As soon as $E_t < 0$, the bank is liquidated at no cost, and D is repaid to depositors. Shareholders walk away empty-handed in the event of bankruptcy. Financial frictions are once again captured by the fact that no additional debt or equity may be issued. Therefore, the bank's investment strategies must be self-financing.

4.2.1 Setting up the stochastic-control problem

As in the previous chapters, the bank's manager decides on the cumulative dividend-distribution process $L = \{L_t, t \geq 0\}$. Here, however, he must also choose the ASSET STRATEGY $A = \{A_t, t \geq 0\}$. The bank's asset portfolio may be continuously rebalanced at no cost. The values A_t and M_t are not allowed to be negative (no short positions), which implies that at every date $t \geq 0$ the relation $A_t \in [0, E_t + D]$ must hold. The book value of equity evolves according to the following stochastic differential equation:

$$dE_t = \underbrace{A_t(\mu dt + \sigma dZ_t)}_{\text{cashflows from risky asset}} + \underbrace{r(M_t - D)dt}_{\text{net interest revenue}} - \underbrace{dL_t}_{\text{dividends}} , \quad E_0 = \epsilon.$$

Using the BALANCE-SHEET EQUATION $E_t + D = A_t + M_t$ we may rewrite dE_t as

$$dE_t = A_t(\mu dt + \sigma dZ_t) + r(E_t - A_t)dt - dL_t, \quad E_0 = \epsilon. \quad (4.2.1)$$

We define the bankruptcy time as

$$\tau := \inf\{t \geq 0 \mid E_t \leq 0\}$$

and we show below that the optimal financial decisions result in $\tau = \infty$. The set of all admissible strategies is

$$\mathscr{A} := \{(A, L)|(A_t, L_t) \in \mathcal{F}_t, dL_t \geq 0 \text{ and } 0 \leq A_t \leq E_t + D \text{ for all } t \geq 0\}.$$

The manager's problem is to maximize shareholder value:

$$V(\epsilon) = \max_{(A,L)\in\mathscr{A}} \mathbb{E}\left[\int_0^\tau e^{-\rho t}dL_t\Big|E_0 = \epsilon\right].$$

Here ρ is the shareholders' discount rate, which we assume satisfies $\rho > \mu$. The evolution of the state variable is as in Expression (4.2.1).

Observation. *If the shareholders discounted the future at a rate smaller than μ, then the manager's problem would lack a well-defined solution. To see this, choose $\delta \in (0, \mu - \rho)$ and set*

$$L_t = \int_0^t \delta E_t dt, \quad A_t = E_t.$$

This would result in

$$dE_t = E_t((\mu - \delta)dt + \sigma dZ_t),$$

a Geometric Brownian Motion that never reaches zero in finite time, and

$$V(\epsilon) \geq \delta\epsilon \int_0^\infty e^{(\mu-\rho-\delta)t}dt = \infty.$$

4.2.2 The value function and the first-best

An additional assumption on the model's parameters is that μ must be strictly greater than r. This implies that, in the absence of retail-deposit financing, shareholders would prefer to consume immediately instead of investing in the risky asset. Being leveraged, however, allows the shareholders to make a profit. In particular, if we were to disregard the restriction that $t \mapsto L_t$ must be nondecreasing, then we could parallel Section 3.1.2 and obtain the first-best outcome as follows: distribute all equity e as an exceptional dividend; hold no cash reserves ($M_t \equiv 0$); set $A_t \equiv D$; offset profits/losses via payments to/from the shareholders. The resulting value function would be

$$V_{\mathrm{fb}}(\epsilon) = \epsilon + \frac{\mu - r}{\rho} D.$$

Notice that in this first-best situation, there is again no need for cash reserves, but the second term is now the expected present value of investing D in the risky technology. The term $\mu - r$ is the net expected margin on assets, once interest payments to depositors have been deducted.

When L is restricted to be nondecreasing (no new issues of equity), the value function is again concave and twice continuously differentiable. As before, there is a dividend-distribution barrier ϵ_1^* that coincides with the point where the marginal value of equity first equals one. In the current setup, though, the structure of the value function on $[0, \epsilon_1^*]$ also takes into account the asset strategies for different levels of equity value. In order to study this, let us define the operator

$$\mathcal{L}(A)V(\epsilon) := -\rho V(\epsilon) + V'(\epsilon)\left(r\epsilon + A(\mu - r)\right) + \frac{\sigma^2 A^2}{2} V''(\epsilon).$$

The Hamilton-Jacobi-Bellman variational inequality is now

$$\max\left\{ \max_{0 \le A \le \epsilon + D} \mathcal{L}(A)V(\epsilon),\, 1 - V'(\epsilon) \right\} = 0. \qquad (4.2.2)$$

As before it is precisely at ϵ_1^* where the inequality $1 \ge V'(\epsilon)$ becomes binding. This fully characterizes the cumulative dividend process. Now, however, the manager is active on $(0, \epsilon_1^*)$, where he must rebalance the bank's asset portfolio. This amounts precisely to the maximization problem

$$\max_{A \in [0, \epsilon + D]} \mathcal{L}(A)V(\epsilon), \quad \epsilon \in (0, \epsilon_1^*). \qquad (4.2.3)$$

We have that, in general, there is an intermediate level $\epsilon_0^* < \epsilon_1^*$ such that the maximization problem (4.2.3) has an interior solution (and $V' > 1$) for all $\epsilon \in (0, \epsilon_0^*)$. In particular, this implies that if the level of equity is small enough, then $A_t < E_t + D$, which in turn means that $M_t > 0$. In other words, for low levels of capitalization, the bank holds a positive level of reserves as a precautionary measure. On $(0, \epsilon_0^*)$ we may find A^* using the first-order condition

$$\frac{\partial}{\partial A} \mathcal{L}(A)V(\epsilon) = 0,$$

which yields

$$A^*(\epsilon) = \frac{\mu - r}{\sigma^2}\left(-\frac{V'(\epsilon)}{V''(\epsilon)}\right). \qquad (4.2.4)$$

This formula is similar to the one obtained in Merton (1969) but here the bank's risk tolerance, namely $-V'(\epsilon)/V''(\epsilon)$, is endogenous. By contrast the investor's risk tolerance in Merton (1969) is exogenous.

Lemma 4.2.1. *The general solution to the differential equation*

$$\mathcal{L}(A^*(\epsilon))V(\epsilon) = -\rho V(\epsilon) + r\epsilon V'(\epsilon) - \frac{1}{2}\left(\frac{\mu - r}{\sigma}\right)^2\frac{(V'(\epsilon))^2}{V''(\epsilon)} = 0,$$

with boundary condition $V(0) = 0$, is

$$V(\epsilon) = K\epsilon^\alpha, \qquad (4.2.5)$$

where $K > 0$ and $\alpha \in (0,1)$ is the smallest solution to

$$r\alpha^2 - \left(r + \rho + \frac{1}{2}(\frac{\mu - r}{\sigma})^2\right)\alpha + \rho = 0.$$

Proof. See Appendix A.4.

Inserting Function (4.2.5) in Expression (4.2.4) we obtain

$$A^*(\epsilon) = \left(\frac{\mu - r}{\sigma^2}\right)\frac{\epsilon}{1 - \alpha} =: \frac{\epsilon}{k}.$$

Observation. *Since $dL_t = 0$ whenever $E_t < \epsilon_1^*$, if we substitute $A^*(E_t)$ into dE_t we obtain that on $(0, \epsilon_0^*)$ the value of equity evolves according to*

$$dE_t = \frac{E_t}{k}\Big[(\mu + r(k - 1))dt + \sigma dZ_t\Big].$$

The factor $\mu + r(k - 1)$ is strictly positive, as $\mu > r$; thus, in this "distress" region E_t evolves like a geometric Brownian motion. This implies that the bank never goes bankrupt. In terms of the value function, this is reflected by the fact that, since $\alpha < 1$, $V'(0) = \infty$.

Lemma 4.2.2. *When $\epsilon \in (0, \epsilon_0^*)$ the bank maintains a constant equity-to-assets (or capital) ratio $\epsilon/A^*(\epsilon) = k$ that is smaller than one.*

Proof. See Appendix A.4.

From Lemma 4.2.2 we have that on $(0, \epsilon_0^*)$ the manager's optimal strategy is to invest a multiple of the bank's equity in the risky technology. Moreover, ϵ_0^* can be computed by solving $\epsilon_0^*/k = \epsilon_0^* + D$, which yields

$$\epsilon_0^* = \frac{kD}{1-k}.$$

For all $e \in (\epsilon_0^*, \epsilon_1^*)$ the maximization problem

$$\max_{A \in [0, \epsilon + D]} L(A)V(\epsilon)$$

has the corner solution $A^*(\epsilon) = \epsilon + D$. This is similar to the scenario presented in Section 2.1 in the sense that the portfolio weight on the risky asset is maximal. On $(\epsilon_0^*, \epsilon_1^*)$ we have to solve

$$\rho V(\epsilon) = \big(\mu \epsilon + (\mu - r)D\big)V'(\epsilon) + \frac{\sigma^2}{2}(\epsilon + D)^2 V''(\epsilon),$$

with boundary conditions $V'(\epsilon_1^*) = 1$ and $V''(\epsilon_1^*) = 0$, and the choice of ϵ_1^* must be such that the resulting solution pastes in $\mathcal{C}^2$ fashion at ϵ_0^*. First we require the following auxiliary result:

Lemma 4.2.3. *For all* $e \in \mathbb{R}_+$ *there exists a unique function* $V(\cdot; e) \in \mathcal{C}^2$ *(parametrized by* e*) that solves*

$$\rho V(\epsilon; e) = \big(\mu \epsilon + (\mu - r)D\big)V'(\epsilon; e) + \frac{\sigma^2}{2}(\epsilon + D)^2 V''(\epsilon; e),$$

with boundary conditions $V'(e; e) = 1$ *and* $V''(e; e) = 0$.

Proof. See Appendix A.4.

From the conditions $V'(e; e) = 1$ and $V''(e; e) = 0$ we get

$$V(e; e) = \frac{D(\mu - r)}{\rho} + \frac{\mu}{\rho}e.$$

This determines the value function on $[\epsilon_1^*, \infty)$, and we have the following result:

Proposition 4.2.4. *There exists a unique* ϵ_1^* *such that the piecewise-defined function*

$$V(\epsilon) := \begin{cases} K\epsilon^\alpha, & \epsilon \in [0, \epsilon_0^*]; \\ V(\epsilon; \epsilon_1^*), & \epsilon \in (\epsilon_0^*, \epsilon_1^*); \\ (\epsilon - \epsilon_1^*) + \frac{D(\mu-r)}{\rho} + \frac{\mu}{\rho}\epsilon_1^*, & \epsilon \in [\epsilon_1^*, \infty), \end{cases} \quad (4.2.6)$$

is twice continuously differentiable and corresponds to the shareholders' value function.

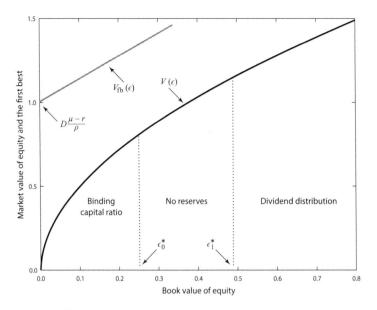

Figure 4.2: The value function and the first best

Proof. See Appendix A.4.

We have established that the optimal investment policy of the bank is

$$A^*(\epsilon) = \min\left\{\frac{\epsilon}{k}, \epsilon + D\right\},$$

i.e, invest a multiple $1/k$ of the bank's equity E_t into risky assets, up to when this exhausts cash reserves. k can be interpreted as a minimum capital ratio

$$\frac{\text{equity}}{\text{assets}}$$

chosen by the shareholders. It is reminiscent of regulatory capital requirements, but here it is purely the result of market discipline imposed by shareholders.

Proposition 4.2.5. *Ceteris paribus, the minimum capital ratio*

$$k = \frac{(1-\alpha)\sigma^2}{\mu - r}$$

optimally chosen by the bank satisfies the following properties:
  i) it decreases with the cost of capital $(\rho - r)$;
  ii) it increases with the volatility of assets σ and

iii) it is single peaked with respect to the expected excess return on assets ($\mu - r$).

Proof. See Appendix A.4.

In the region where its investment policy is not constrained, the bank behaves like a Von Neumann-Morgenstern investor with constant relative risk aversion (CRRA) $1 - \alpha$.

Proposition 4.2.6. *Ceteris paribus, the risk aversion coefficient* $1-\alpha$ *of the bank satisfies the following properties:*
 i) it decreases with the cost of capital ($\rho - r$);
 ii) it decreases with the volatility of assets σ and
 iii) it increases with the expected excess return on assets ($\mu - r$).

Proof. See Appendix A.4.

4.3 Optimal bank funding

We have so far studied the optimal managerial decisions concerning dividend distribution and the structure of the asset portfolio of a deposit-taking bank. In this section, based on Klimenko and Moreno-Bromberg (2016), we present a "dual" model where the bank's assets are given and the focus of attention is on the liability side. This setup is relevant because empirical evidence suggests that the composition of banks' liabilities is richer than a simple mix of equity and insured deposits as assumed in Section 4.2.

4.3.1 The model

A group of equity investors holds a banking license and has to decide on the financing structure of a new bank. The bank's portfolio of risky assets A has a fixed size. A fraction ηA, for $\eta \in (0,1)$ given, corresponds to assets that hold their value in the case of liquidation and can be used as collateral for secured borrowing (e.g. sovereign bonds). We assume all liability holders are risk-neutral and discount the future at rate $\rho > 0$. On the liability side, the bank has obligations toward:

1. Shareholders who earn the dividend flows dL_t and are protected by limited liability.

2. Long-term creditors who hold perpetual debt issued by the bank. It has face value D_l and pays interest at a constant rate r_l, which is determined endogenously.

3. Depositors who are passive: their debt has face value D_d and it accrues interest at a rate r_d, both of which are taken as given. In the case of liquidation, deposits are senior to long-term debt, but junior to short-term debt. We assume that $D_d \geq \eta A$, which implies that long-term debt is risky even if there are no other types of debt.

4. Short-term creditors who hold instantaneously maturing debt. Short-term debt has face value D_s and pays interest at rate r_s. Short-term creditors may decide at any time to stop rolling their debt over, an event that we refer to as a RUN. We assume that short-term debt: i) is fully collateralized, which requires that $D_s \leq \eta A$; ii) is senior to all other types of debt.[4] As a consequence, the interest rate r_s on short-term debt is insensitive to the bank's liquidation risk. We assume $r_s < \rho$, which is interpreted as a LIQUIDITY PREMIUM that short-term creditors are willing to pay in exchange for immediate access to their funds.

The bank's balance sheet at date t is depicted in Figure 4.3.

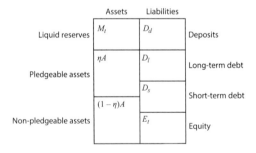

Figure 4.3: The bank's balance sheet

The bank's creditors are subject to exogenous liquidity shocks, whose arrivals are described by a Poisson process $N = \{N_t, t \geq 0\}$ with intensity λ. When hit by a liquidity shock, short-term creditors stop rolling their debt over, but long-term creditors are "locked in." We define the run time as

$$\tau_r := \inf \{t > 0 | N_t = 1\}.$$

After τ_r, the bank (if still in operation) has no short-term debt left on its balance sheet. To account for this in the dynamics of the bank's

---

[4]This feature of short-term debt, commonly known as a SAFE-HARBOR provision, is one of the reasons why short-term debt was widely used in the buildup of the Global Financial Crisis.

liquid reserves, we define the stopped process $\overline{N}$ as $\overline{N}_t = N_t$ for $t \le \tau_r$ and $\overline{N}_t \equiv 1$ for $t > \tau_r$. As in Section 1.4, the bank's revenues are taxed at a fixed rate $\theta \in (0,1)$. For a given structure of debt funding (D_d, D_l, D_s), the bank's after-tax net earnings are

$$dY_t = (1-\theta)[(\mu - r_d D_d - r_l D_l - (1-\overline{N}_t)r_s D_s)dt + \sigma dZ_t], \quad Y_0 = 0.$$

Given a strategy $\pi = (D_s, D_l, L)$, liquid reserves satisfy

$$dM_t^\pi = dY_t - dL_t - D_s d\overline{N}_t, \quad M_0^\pi = m. \tag{4.3.1}$$

The liquidation time corresponding to a strategy π is

$$\tau_\pi := \inf\left\{t > 0 \,|\, M_t^\pi < 0\right\}.$$

Observe that liquidation is triggered by a bank run if the latter occurs when $M^\pi \in [0, D_s)$.

The market value of equity corresponding to a strategy π and an initial level of liquid reserves m is

$$\mathcal{E}^\pi(m) := \mathbb{E}\left[\int_0^{\tau_\pi} e^{-\rho t} dL_t \,\Big|\, M_0^\pi = m\right].$$

Shareholders maximize the market value of their equity, net of their initial investment:

$$\max_{m \ge 0, \pi \in \mathscr{A}} V^\pi(m) := \left\{\mathcal{E}^\pi(m) - (A + m - D_d - D_l - D_s)\right\},$$

where

$$\mathscr{A} := \left\{(D_l, D_s) \,|\, 0 \le D_l, 0 \le D_s < \eta A\right\}.$$

Observe that, in contrast with previous models, the shareholders' maximization problem includes choosing the initial level of liquid reserves m. This is because, as we show below, the level m affects the bank's default risk and, therefore, the interest paid on long-term debt.

The market value of long-term debt under strategy π is the sum of the discounted stream of interest payments until the liquidation:

$$\mathcal{D}^\pi(m) := \mathbb{E}\left[\int_0^{\tau_\pi} e^{-\rho t} r_l D_l dt \,\Big|\, M_0^\pi = m\right].$$

We assume that long-term debt is issued at par in a competitive market with rational investors. In other words, r_l must be such that, at date $t = 0$, the face and market values of long-term debt coincide:

$$\mathcal{D}^\pi(m) = D_l. \tag{4.3.2}$$

It is via Expression (4.3.2) that the endogenous value of r_l is determined.

4.3.2 The optimal funding strategies

Shareholders form rational expectations about the value of equity **after** the run has occurred when they make their funding decisions at date $t = 0$. When computing the post-run value of equity, they take D_l and r_l as given and liquid reserves evolve, given a dividend policy L, according to

$$dM_t = (1 - \theta)[(\mu - f_0)dt + \sigma dZ_t] - dL_t, \quad M_0 = m, \qquad (4.3.3)$$

where $f_0 := r_d D_d + r_l D_l$. For an initial liquidity level m, the post-run value of equity is

$$\mathcal{E}_0(m) = \max_L \mathbb{E}\left[\int_0^\tau e^{-\rho t} dL_t \,\Big|\, M_0 = m\right],$$

with the liquid reserves evolving according to Expression (4.3.3) and

$$\tau := \inf\{t \geq 0 | M_t < 0\}.$$

This is precisely the setup of the base liquidity-management model, with $(1 - \theta)(\mu - f_0)$ being the drift and $(1 - \theta)\sigma$ the volatility of the net-earnings process. Therefore, we know there is a target liquidity level $m_0^*(D_l)$ such that $\mathcal{E}_0$ satisfies

$$\rho \mathcal{E}_0(m) = (1 - \theta)(\mu - f_0)\mathcal{E}_0'(m) + (1 - \theta)^2 \frac{\sigma^2}{2} \mathcal{E}_0''(m)$$

for $c \in \big(0, m_0^*(D_l)\big)$, together with the boundary conditions

$$\mathcal{E}_0(0) = 0 \quad \text{and} \quad \mathcal{E}_0'\big(m_0^*(D_l)\big) = 1.$$

The target cash level is again determined by the supercontact condition $\mathcal{E}_0''\big(m_0^*(D_l)\big) = 0$. As we saw in Section 2.3.3, the magnitude of the drift in the cash-reserves process affects the value of the dividend-distribution barrier, which is why the choice of D_l impacts $m_0^*(D_l)$.

Using the valuation equation of Chapter 1, we have that the post-run value of long-term debt $\mathcal{D}_0$ satisfies

$$\rho \mathcal{D}_0(m) = (1 - \theta)^2 \frac{\sigma^2}{2} \mathcal{D}_0''(m) + (1 - \theta)(\mu - f_0)\mathcal{D}_0'(m) + r_l D_l$$

for $m \in (0, m_0^*(D_l))$, where $r_l D_l$ is the flow of interest payments. The boundary conditions are

$$\mathcal{D}_0(0) = 0 \quad \text{and} \quad \mathcal{D}_0'\big(m_0^*(D_l)\big) = 0.$$

The condition at $m = 0$ reflects the seniority of deposits over long-term debt (recall that $\eta A \leq D_d$) and the shareholders' limited liability.

In order to study the optimal strategies before the run, we first take arbitrary values of r_l, D_l and D_s, which result in the following evolution of cash reserves given a dividend policy L :

$$dM_t = (1 - \theta)[(\mu - f_0 - (1 - \overline{N}_t)r_sD_s)dt + \sigma dZ_t] - dL_t - D_sd\overline{N}_t, \; M_0 = m.$$

The pre-run value of equity is then

$$\mathcal{E}_1(m) := \max_L \mathbb{E}\left[\int_0^\tau e^{-\rho t}dL_t \Big| M_0 = m\right], \quad c \geq 0,$$

but now we have to take into account that there could be run-driven liquidation or a significant change in the bank's balance sheet if it is hit by a run. The former case occurs if $M_t \leq D_s$ when short-term creditors run. The bank is forced to sell ηA of its assets to cover the shortfall $M_t - D_s$. Any remaining funds are first used to pay back the face value of deposits, after which no funds remain. In other words, shareholders walk away empty-handed. The bank survives a run if it occurs when $M_t > D_s$. It is in this case that we use the function $\mathcal{E}_0$ obtained above: let $m_1^*(D_s, D_l)$be the pre-run target liquidity level, then the equity value function $\mathcal{E}_1$ satisfies

$$\rho\mathcal{E}_1(m) = \begin{cases} \mathcal{L}\mathcal{E}_1(m) - \lambda\mathcal{E}_1(m), & m \in (0, D_s); \\ \mathcal{L}\mathcal{E}_1(m) - \lambda[\mathcal{E}_1(m) - \mathcal{E}_0(m - D_s)], & m \in (D_s, m_1^*), \end{cases} \tag{4.3.4}$$

where, for any twice-continuously differentiable function g, we define

$$\mathcal{L}g := (1 - \theta)^2 \frac{\sigma^2}{2}g'' + (1 - \theta)(\mu - f_0 - r_sD_s)g'.$$

As before, the value function is linear for $m \geq m_1^*$: $\mathcal{E}_1(m) = \mathcal{E}_1(m_1^*) + (m - m_1^*)$, and the boundary conditions are $\mathcal{E}_1(0) = 0$ and $\mathcal{E}_1'(m_1^*) = 1$. The JUMP TERMS

$$\lambda\mathcal{E}_1(m) \quad \text{and} \quad \lambda[\mathcal{E}_1(c) - \mathcal{E}_0(c - D_s)]$$

in Expression (4.3.4) reflect liquidation and regime change, respectively. Observe that the drift in the evolution of the bank's liquid reserves increases from $\mu - f_0 - r_sD_s$ before the run to $\mu - f_0$ after the run, i.e. there is a trade-off between the immediate loss D_s and larger expected profits.

As before, $\mathcal{E}_1$ is an increasing function that is strictly concave up to the target cash level $m_1^*(D_s, D_l)$. In the sequel we assume

$m_1^*(D_s, D_l) \in (D_s, D_s + m_0^*(D_l)]$, which is the only case that manifests itself in the numerical analysis below.[5]

When it comes to long-term debt, if the bank survives a run when its reserves are at level m, then its market value drops to $\mathcal{E}_0(m - D_s)$. On the other hand, if the run forces the bank to liquidate, then long-term creditors walk away empty-handed (due to our assumptions in debt seniority and the magnitude of ηA). Therefore, the pre-run market value of long-term debt solves the following boundary-value problem:

$$\rho \mathcal{D}_1(m) = \begin{cases} \mathcal{L}\mathcal{D}_1(m) + r_l D_l - \lambda \mathcal{D}_1(m), & m \in (0, D_s); \\ \mathcal{L}\mathcal{D}_1(m) + r_l D_l - \lambda[\mathcal{D}_1(m) - \mathcal{D}_0(m - D_s)], & m \in (D_s, m_1^*), \end{cases}$$

together with the boundary conditions $\mathcal{D}_1(0) = 0$ and $\mathcal{D}_1'(m_1^*) = 0$.

The following result provides us with the first step in solving the shareholders' financing problem. It is obtained in similar fashion to the optimal equity-issuance level studied in Chapter 3.

Lemma 4.3.1. *The optimal initial level of liquid reserves is $m = m_1^*$. In words, shareholders optimally choose to start the bank with cash reserves at the target cash level.*

In light of this result, the shareholders' funding problem reduces to the choice of debt structure:

$$\max_{(D_s, D_l) \in \mathscr{A}} V_1^*(D_l, D_s) = \left\{ \mathcal{E}_1(m_1^*) - m_1^* - (A - D_d - D_l - D_s) \right\}. \quad (4.3.5)$$

Recall that $\mathcal{E}_1(m_1^*)$ depends on r_l, which itself depends on m_1^*. For a given debt structure (D_d, D_l, D_s), the equilibrium interest rate on long-term debt r_l^* and the optimal dividend barrier $m_1^*(D_l, D_s)$ are jointly determined by the system of equations

$$\mathcal{D}_1(m_1^*) = D_l \quad \text{and} \quad \mathcal{D}_1''(m_1^*) = 0.$$

The first of these expressions represents the condition that long-term debt is issued at par and the second is the supercontact condition. With this in hand, we may (numerically) compute the solution to Problem (4.3.5). Qualitatively, we have

1. Default is more likely when the magnitude of the run of short-term creditors is larger.

---

[5] The cases $m_1^*(D_s, D_l) \leq D_s$ and $m_1^*(D_s, D_l) > m_0^*(D_l)$ are somewhat pathological. The former guarantees that the bank never holds enough liquid reserves to survive a run, whereas the latter means that shareholders enjoy a lump-sum dividend payout after a run.

2. Default is more likely when the magnitude of f_0, is large, because the drift of the cash-reserves process is small.

These two effects require shareholders to trade off between issuing a larger D_s, which pays a lower interest r_s, and issuing a smaller D_s, which results in a smaller interest rate $r_l(D_s, D_l)$, given that the probability of default is reduced.

4.3.3 Numerical analysis

Even though this model allows for less qualitative results than the ones in the previous two sections, it is flexible enough to calibrate it to data and conduct numerical analyses.[6] In Table 4.1 we look at the impact that the "intrinsic profitability" μ and the cost of deposit funding r_d have on bank leverage, on the composition of bank liabilities and on bank value. We take: proportion of liquid assets $\eta = 0.3$; run intensity $\lambda = 0.05$; discount rate $\rho = 5\%$; cost of short-term debt $r_s = 2.5\%$; volume of deposits $D_d = 2$; tax rate $\theta = 35\%$; volatility $\sigma = 18\%$ and asset value $A = (1 - \theta)\mu/\rho$. Leverage, i.e. debt over total assets, is computed at the target cash level m_1^* :

$$\text{leverage} = \frac{D_d + D_l + D_s}{A + m_1^*}.$$

We observe that leverage moves in the same direction as expected profitability and opposite to the cost of deposit funding. For comparison, we also present the case where $D_d = 0$ (first and fourth rows of Table 4.1), where the bank is closer to a "general" financial firm that takes no deposits. We see that, absent deposits, the bank relies less on short-term debt (the overall volume of short-term debt is lower, as is the ratio $D_s/(D_s + D_l)$). Furthermore, without deposits in its balance sheet, the bank is less leveraged, which suggests that the presence of deposits is one of the reasons for the high leverage observed in banks.

We may also see in Table 4.1 that banks with a lower expected profitability μ have a higher reliance on short-term debt funding, as seen in from the ratio

$$\frac{D_s}{D_s + D_l}.$$

---

[6]Klimenko and Moreno-Bromberg (2016) allow for deposits to be junior to long-term debt and also study the optimal capital structure of a non-deposit-taking institution. They find that access to deposit funding exacerbates leverage and increases bank value. Moreover, the implementation of the depositor seniority rule reduces leverage bank value. The reduction in leverage that follows the depositor preference rule is consistent with the numerical findings of Hugonnier and Morellec (2015b) and the empirical evidence documented by Danisewicz et al. (2015).

		D_s	D_l	$\frac{D_s}{D_s+D_l}$	r_l	Leverage
	$D_d = 0$	0.09	1.99	4.17%	5.47%	0.67
$\mu = 20\%$	$r_d = 2.5\%$	0.12	1.07	10.34%	5.83%	1.02
	$r_d = 4.5\%$	0.15	0.56	21.04%	6.29%	0.87
	$D_d = 0$	0.07	3.59	2.02%	5.33%	0.83
$\mu = 30\%$	$r_d = 2.5\%$	0.09	2.55	3.45%	5.47%	1.05
	$r_d = 4.5\%$	0.10	1.93	4.93%	5.56%	0.91

Table 4.1: The impact of profitability and cost of deposits

Moreover, for μ given, a higher cost of deposits also results in a larger proportion of short-term debt in the bank's liabilities.

4.4 Further reading

Similar to Jiang and Pistorius (2012), Gryglewicz (2011) assumes that the drift of a firm's EBIT (earnings before interest and taxes) can take two values. The true value of the drift is unknown and market participants update their beliefs μ_t about this value. This results in two potential sources of corporate distress. On the one hand, the unpredictability of earnings that results from the presence of the Brownian driver may result in short-term liquidity risk. On the other, the drift's uncertainty may result in solvency risk and, eventually, in default. As in Section 4.3, the author studies the optimal way to manage the bank's cash holdings and its dividend strategy when external financing is only available at initiation. The drift uncertainty results in smooth dividend payments that take place at a threshold that varies with μ_t. This model allows for an interesting study of the interaction between liquidity and solvency, as well as capital structure, default and credit spreads.

Bolton et al. (2014) analyze a model that shares many similarities with the one studied in Section 4.3. Their aim is also to delve into issues of optimal capital structure and liquidity choice. The authors consider the financing problem of an entrepreneur who must raise the total costs required to initiate a limited-liability project. Once in place, the firm's assets generate cashflows that follow an Arithmetic Brownian Motion. They consider a realistic tax structure, where corporate income tax, taxes on interest payments and on income from equity have different rates. Just as in Section 4.3, decisions regarding the (costly) issuance of equity and debt (consol bond) so as to finance the investment can only be made at $t = 0$. Here there is no debt-maturity issue; instead, the firm has access to a credit line that can be used when its liquidity reserves are depleted and whose limit is also decided upon at initiation. Bankruptcy may occur in the scenario where both liquidity and the sources of credit are depleted, which implies that long-term debt is risky. The authors analyze how variations in tax policies or in the characteristics of the cashflow process impact the leverage arising from the optimal choice of capital structure. A result that should be highlighted is that more volatile cashflows result not only in higher reserves levels, but also in an increase in the use of debt, i.e. in contrast with what the classical trade-off theory predicts, a riskier firm is more leveraged.

Hugonnier and Morellec (2015a) make use of an extension of the base liquidity-management model in order to assess the effects of liquidity and leverage requirements on banks' insolvency risk. The sources of bank financing are equity, insured deposits and risky long-term debt. Their model considers no short-term debt as in Section 4.3 but instead the cashflows are subject to large losses (say defaults on large credits) that are modeled using a compound Poisson process with exponentially distributed losses. They also allow for costly liquidity injections as in Section 3.1, which, given the possibility of strictly negative reserves levels, result in a value function that is linear in the "distress region"; thus, it is not globally concave. The authors conclude that liquidity requirements may increase short-term default risk without having any effect on the long run, whereas capital requirements reduce default risk but may also significantly reduce bank value.

Auh and Sundaresan (2015) is, loosely speaking, a Geometric Brownian Motion based version of the model presented in Section 4.3, with the capital structure of the bank containing equity, short-term collateralized debt and long-term unsecured debt. Given that cashflows are always positive, there is no liquidity-driven bankruptcy. Instead, in the spirit of the trade-off model of Section 1.4, an optimal restructuring barrier is determined. A crucial insight provided by the authors is that safe-harbor provisions on short-term debt may actually emerge as part of the bank's optimal liability structure.

Sundaresan and Wang (2015) study the impact of deposit insurance and regulation on the optimal leverage choice of banks. The authors consider a Leland-type model with insured deposits and subordinated, long-term debt. Given the risky nature of the latter, its yield includes a credit spread that is determined endogenously. They model the deposit-insurance institution (e.g. the FDIC) explicitly and bankruptcy costs may vary depending on whether liquidation is triggered by shareholders or by the deposit insurer. The latter happens at the point where depositors would have run in the absence of deposit insurance. The determination of the bank's optimal capital structure has an impact on the value of the fair deposit-insurance premium. The authors conclude that the presence of deposit insurance and the corresponding possibility of charter-enacted bankruptcy leads to an increase of the bank value and leverage through an expansion of deposits, even if the deposit insurance premium is fair.

5 Applications to Insurance

THIS CHAPTER PRESENTS applications of the base liquidity-management model to the insurance industry. Two essential components of the insurance business are the possibility of large losses and the use of reinsurance (as an instrument for risk management). A traditional approach to model the net earnings of an insurance firm is the so-called Cramér-Lundberg model, where risk is not represented by a Brownian motion, but rather by a compound Poisson process. Here we study models with both types of risks. We look at the use of reinsurance as a way of maximizing the value of the firm (instead of minimizing the insurer's probability of ruin, as the models of the first generation).

5.1 The base liquidity-management model with large losses

Certain types of insurance contracts may be subject to sudden large losses. This is the case, for instance, if the company underwrites policies to cover natural catastrophes (Nat Cat insurance). Such a scenario is not covered by (Brownian) diffusion models. In this section, besides the Brownian motion Z, corresponding to standard operating losses, we introduce a process of large losses in the following way: let $N = \{N_t, t \geq 0\}$ be a Poisson process with intensity λ.[1] We identify each arrival of N with the times at which large losses occur. For simplicity we assume that all large losses are of the same magnitude $l > 0$.[2] The probability that a large loss happens over an interval $[t, t+dt]$ is λdt and the corresponding expected large losses $l\lambda dt$. For a given cumulative dividend process $L = \{L_t, t \geq 0\}$, the firm's cash reserves evolve according to

$$dM_t^L = \mu dt + \sigma dZ_t - dL_t - l dN_t, \quad M_0 = m.$$

As in the base liquidity-management model, the manager's objective

---

[1] In this section we redefine $\mathbb{F}$ to be the filtration generated by the processes N and Z, i.e. $\mathbb{F} = \sigma(N, Z)$.

[2] It is possible to incorporate stochastic loss sizes (see, e.g. Hugonnier and Morellec (2015a)).

is to maximize the present value of the stream of dividends paid out until liquidation. Note that if a loss occurred when $m \in (0, l)$, then the post-loss level of cash reserves would be strictly negative.

5.1.1 The variational inequality in the presence of large losses

How do large losses impact the structure of the variational inequality that characterizes the value function V? The complementarity condition $1 - V'(m) \leq 0$, implied by the possibility of dividend distributions, remains unaltered. Assuming that V is concave, which we verify ex-post, we have that dividends are distributed when cash reserves reach some target cash level. We denote this target cash level by m_η^*, where $\eta := (\lambda, l)$ parametrizes losses: the firm's dividend strategy depends both on the intensity of losses λ as well as on their size l. The Hamilton-Jacobi-Bellman equation has to take the probability of large losses into account. Let us assume there is a loss l when the level of liquid reserves is m. Then, the change in shareholder value is $V(m - l) - V(m)$. As the instantaneous probability of an arrival is λdt, the JUMP TERM $\lambda\big(V(m - l) - V(m)\big)$ has to be added to the Hamilton-Jacobi-Bellman equation of the base liquidity-management model:

Proposition 5.1.1. *The value function V is concave, twice continuously differentiable and satisfies the following variational inequality for $m > 0$:*

$$\max\left\{\frac{\sigma^2}{2}V''(m) + \mu V'(m) + \lambda\big(V(m - l) - V(m)\big) - \rho V(m),\right.$$
$$\left. 1 - V'(m)\right\} = 0;$$

whereas $V(m) = 0$ for $m \leq 0$.

5.1.2 The value function

A differential equation of the form

$$\rho V(m) = \frac{\sigma^2}{2}V''(m) + \mu V'(m) + \lambda\big(V(m - l) - V(m)\big)$$

is called a DELAY EQUATION.[3] It relates the values of V, V' and V'' at m to the value of V at $m - l$. Observe that on $(0, l)$ the value

---

[3]When m is a time variable, l corresponds to a delay, hence the name of this type of equation.

function solves

$$(\rho + \lambda)V(m) = \frac{\sigma^2}{2}V''(m) + \mu V'(m) \qquad (5.1.1)$$

with the boundary condition $V(0) = 0$. This is because $V(m - l) = 0$ if $m \leq l$. If we let $\beta_1 < 0 < \beta_2$ be the solutions to the characteristic equation $\rho + \lambda = (\sigma^2/2)\beta^2 + \mu\beta$, then the general solution to Equation (5.1.1) is

$$V(m) = A\big(e^{\beta_1 m} - e^{\beta_2 m}\big).$$

With this in hand, we can rewrite the delay equation on $(l, 2l)$ as

$$(\rho+\lambda)V(m) = \frac{\sigma^2}{2}V''(m)+\mu V'(m)+\lambda A\big(e^{\beta_1(m-l)}-e^{\beta_2(m-l)}\big), \quad (5.1.2)$$

subject to the smooth pasting condition

$$V(l_-) = V(l_+) \quad \text{and} \quad V'(l_-) = V'(l_+).$$

Once we solve Equation (5.1.2), we may rewrite the delay equation for $m \in (2l, 3l)$ and so on, up to the point that $nl \geq m_\eta^*$.

We have from the previous argument that the relationship between the values of l and m_η^* has a marked influence on the value function's structure. For instance, let us first assume that $m_\eta^* < l$. This could be interpreted as the firm being exposed to a catastrophic loss, e.g. an insurer of a nuclear power plant that, with a small probability, can have a meltdown leading to enormous losses. In such case the value function is analogous to that of the base liquidity-management, as $V(m-l) = 0$ for all $m \in [0, m_l]$, but the shareholder's "discount rate" grows from ρ to $\rho + \lambda$. In other words, they become more impatient. Recall that the dividend-distribution threshold in the base liquidity-management model is

$$m^* = \frac{2}{r_1 - r_2} \log\left(-\frac{r_2}{r_1}\right),$$

with $r_1 < 0 < r_2$ the solutions to the characteristic equation $\rho + \lambda = (\sigma^2/2)r^2 + \mu r$. If $m_\eta^* < l$, then

$$m_\eta^* = \frac{2}{\beta_1 - \beta_2} \log\left(-\frac{\beta_2}{\beta_1}\right).$$

We leave it as an exercise to prove that, in this case, $m_\eta^* \leq m^*$, with equality only when $\lambda = 0$. This means that shareholders hoard less

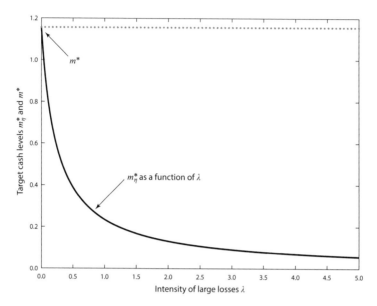

Figure 5.1: m_η^* as a function of λ when $m_\eta^* < l$

cash to hedge against the Brownian risk of liquidation than when there is no Poisson risk. Avoiding the Poisson risk is too costly and waiting too long to distribute dividends is value decreasing. We present an example with $\mu = 0.3, \sigma = 0.5$ and $\rho = 0.15$ in Figure 5.1, with λ varying from 0 to 5.

Let us now assume that $l < m_\eta^* \leq 2l$. In this case, the value function satisfies

$$(\rho + \lambda)V(m) = \begin{cases} \dfrac{\sigma^2}{2}V''(m) + \mu V'(m), & m \in (0, l); \quad (5.1.3a) \\[2mm] \dfrac{\sigma^2}{2}V''(m) + \mu V'(m) + \lambda A\psi(m), & m \in (l, m_l^*), \quad (5.1.3b) \end{cases}$$

where $\psi(m) := e^{\beta_1(m-l)} - e^{\beta_2(m-l)}$, subject to the smooth pasting condition at $m = l$, and the boundary conditions

$$V(0) = 0 \quad \text{and} \quad V'(m_l^*) = 1.$$

We already know the general solution to Equation (5.1.3a) is

$$V(m) = A\big(e^{\beta_1 m} - e^{\beta_2 m}\big).$$

The general solution V_h to the homogeneous part of Equation (5.1.3b) is

$$V_h(m) = Be^{\beta_1 m} + Ce^{\beta_2 m}.$$

In order to find a particular solution to Equation (5.1.3b), notice that, for $i = 1, 2$, a particular solution to

$$(\rho + \lambda)V(m) = \frac{\sigma^2}{2}V''(m) + \mu V'(m) + De^{\beta_i m}$$

is given by[4]

$$V_i = -\frac{D}{\mu + \sigma^2 \beta_i} me^{\beta_i m}.$$

As a result, if we define for $i = 1, 2$, $D_i := \lambda A e^{-\beta_i l}$, then a particular solution to Equation (5.1.3b) is

$$V_p(m) = -\frac{D_1}{\mu + \sigma^2 \beta_1} me^{\beta_1 m} + \frac{D_2}{\mu + \sigma^2 \beta_2} me^{\beta_2 m}$$

and, on (l, m_l^*), the general solution to Equation (5.1.3b) is

$$V(m) = V_h(m) + V_p(m) = \left(B - \frac{D_1 m}{\mu + \sigma^2 \beta_1}\right)e^{\beta_1 m} + \left(C + \frac{D_2 m}{\mu + \sigma^2 \beta_2}\right)e^{\beta_2 m}.$$

Summarizing, we have

$$V(m) = \begin{cases} A\left(e^{\beta_1 m} - e^{\beta_2 m}\right), & m \in (0, l]; \\ \left(B - \frac{D_1 m}{\mu + \sigma^2 \beta_1}\right)e^{\beta_1 m} + \left(C + \frac{D_2 m}{\mu + \sigma^2 \beta_2}\right)e^{\beta_2 m}, & m \in (l, m_l^*). \end{cases}$$

The final step is to find A, B, C and m_l^* such that the resulting V is twice continuously differentiable on $(0, m_l^*)$. This cannot be done in closed form, but it is simple to do numerically, as we show in the next section.

5.1.3 Computing the value function

Making use of the conditions $V'(m_l^*) = 1$ and $V''(m_l^*) = 0$ we can find B and C as functions of m_l^* and A (as D_1 and D_2 depend themselves on A). The closed-form expressions for $B(A, m_l^*)$ and $C(A, m_l^*)$ are cumbersome, so we only provide them in Appendix A.5. If we define

$$\mathbf{B}(A, m_l^*) := \frac{B(A, m_l^*)}{A} - \frac{D_1 m_l^*}{A(\mu + \sigma^2 \beta_1)}$$

---

[4] This is because $[me^{\beta_i m}]' = e^{\beta_i m}[1 + \beta_i m]$, $[me^{\beta_i m}]'' = e^{\beta_i m}[2\beta_i^2 + \beta_i^2 m]$ and β_i solves $\rho + \lambda = (\sigma^2/2)\beta^2 + \mu\beta$.

and

$$C(A, m_l^*) := \frac{C(A, m_l^*)}{A} + \frac{D_2 m_l^*}{A(\mu + \sigma^2 \beta_2)},$$

then the smooth pasting condition at $m = l$ yields the following system of equations on m_l^* and A :

$$
\begin{aligned}
e^{\beta_1 l} - e^{\beta_2 l} &= B(A, m_l^*) e^{\beta_1 l} + C(A, m_l^*) e^{\beta_2 l}, \\
\beta_1 e^{\beta_1 l} - \beta_2 e^{\beta_2 l} &= B(A, m_l^*) \beta_1 e^{\beta_1 l} + C(A, m_l^*) \beta_2 e^{\beta_2 l}.
\end{aligned}
\tag{5.1.4}
$$

It must be kept in mind that the system of equations (5.1.4) only has a (feasible) solution if the choice of parameters is such that $l < m_\eta^* < 2l$.

In Figure 5.2 we depict the impact that a loss of magnitude $l = 0.2$ with intensity $\lambda = 0.15$ has on the value function of the base liquidity-management model with $\mu = 0.3, \sigma = 0.15$ and $\rho = 0.2$. The solution to System (5.1.4) is $A \approx -0.917$ and $m_\eta^* \approx 0.366$. We observe in Figure 5.2(a) how the possibility of a large loss decreases shareholder value and postpones the distribution of dividends. In Figure 5.2(b) we have plotted the difference between the two value functions, which becomes constant after $m = m_\eta^*$.

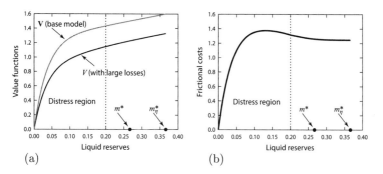

Figure 5.2: Comparison with the base model. (a) Value functions with(out) large losses. (b) Frictional costs of large losses.

5.2 Reinsuring Brownian risks

This section is based on the seminal article of Hoejgaard and Taksar (1998), which has led to a large academic literature. In this article, on top of liquidity-management decisions, the manager decides on risk exposure through the choice of REINSURANCE STRATEGY. By this we mean the following: The net-earnings process represents the balance between policy income and claims paid out. At each date t, it is possible for the insurer (usually called the CEDENT in the reinsurance terminology) to cede a fraction $(1-\alpha_t)$ of all premia to the reinsurance company. In exchange, the reinsurer pays $(1-\alpha_t)$ of each claim. Doing this scales down the firm's income from selling policies, thus, making it less profitable in expected terms. The upside, however, is that the volatility is also reduced, leading to a smaller exposure to losses. This is relevant when the levels of liquidity are low, a situation in which sharp decreases in the firm's cash reserves have a starker impact on shareholder value than movements in the positive direction. In this sense, the choice of an EXPOSURE STRATEGY, which is any predictable process $\alpha = \{\alpha_t, t \geq 0\}$ that satisfies $\alpha_t \in [0,1]$ for all $t \geq 0$, is a component of the firm's risk-management policies.

5.2.1 The dynamics of liquid reserves and the variational inequality

Liquidity management and, more important, how it interacts with risk management is a central component of the day-to-day operations of insurance companies. As before, we model it via a cumulative dividend process $L = \{L_t, t \geq 0\}$, which leads to strategies of the form $\pi = (\alpha, L) \in \mathscr{A}_p$ (the subindex "p" stands for "proportional" reinsurance). The choice of $\pi \in \mathscr{A}_p$ results in the following dynamics of the firm's cash reserves:

$$dM_t^\pi = \alpha_t(\mu dt + \sigma dZ_t) - dL_t, \quad M_0^\pi = m.$$

The liquidation time τ_π corresponds again to $\inf\{t > 0 \mid M_t^\pi < 0\}$. Shareholder value corresponding to a strategy π and an initial level of liquid reserves m is

$$V^\pi(m) := \mathbb{E}\left[\int_0^{\tau_\pi} e^{-\rho t} dL_t \Big| M_0^\pi = m\right].$$

The value function corresponds to the maximization over all admissible strategies:

$$V(m) = \max_{\pi \in \mathscr{A}_p} V^\pi(m), \quad m \geq 0 \tag{5.2.1}$$

and, under the simplifying assumption that the firm's liquidation value is zero, we have as before that $V(0) = 0$.

The Hamilton-Jacobi-Bellman variational inequality that characterizes the value function bears a stark resemblance to that in Expression (4.2.2) in Chapter 4. In the current case, however, the absence of interest accruing on retained earnings, together with the fact that the choice set for α is independent of the current reserves level, results in closed-form solutions.

Proposition 5.2.1. *The value function V is concave, twice continuously differentiable and it satisfies the following variational inequality for $m > 0$:*

$$\max\left\{\max_{\alpha\in[0,1]}\left\{\frac{1}{2}\sigma^2\alpha^2 V''(m) + \mu\alpha V'(m) - \rho V(m)\right\}, 1 - V'(m)\right\} = 0.$$

Together with the boundary condition $V(0) = 0$.

5.2.2 The partial-exposure region

By analogy with Section 4.2, we conjecture (and verify ex-post) the existence of a REINSURANCE BOUNDARY m_0^* such that, for $m \in (0, m_0^*)$ (the PARTIAL-EXPOSURE region) we have an interior solution to

$$\max_{\alpha\in[0,1]}\left\{\frac{1}{2}\sigma^2\alpha^2 V''(m) + \mu\alpha V'(m) - \rho V(m)\right\}. \qquad (5.2.2)$$

In other words in this region the manager optimally makes use of reinsurance. We study the level of reinsurance as a function of the current level of liquid reserves m: in order to find $\alpha(m)$ we use the first-order condition of Problem (5.2.2) to get

$$\alpha(m) = -\frac{\mu}{\sigma^2}\frac{V'(m)}{V''(m)}. \qquad (5.2.3)$$

Observe the close resemblance between Equations (5.2.3) and (4.2.4). Inserting $\alpha(m)$ into the Hamilton-Jacobi-Bellman equation results in the expression

$$V(m) = -\frac{\mu^2}{2\sigma^2\rho}\frac{[V'(m)]^2}{V''(m)}, \qquad (5.2.4)$$

whose general solution is[5]

$$V(m) = c_1\left(m\frac{\rho}{\gamma} + c_2\right)^{\gamma}, \qquad (5.2.5)$$

---

[5] To see this, set $V(m) = \exp\{U(m)\}$, so that $V' = U'V$ and $V'' = U''V + (U')^2 V$. Then, Equation (5.2.4) becomes

$$V = -\frac{\mu^2}{2\sigma^2\rho}\frac{(U')^2 V^2}{U''V + (U')^2 V}.$$

After simplification we get

$$-\frac{U''}{(U')^2} = \frac{\mu^2 + 2\sigma^2\rho}{2\sigma^2\rho} = \frac{1}{\gamma};$$

thus, $1/U'(m) = (m/\gamma) +$ constant, which yields Expression (5.2.5) after one more integration.

where c_1 and c_2 are constants to be determined and

$$\gamma := \frac{2\sigma^2\rho}{\mu^2 + 2\sigma^2\rho}.$$

From the boundary condition $V(0) = 0$ we obtain that $c_2 = 0$; thus,

$$\alpha(m) = -\frac{\mu V'(m)}{\sigma^2 V''(m)} = -\left(\frac{c_1\mu\rho}{\sigma^2}\left(m\frac{\rho}{\gamma}\right)^{\gamma-1}\right)\bigg/\left(\frac{c_1\rho^2(\gamma-1)}{\gamma}\left(m\frac{\rho}{\gamma}\right)^{\gamma-2}\right)$$

$$= \frac{m\mu}{\sigma^2(1-\gamma)},$$

$$(5.2.6)$$

which is independent of c_1. In order to find m_0^*, we set $\alpha(m) = 1$ and obtain

$$m_0^* = \frac{\sigma^2(1-\gamma)}{\mu} = \frac{\sigma^2\mu}{\mu^2 + 2\sigma^2\rho} > 0. \qquad (5.2.7)$$

This yields the following result:

Proposition 5.2.2. *For any choice of parameters μ, ρ and σ, the partial-exposure region $(0, m_0^*)$ is nonempty.*

The optimal structure of the exposure strategy given in Expression (5.2.6) implies that, as long as $M_t \in (0, m_0^*)$ where all earnings are retained, the dynamics of the cash reserves are

$$dM_t = \frac{\mu}{\sigma^2}\frac{M_t}{1-\gamma}(\mu dt + \sigma dZ_t).$$

Observe that, in the partial-exposure region, cash reserves evolve according to a geometric Brownian motion; therefore, liquidation never occurs:

Lemma 5.2.3. *The optimal exposure strategy*

$$\alpha(m) = \min\left\{1, \frac{\mu}{\sigma^2}\frac{m}{1-\gamma}\right\}$$

yields $\tau^\pi = \infty$.

In terms of the marginal value of cash in the firm, we have that

$$\lim_{m \searrow 0} V'(m) = \lim_{m \searrow 0} c_1\gamma\left(m\frac{\rho}{\gamma}\right)^{\gamma-1} = \infty,$$

where the second equality follows from the fact that $\gamma - 1 < 0$. In other words, for very low levels of liquidity, additional cash is highly desirable for the shareholders, who would like the firm to operate in a higher-profitability mode.

5.2.3 The full-exposure region

Clearly no dividends are distributed as long as $m < m_0^*$, as this would decrease liquidity in a region where the manager has chosen to use reinsurance. Therefore, the dividend-distribution barrier m_1^* must satisfy $m_0^* < m_1^*$, which we verify below. In the region (m_0^*, m_1^*) the maximization Problem (5.2.2) has the corner solution $\alpha \equiv 1$. In other words, no reinsurance takes place when $m \in (m_0^*, m_1^*)$; we call this the FULL-EXPOSURE (or zero-reinsurance) region. As long as $m \in (m_0^*, m_1^*)$, the value function has the same structure as that of the base liquidity-management model:

$$V(m) = \frac{1}{r_1 r_2}\left(\frac{r_2^2}{r_2 - r_1}e^{r_1(m - m_1^*)} - \frac{r_1^2}{r_2 - r_1}e^{r_2(m - m_1^*)}\right), \quad m \in (m_0^*, m_1^*).$$

The optimal pair (c_1^*, m_1^*) must be chosen to satisfy the smooth-pasting condition

$$V(m_{0-}^*) = V(m_{0+}^*) \quad \text{and} \quad V'(m_{0-}^*) = V'(m_{0+}^*).$$

Proposition 5.2.4. *For μ, ρ and σ given there exist $c_1^* > 0$ and $m_1^* > m_0^*$ such that the piecewise-defined function*

$$V(m) = \begin{cases} c_1^*\left(m\frac{\rho}{\gamma}\right)^\gamma, & m \in [0, m_0^*); \\ \frac{1}{r_1 r_2}\left(\frac{r_2^2}{r_2 - r_1}e^{r_1(m - m_1^*)} - \frac{r_1^2}{r_2 - r_1}e^{r_2(m - m_1^*)}\right), & m \in [m_0^*, m_1^*]; \\ V(m_1^*) + (m - m_1^*), & m \in (m_1^*, \infty) \end{cases}$$

is twice continuously differentiable and corresponds to the value function in Expression (5.2.1).

Proof. See Appendix A.5.

We observed in Chapter 3 that the possibility of avoiding liquidation by means of equity issuance resulted in a smaller target liquidity level compared to the base liquidity-management model, as it reduced the risk of liquidation. In the current setting, reinsurance also serves the purpose of reducing (in fact, eliminating) this risk. Therefore, we should expect that, all other things being equal, $m_1^* < m^*$. In Figure 5.3 we revisit the value function of the base liquidity-management model with $\mu = 3$, $\rho = 1.5$ and $\sigma = 1$ and compare it to the value function for the reinsurance case. Observe that $m_1^* < m^*$ and that the use of reinsurance is value increasing.

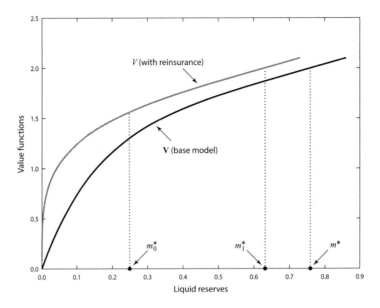

Figure 5.3: The gains from reinsurance

5.2.4 Sensitivity analysis

Let us analyze the dependence of the reinsurance boundary m_0^* on the problem's parameters. Recalling that

$$m_0^* = \frac{\sigma^2 \mu}{\mu^2 + 2\sigma^2 \rho},$$

we readily compute

$$\frac{\partial m_0^*}{\partial \mu} = \frac{2\sigma^4 \rho - \mu^2 \sigma^2}{(\mu^2 + 2\sigma^2 \rho)^2}.$$

From this expression it is immediate to see that the mapping $\mu \mapsto m_0^*$ has a unique critical point at $\mu = \sigma\sqrt{2\rho}$. Moreover, as a function of μ we have

$$\lim_{\mu \to \infty} m_0^*(\mu) = m_0^*(0) = 0.$$

We conclude that the mapping $\mu \mapsto m_0^*$ is increasing over the range $[0, \sigma\sqrt{2\rho})$ and decreasing over $(\sigma\sqrt{2\rho}, \infty)$. This accepts a simple interpretation: if potential profits (as measured by the magnitude of μ) are high, there is no need to manage risk unless the reserves level is very low. On the other hand, if potential profits are very small, the firm must take a riskier stance so as to be able to distribute dividends at low levels of reserves. In terms of the dependence of m_0^* with respect to σ, we have

$$\frac{\partial m_0^*}{\partial \sigma} = \frac{2\mu^3 \sigma}{(\mu^2 + 2\sigma^2 \rho)^2},$$

which is always positive. This is not too surprising, since it simply means that the riskier the firm is (as measured by the volatility of its net earnings), the more liquid reserves it should hold. Notice that

$$\lim_{\sigma \to \infty} m_0^*(\sigma) = \frac{\mu}{2\rho},$$

in other words, regardless of how risky the firm is, the reinsurance boundary is bounded above by half the expected present value of future cash flows. The qualitative patterns of m_1^* with respect to μ and σ are analogous to those of m^*: inverted U-shaped in μ and increasing in σ. In Figure 5.4 we showcase these patterns.

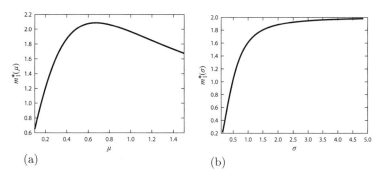

(a)   (b)

Figure 5.4: Sensitivity of the target cash level m_1^* with respect to μ and σ for $\rho = 0.15$. (a) m_1^* as a function of μ for $\sigma = 1$. (b) m_1^* as a function of σ for $\mu = 0.3$.

Finally, we may draw some intuition regarding what shareholders gain from reinsurance for different levels of the discount rate. As we observed in Figure 5.3, the reinsurance option is valuable to the shareholders. However, since

$$\lim_{\rho \to \infty} m_0^* = \lim_{\rho \to \infty} \frac{\sigma^2 \mu}{\mu^2 + 2\sigma^2 \rho} = 0,$$

when the shareholders are very impatient the partial-exposure region becomes very small. As a consequence the gap between the value functions with and without proportional reinsurance also tightens.

This is because of the fact that the more impatient shareholders are, the sooner they demand to receive payouts. Hence, they assign less value to risk management than more patient shareholders would.

5.3 Reinsuring large losses

This section, based on Rochet and Villeneuve (2011), revisits the liquidity-management model with large losses of Section 5.1 and addresses the reinsurance problem faced by the manager of an insurance company exposed to large losses.[6]

5.3.1 The cash-reserves dynamics

Recall that, in the absence of reinsurance, the firm's cash reserves evolve according to

$$dM_t^L = \mu dt + \sigma dZ_t - dL - l dN_t, \quad M_0^L = m,$$

for a given cumulative dividend process L. Now we allow for the reinsurance of large losses at an ACTUARIALLY FAIR PRICE, by which we mean the following: if the manager decides to reduce the firm's exposure to large losses over the interval $[t, t+dt]$ to $(1-i)l dN_t$, the amount $i l \lambda dt$ must be paid to the reinsurer. Formally, a REINSURANCE PROCESS is any $\mathbb{F}$-predictable process $i = \{i_t \in [0,1], t \geq 0\}$. Strategies are pairs $\pi = (i, L)$, for which the dynamics of liquid reserves are

$$dM_t^\pi = (\mu - i_t l \lambda)dt + \sigma dZ_t - dL_t - (1-i_t)l dN_t, \quad M_0^\pi = m > 0.$$

We make the following parametric assumption:

Assumption. *The firm's expected net earnings exceed expected losses:* $\mu > l\lambda$.

Given that on $(0, m^*)$ no dividends are paid out, in this region the Hamilton-Jacobi-Bellman equation is (compare to those in Section 5.1.2)

$$(\rho+\lambda)V(m) = \frac{\sigma^2}{2}V''(m) + \max_{i\in[0,1]} \left\{ (\mu-i\,l\lambda)V'(m) + \lambda V(m-(1-i)l)) \right\}$$

with $V(0) = 0$ and the target level m_i^* being characterized, as before, by the supercontact condition

$$V'(m_i^*) = 1 \quad \text{and} \quad V''(m_i^*) = 0.$$

---

[6]In Rochet and Villeneuve (2011), the authors also allow for fixed equity issuance and reinsurance of Brownian losses. We abstract from these features for simplicity.

5.3.2 The optimal reinsurance strategy

As in our model of proportional reinsurance of Brownian risk, here there is also a reinsurance boundary m_0^*. However, this is where similarities end. First, reinsurance is only used when cash reserves are **larger** than m_0^*. Second, there is no partial reinsurance, i.e. $i \in \{0, 1\}$. In order to see this last point, define

$$R(i; m) := (\mu - i l \lambda)V'(m) + \lambda V(m - (1 - i)l).$$

The quantity $R(i; m)$ measures the impact of reinsurance at level i on firm value when cash reserves are m, with the first summand being the marginal cost of reinsurance and the second its marginal benefit. The optimal reinsurance strategy $i^*(m)$ is found by maximizing $R(\cdot; m)$. The first-order condition for an interior solution is

$$R'(i; m) = \lambda l \big(V'(m - (1 - i)l) - V'(m) \big) = 0.$$

Given that V' is decreasing, this first-order condition can only be satisfied if $m - (1 - i)l = m,$[7] which implies $i = 1$. Therefore, the solution can never be interior, and we just have to compare $R(0; m)$ and $R(1; m)$ for each m. It is easy to prove that $R(0; m) > R(1; m)$ when m is smaller that a certain threshold m_0^*. The following lemma shows that $m_0^* < l$:

Lemma 5.3.1. *The level of cash reserves m_0^* at which the manager optimally switches from zero to full reinsurance satisfies $m_0^* < l$.*

Proof. See Appendix A.5.

This result is not surprising: why wait until the risk of liquidation through the arrival of a large loss is fully mitigated by the cash reserves before engaging in reinsurance? For $m > m_0^*$ we have $R(0) < R(1)$; thus, the optimal reinsurance strategy is

$$i^*(m) = \begin{cases} 0, & \text{if } m \leq m_0^*; \\ 1, & \text{if } m \in (m_0^*, m_l^*]. \end{cases}$$

This can be interpreted as the manager "gambling for resurrection" in the low-liquidity region $(0, m_0^*)$. The manager behaves this way because the value function is **not concave** around $m = 0$ because $m < 0$ is possible after a large loss. The value function satisfies

$$\rho V(m) = \begin{cases} \frac{\sigma^2}{2}V''(m) + \mu V'(m) - \lambda V(m), & \text{if } m \leq m_0^*; \\ \frac{\sigma^2}{2}V''(m) + (\mu - l\lambda)V'(m), & \text{if } m \in (m_0^*, m_l^*]. \end{cases} \quad (5.3.1)$$

---

[7]We rule out the uninteresting case where $m - (1 - i)l > m_\eta^*$ (so that $V'(m - (1 - i)l) = V'(m) = 1$) because it can only occur at $t = 0..$

We observe that on $(0, m_0^*)$ we have the same differential equation as in the no-reinsurance setting of Section 5.1 when the firm is in distress, whereas on $(m_0^*, m_l^*]$ we are in the setting of the base liquidity-management model, with the expected net earnings being $\mu - l\lambda$. If we let $\gamma_1 < 0 < \gamma_2$ be the solutions to the characteristic equation $\rho = (\sigma^2/2)\gamma^2 + (\mu - l\lambda)\gamma$, then

$$
V(m) = \begin{cases}
A\big(e^{\beta_1 m} - e^{\beta_2 m}\big), & \text{if } m \leq m_0^*; \\
\frac{1}{\gamma_1\gamma_2}\Big(\frac{\gamma_2^2}{\gamma_2-\gamma_1}e^{\gamma_1(m-m_\eta^*)} - \frac{\gamma_1^2}{\gamma_2-\gamma_1}e^{\gamma_2(m-m_\eta^*)}\Big), & \text{if } m \in (m_0^*, m_l^*]; \\
\frac{\mu-l\lambda}{\rho} + (m - m_l^*), & \text{if } m > m_l^*,
\end{cases}
$$

where $V(m_l^*) = (\mu - l\lambda)/\rho$ follows from the supercontact condition at m_l^*. We observe from Expression (5.3.1) that the differential equations for V do not coincide at m_0^*. In order to guarantee the twice-differentiability of V, we must choose A, m_0^* and m_η^* such that

$$
V(m_{0-}^*) = V(m_{0+}^*), \ V'(m_{0-}^*) = V'(m_{0+}^*) \text{ and } V''(m_{0-}^*) = V''(m_{0+}^*).
$$

From the above, one can derive closed-form expressions for m_0^* and m_η^* :

Lemma 5.3.2. *If the condition $\mu - \lambda l > 0$ holds, then*

$$
m_0^* = \frac{1}{\beta_2 - \beta_1} \log\left(\frac{1 - l\beta_1}{1 - l\beta_2}\right) \quad and
$$

$$
m_\eta^* = m_0^* + \frac{1}{\gamma_2 - \gamma_1} \log\left(\frac{\gamma_1^2(1 - l\gamma_2)}{\gamma_2^2(1 - l\gamma_1)}\right).
$$

Notice that when $\mu - \lambda l = 0$ then $\gamma_1 = -\gamma_2$ and, from Lemma 5.3.2, this implies $m_0^* = m_\eta^*$. In other words, if the size of the large losses l and/or their frequency λ are large enough, the firm abstains from buying reinsurance, even if it is fairly priced.

Summarizing, reinsurance against large (Poisson) losses is only used when the firm has enough liquidity. This is in contrast with reinsurance of small (Brownian) losses as in Section 5.2, in which case the firm only uses reinsurance when its cash reserves are low.

5.4 Further reading

Before De Finetti (1957), the usual way to go about modeling risk management in insurance companies was to study the minimization of the probability of ruin. It was De Finetti who originally suggested the maximization of the discounted stream of dividends as an alternative managerial objective. His work, set in discrete time, is the point of origin of the liquidity-management models studied throughout this book. A modern exposition of De Finetti's model can be found in Chapter 1 of Schmidli (2008), a book that provides a systematic presentation of the use of stochastic-control techniques in insurance problems. It should be noted that a large part of the literature on dynamic models of insurance firms uses the classical risk model (also called the Cramer-Lundberg model) mentioned in Section 3.4, as the arrival of large losses is an issue that many insurers must face. The model presented in Section 5.3 can, in fact, be seen as a modification of the classical risk model to allow for Brownian risk, even though the size of large losses is assumed to be constant.

Asmussen and Taksar (1997) study the optimal-dividends problem under the assumption that the rate at which dividends are paid is bounded above by $a_0 > 0$. The authors show that the dividend-distribution strategy that maximizes shareholder value is the following: i) if a_0 is small enough, then dividends are paid out constantly at rate a_0; ii) for larger values of a_0, the optimal strategy is of threshold type. There is a threshold m^* such that no payouts take place if the liquid reserves are smaller than m^*, whereas dividends are continuously paid out at the maximal rate whenever the liquid reserves exceed m^*. In a second step, Asmussen and Taskar consider the limit case when a_0 tends to infinity, and they recover the localized strategy of our base liquidity-management model.

Gerber and Shiu (2004) model the earnings of a company via a Brownian motion with positive drift. They assume that dividends are distributed according to a barrier strategy and provide an explicit expression for the moment-generating function of the time of ruin and of the sum of the discounted dividends until ruin. The optimal dividend barrier is chosen so as to maximize the expectation of the latter, which results in the classical supercontact condition. Hoejgaard and Taksar (2004) start with a similar model, but then allow for risk control in terms of proportional reinsurance and for investment of the liquid reserves in a Black-Scholes financial market.

Azcue and Muler (2005) and Albrecher and Thonhauser (2008) study the dividend-distribution problem using a Cramér-Lundberg model. The former authors also study several types of reinsurance possibilities. In both cases the value functions are identified using the viscosity solutions[8] of the associated Hamilton-Jacobi-Bellman equa-

---

[8] The definition and properties of viscosity solutions can be found in Fleming and Soner (2006).

tions. Interestingly, unlike the Brownian case, the optimal dividend-distribution strategies are, in general, of band type (Albrecher and Tonhauser show that if losses are exponentially distributed, then the optimal payout strategy is of barrier type).

Similar to our Section 3.2, Eisenberg and Schmidli (2011) study dynamic proportional reinsurance strategies. They do so both in a diffusion setup and using the classical risk model. Instead of maximizing the discounted stream of dividends until bankruptcy, however, here the manager's aim is to minimize the ruin probability. Taksar (2000) and Avanzi (2009) offer comprehensive overviews of the dividend-distribution and risk-control problems in insurance.

6 Applications to Investment

THUS FAR, WE have only considered firms that do not invest. This chapter addresses the important question of the determinants of corporate investment. The first two sections are based on Hayashi (1982) and Bolton et al. (2011) where the purpose of investment decisions is to adjust the firm's CAPITAL STOCK over time. This question was studied early on in the seminal paper of Tobin (1969), who showed that optimal investment decisions are determined by the marginal value of the physical capital of a firm (its marginal Tobin's q).[1] Section 6.1 presents Hayashi's (1982) paper, which derives analytically the optimal investment strategy and endogenizes Tobin's q. Section 6.2, based on Bolton et al. (2011), introduces financial frictions into Hayashi's model. Section 6.3 is based on Décamps and Villeneuve (2006) and studies a different kind of investment, namely the adoption of a new (and more productive) technology. The optimal timing for the adoption of the new technology is a real-option problem, but it is complicated by the assumption that no external financing is available. The choice of the optimal investment time interacts with the decisions to distribute dividends, as payouts reduce the availability of funds that must be used to invest in the new technology.

6.1 The "q-model" of corporate investment

This section is based on Hayashi (1982), who clarified the link between the NEOCLASSICAL model, where firms maximize the NPV of their cash flows subject to technological constraints, and Tobin's model of investment as a function of the marginal value of capital q. For the time being we neglect financial frictions and assume that the firm's owners can always inject new funds at no cost. As a consequence, the firm does not need to keep any cash reserves.

---

[1] Originally, Tobin worked with the **average** value of capital, which is easier to estimate empirically.

6.1.1 The stock of capital and its productivity

The neoclassical model considers firms that use labor and capital to produce output. Labor can be adjusted at no cost (and is not explicitly modeled here), while capital adjustment is costly. The production function has constant returns to scale: once labor input has been optimized given the available CAPITAL STOCK, net output is the product of the capital stock times its productivity, which is modeled as an Arithmetic Brownian Motion

$$\mu dt + \sigma dZ_t.$$

In other words, each unit of capital generates an expected output flow μ per unit of time with a volatility σ. Productivity shocks are i.i.d. over time. The capital stock $K = \{K_t, t \geq 0\}$ evolves with time, due to the combination of depreciation at a constant rate $\delta > 0$ and investment I_t. Therefore, the dynamics of K are given by the deterministic equation

$$dK_t = \left(I_t - \delta K_t\right)dt, \quad K_0 = k. \tag{6.1.1}$$

The adjustment cost function is[2]

$$H(I, K) = \frac{\theta}{2} \frac{I^2}{K},$$

with $\theta > 0$ parametrizing the adjustment cost of capital. This means that the total cost of investment is given by $I + H(I, K)$: the physical capital investment plus the corresponding adjustment cost. The INVESTMENT RATE i_t is

$$i_t := \frac{I_t}{K_t}.$$

Then, $i_t + (\theta/2)i_t^2$ is the unitary cost of investment. Due to constant returns to scale, the gross earnings dX_t generated by the firm are proportional to its capital stock:

$$dX_t = K_t\left[\mu dt + \sigma dZ_t\right].$$

The firm's net earnings (taking investment into account) are

$$dY_t^i = K_t\left[\mu dt + \sigma dZ_t - \left(i_t + \frac{\theta}{2}i_t^2\right)dt\right].$$

---

[2]The results extend if H is increasing, convex and has constant returns to scale.

6.1.2 Shareholder value

We assume that shareholders are risk neutral and discount the future at rate $\rho > 0$. Thus, in the absence of financial frictions, shareholder value equals the expected present value of future net earnings (as was the case in Chapter 1). In other words, given initial capital k and an investment rate process i, shareholder value equals

$$V^i(k) := \mathbb{E}\left[\int_0^\infty e^{-\rho t} dY_t^i \big| K_0 = k\right] = K_0 + \int_0^\infty e^{-\rho t} K_t\left[\mu - i_t - \frac{\theta}{2}i_t^2\right]dt. \tag{6.1.2}$$

The shareholders' problem is then to find

$$V(k) := \sup_{i \in \mathscr{A}} V^i(k), \quad k \geq 0.$$

As in the previous chapters, the shareholders' problem is stationary: decisions are based only on the current stock of capital. In particular, Equation (6.1.1) implies that the capital stock at date t is

$$K_t = k \exp\left\{\int_0^t (i_s - \delta) ds\right\}. \tag{6.1.3}$$

This implies that the optimal investment strategy is independent of k, which is only a scaling factor in Expression (6.1.3). Hence, the optimal investment rate is constant: $i_t^* \equiv i^*$, with i^* to be determined. The optimally controlled capital stock grows (or decays) at a constant rate:

$$K_t^* = \exp(i^* - \delta)t.$$

This means that we may restrict our search for the optimal investment rate to finding $i \geq 0$ that maximizes

$$V^i(k) = k\left(\mu - i - \frac{\theta}{2}i^2\right)\int_0^\infty e^{-(\rho+\delta-i)t}dt = k\frac{\mu - i - (\theta/2)i^2}{\rho + \delta - i}. \tag{6.1.4}$$

6.1.3 Tobin's q

An important observation is that $V^i(k)$ is proportional to the current capital stock k. In other words, if we define

$$q(i) := \frac{\mu - i - (\theta/2)i^2}{\rho + \delta - i}, \tag{6.1.5}$$

then $V^i(k) = k \cdot q(i)$. The quantity $q(i)$ is TOBIN'S q. It is the unitary (market) value of capital.

In the absence of financial frictions, the optimal i (the first-best value i_{fb} of the investment policy) is obtained by maximizing the mapping $i \mapsto q(i)$ for $i \in [0, \delta + \rho]$. In order to have a well-defined, interior solution, we require

$$q'(0) = \frac{\mu - (\rho + \delta)}{(\rho + \delta)^2} > 0 \quad \text{and} \quad \mu \le \rho + \delta + \frac{\theta}{2}(\rho + \delta)^2.$$

Therefore, μ must be between $(\rho + \delta)$ and $(\rho + \delta) + (\theta/2)(\rho + \delta)^2$. These conditions guarantee the existence of an interior maximum, characterized by the first-order condition

$$q'(i) = \frac{(\theta/2)i^2 - \theta i(\rho + \delta) + \mu - \rho - \delta}{(\rho + \delta - i)^2} = 0. \tag{6.1.6}$$

The optimal investment rate i_{fb} must be chosen among the roots of the quadratic equation

$$\frac{\theta}{2}i^2 - \theta i(\rho + \delta) + \mu - \rho - \delta = 0,$$

which are

$$\rho + \delta \pm \sqrt{(\rho + \delta)^2 - \frac{2}{\theta}(\mu - \rho - \delta)}.$$

The condition $i_{\text{fb}} < \rho + \delta$ implies that only the smallest of the two roots is a candidate for i_{fb}. The first-best investment rate is then

$$i_{\text{fb}} = \rho + \delta - \sqrt{(\rho + \delta)^2 - \frac{2}{\theta}(\mu - \rho - \delta)}. \tag{6.1.7}$$

Figure 6.1 shows the graph of q for the following parameter values: depreciation rate $\delta = 0.1$, discount rate $\rho = 0.1$, expected productivity of capital $\mu = 0.3$ and adjustment cost of capital $\theta = 10$.

As expected in a frictionless setting, i_{fb} is independent of k and σ[3]. Inserting the value of i_{fb} into Expression (6.1.5) yields, after simplification,

$$q_{\text{fb}} := q(i_{\text{fb}}) = 1 + \theta i_{\text{fb}}.$$

We have that the first-best firm value function is[4]

$$V_{\text{fb}}(k) = k(1 + \theta i_{\text{fb}})$$

[3] In the model with frictions of the upcoming section, the optimal investment-to-capital ratio depends on k and σ.

[4] If we compare V_{fb} to the first-best case of the base model in Section 2.3.3, we see that, although both are affine, here $V_{\text{fb}}(0) = 0$.

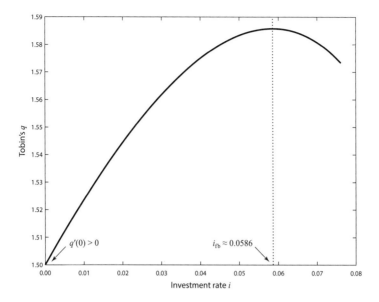

Figure 6.1: Tobin's q for various levels of investment rate.

and the firm's capital stock at date t is

$$K_t = k \exp\left\{\left(\rho - \sqrt{(\rho+\delta)^2 - \frac{2}{\theta}(\mu - \rho - \delta)}\right)t\right\}.$$

Whether or not the firm's capital stock decays to zero, remains constant over time or grows exponentially depends on the sign of $\rho - \sqrt{(\rho+\delta)^2 - (2/\theta)(\mu - \rho - \delta)}$. All other things being equal, if the adjustment cost of capital is high (i.e. θ is large), the firm's capital stock depletes over time. The opposite is true if θ is small. In Figure 6.2 we depict the evolution of the firm's capital stock when $\delta = 0.15, \mu = 0.26, \rho = 0.04, \sigma = 0.11$ and $\theta = 4, \approx 4.05$ and 6. We have set $k = 1$ and the capital stock remains constant at this level when $\theta \approx 4.05$.

6.2 Introducing external financial frictions

Mimicking the transition from problems of insolvency to those of illiquidity that we adopted between Chapters 1 and 2, we assume in this section (based on Bolton et al. (2011)) that the firm must maintain a nonnegative level of cash reserves or instead be forced into liqui-

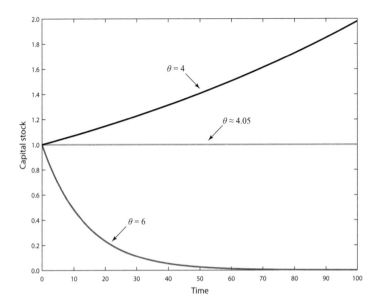

Figure 6.2: The evolution of K_t for different levels of θ

dation.[5] As before, we assume the firm has zero liquidation value. So as to (partially) control the firm's liquidity, the manager chooses not only an investment strategy $i = \{i_t, t \geq 0\}$, but also a dividend-distribution strategy $L = \{L_t, t \geq 0\}$.

6.2.1 The impact of liquidity constraints on firm value

In Section 6.1 the sole state variable was the firm's capital stock K. Introducing liquidity constraints implies that shareholder value is now also a function of the firm's liquid reserves M:

$$V(M, K) = \sup_{L,i} \mathbb{E}\left[\int_0^\tau e^{-\rho} K_t dL_t \Big| M_0 = M, K_0 = K\right],$$

where the capital stock and the cash reserves evolve as

$$dK_t = K_t(i_t - \delta)dt, \qquad\qquad\qquad K_0 = K; \quad (6.2.1)$$

$$dM_t = K_t\left[\left(\mu - i_t - \frac{\theta}{2}i_t^2\right)dt + \sigma dZ_t - dL_t\right], \qquad M_0 = M, \quad (6.2.2)$$

respectively. As in Chapter 2 the liquidation time is defined as

$$\tau := \inf\{t \geq 0 | M_t < 0\}.$$

---

[5]Bolton et al. (2011) allow for costly recapitalization.

Recall that in Section 4.2, where we studied a bank's portfolio problem, the manager could decide on the amount of risky assets (loans) on the bank's balance sheet. Similarly, in the model at hand the manager can decide at each date t on the capital stock K_t (thereby on the firm's "size") through the choice of investment strategy. We stress that now the costs of investment are shouldered by the firm's liquid reserves, as can be seen in Expression (6.2.2), instead of by the shareholders' deep pockets, as in Section 6.1.[6]

The predictable process L corresponds to the cumulative dividends **per unit** of capital. In other words, $K_t dL_t$ represents the (non-negative) flow of dividends. On the other hand, i is the investment-to-capital ratio. Given that the latter depends on the capital stock K, so does the dividend-distribution boundary $M^*(K)$. That is, in contrast with the base liquidity-management model, now the value function is defined in the two-dimensional region

$$\mathcal{D} := \{(M, K) \mid M \in (0, M^*(K)), K > 0\}.$$

6.2.2 The size-adjusted value function

Away from the boundaries of $\mathcal{D}$, where neither dividend distribution nor liquidation take place, the value function V satisfies the Bellman equation

$$\rho V(M, K) = \max_{i \geq 0} \left\{ K\left(\mu - i - \frac{\theta}{2} i^2\right) \frac{\partial V}{\partial M}(M, K) + \frac{\sigma^2}{2} K^2 \frac{\partial^2 V}{\partial M^2}(M, K) \right.$$
$$\left. + K(i - \delta) \frac{\partial V}{\partial K}(M, K) \right\},$$
$$(6.2.3)$$

together with the boundary conditions

$$V(0, K) = 0, \text{ for all } K > 0 \quad \text{and} \quad \frac{\partial V}{\partial M}(M^*(K), K) = 1.$$

---

[6] As in Décamps et al. (2011), Bolton et al. (2011) allow for external, costly financing. Equity again dominates debt because there are neither informational issues nor tax advantages of debt. Issuing securities involves a fixed cost κ; therefore, it is only done in a lumpy and infrequent fashion. The firm's cash reserves then evolve according to

$$dM_t = K_t \left[\left(\mu - i_t - \frac{\theta}{2} i_t^2\right) dt + \sigma dZ_t - dL_t + dJ_t\right], \quad M_0 = M,$$

where the predictable process $J = \{J_t, t \geq 0\}$ is the cumulative equity-issuance process per unit of capital stock. In other words, $K_t dJ_t$ represents the (non-negative) new equity issuances. Just as in Section 3.1, this process is driven by an impulse control that is activated when cash reserves hit an equity issuance barrier $\underline{M}$.

In general, determining the free boundary $M^* = \{M^*(K), K > 0\}$; thus, finding V is quite complicated (see, e.g Barth et al. (2016) for a description of a numerical approach). This is due to the fact that, unlike the models in Chapters 2–5, we now have to determine a curve in two-dimensional space $(M \times K)$ instead of a threshold $m^* \geq 0$. However, as in the frictionless model of Section 6.1, analyzing shareholder value is greatly simplified by the fact that it is homogeneous of degree one in (M, K):

$$V(M, K) = K V\left(\frac{M}{K}, 1\right) =: K\, v(m),$$

where the size-adjusted variable $m := M/K$ denotes the liquidity-to-assets ratio. The size-adjusted value function v satisfies the one-dimensional Bellman equation

$$\rho v(m) = \max_{i \geq 0}\left\{\left(\mu - i - \frac{\theta}{2}i^2\right)v'(m) + \frac{\sigma^2}{2}v''(m) + \left(i - \delta\right)\left(v(m) - mv'(m)\right)\right\}.$$
(6.2.4)

This equation can be deduced from Expression (6.2.3) by observing that

$$\frac{\partial V}{\partial M} = v'(m), \quad \frac{\partial^2 V}{\partial M^2} = \frac{v''(m)}{K} \quad \text{and} \quad \frac{\partial V}{\partial K} = v(m) - mv'(m).$$

Under the assumption that v is concave, there is a size-adjusted dividend-distribution threshold $m^* > 0$; thus, we have the boundary conditions
$$v(0) = 0 \quad \text{and} \quad v'(m^*) = 1.$$

Observe that the proportionality of the value function with respect to K implies that $M^*(K) = m^*K$: the dividend-distribution barrier is linear in K.

In the retention region $(0, m^*)$ there is no dividend distribution. In order to determine the optimal investment rule $i^*(m)$ as a function of the size-adjusted liquid reserves, we use the first-order condition with respect to i in the maximization problem in Expression (6.2.4):

$$v(m) - mv'(m) - (1 + \theta i)v'(m) = 0. \tag{6.2.5}$$

There is a parallel with the determination of the optimal investment (in risky assets) rule $A^*(\epsilon)$, in Section 4.2.2, as a function of the bank's equity. From Expression (6.2.5) we have that the optimal investment rule can be expressed as a function of $m, v(m)$ and $v'(m)$:

$$i^*(m) = \frac{1}{\theta}\left[\frac{v(m)}{v'(m)} - m - 1\right].$$

Inserting the above in Expression (6.2.4) we have that, after simplification, the size-adjusted value function satisfies the Hamilton-Jacobi-Bellman equation

$$(\rho + \delta)v(m) = (\mu + \delta m)v'(m) + \frac{\sigma^2}{2}v''(m) + \frac{\big(v(m) - (m+1)v'(m)\big)^2}{2\theta v'(m)}$$

$$(6.2.6)$$

with boundary conditions $v(0) = 0$ and $v(m^*) = 1$. As before, the size-adjusted target liquidity level m^* is pinned down making use of the supercontact condition $v''(m^*) = 0$.

Solutions to Equation (6.2.6) can only be found numerically (something we do in the next section). However, by computing the derivative of i^* with respect to m, we have

$$(i^*)'(m) = -\frac{1}{\theta}\left[\frac{v(m)v''(m)}{(v'(m))^2}\right] > 0,$$

where the inequality follows from the fact that v is a concave function of m. In other words, the model predicts that firms that are more liquid should invest more, which is something that is not rejected by empirical studies.

Tobin's q is defined as the rate of change of the firm's enterprise value $V(M, K)$ with respect to its capital stock. In other words,

$$q = q(m) = \frac{\partial V(M, K)}{\partial K} = v(m) - mv'(m).$$

Once we have solved Equation (6.2.6), we may compute $q(m)$ and compare it to the first-best case.

6.2.3 Optimal investment and Tobin's q

In the simulations that we show below we use, as before, $\delta = 0.15, \mu = 0.26, \theta = 6, \rho = 0.04$ and $\sigma = 0.11$.[7] For these values the size-adjusted target cash level is $m^* \approx 0.25$. We abstain from plotting the size-adjusted value function, as its shape is very similar to the ones in the previous chapters.

Figure 6.3(a) presents Tobin's q and the corresponding first-best value q_{fb}, whereas Figure 6.3(b) depicts the optimal investment-to-capital ratio in both the frictions and first-best cases. We observe that financial frictions lead to underinvestment. In fact, for sufficiently low levels of m the firm divests so as to keep its size-adjusted cash reserves away from the liquidation boundary.

---

[7]In Bolton et al. (2011) the carry cost of cash is less than the 100% that we consider here.

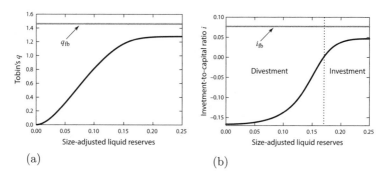

Figure 6.3: Tobin's q and the investment rate. (a) Tobin's q.
(b) Investment-to-capital i.

6.3 Adopting a new technology

The models in the previous two sections study investment that is
(mostly) used to counteract depreciation of the firm's capital stock.
An alternative scenario is investment that is lumpy and is used to
adopt a more productive technology. In this section, based on Décamps
and Villeneuve (2006), we analyze such a scenario. More specifically,
the manager has to decide when to exercise an investment opportunity that is always available but must be financed out of the firm's
liquid reserves. This introduces a real-options type component in the
base liquidity-management model.

6.3.1 The model

At date $t = 0$ the firm is exactly as in the base model. As long as
there is no investment, its net earnings are

$$\mu dt + \sigma dZ_t,$$

and the firm operates under the old technology. The firm has a single
INVESTMENT OPTION whose fixed cost is $I > 0$. We assume that the
firm has no access to credit, so that investment must be fully internally
financed. We explain below the effect of exercising the investment
option on firm profitability. The manager still chooses a cumulative-
dividend process L, but now he also decides on the INVESTMENT TIME
$\tau_i \geq 0$. On the time interval $[0, \tau_i]$, the firm's cash reserves have
dynamics

$$dM_t^L = \mu dt + \sigma dZ_t - dL_t, \quad M_0^L = m,$$

for a given cumulative-dividend process L. When $t = \tau_i$ the firm's
reserves drop from $M_{\tau_i}^L$ to $M_{\tau_i}^L - I$. On the other hand, the firm's

expected profitability jumps up from μ to $\bar{\mu} > \mu$. That is, for $t > \tau_i$, the firm's net earnings are

$$\bar{\mu}dt + \sigma dZ_t,$$

and the firm operates under the new technology. We can summarize the above by writing the evolution of cash reserves for a strategy $\pi = (L, \tau_i)$ as follows:

$$dM_t^\pi = \begin{cases} \mu dt + \sigma dZ_t - dL_t, & t < \tau_i; \\ -I, & t = \tau_i; \\ \bar{\mu}dt + \sigma dZ_t - dL_t & t > \tau_i, \end{cases} \quad M_0 = m.$$

For a strategy π and an initial level of liquid reserves m, shareholder value is given by

$$V^\pi(m) = \mathbb{E}\left[\int_0^{\tau_\pi} e^{-\rho t}dL_t \,\middle|\, M_0^\pi = m\right],$$

where

$$\tau_\pi = \inf\{t \geq 0 | M_t^\pi \leq 0\}.$$

As in the base model, the value function is defined, for $m \geq 0$, as

$$V(m) = \max_\pi V^\pi(m).$$

However, a crucial departure from the base model (in fact from all the models in Chapters 2–5) is that now retaining earnings is not only precautionary: besides acting as a buffer against liquidation, here cash reserves can be put to use to make the firm more profitable. The flip side is that, in the short run, taking the investment option exposes the firm to a higher risk of liquidation, as its liquid reserves are partially depleted. We study below the way in which the manager optimally makes this compromise and how the choices of τ_i and L interact.

6.3.2 The interaction between investment and dividend payouts

All the models studied in Chapters 2-5 fall under the umbrella of stochastic control. The evolution of the state variables (capital stock, cash reserves, etc.) is controlled by the manager via his choice of strategies (dividend payouts, equity issuance, etc.). These strategies affect shareholder value; in particular, the time of liquidation τ is a consequence of the choice of strategy but it is **not** chosen directly by the manager. In contrast, solving the current dividend-investment problem does include making a direct choice of the investment time τ_i. This is commonly called an OPTIMAL-STOPPING PROBLEM.[8]

The first step to determine the optimal τ_i is establishing shareholder value **after** investment. In our case, this is closely related to $\mathbf{V}$, the value function of the base model. Indeed, if the firm's liquid reserves at the time of investment are $m > I$ (given that investment has to be financed using the firm's reserves, it can only happen if the latter exceed I), then after investment we have a firm with $m - I$ in cash reserves, whose net earnings are $\bar{\mu}dt + \sigma dZ_t$ and whose manager has to choose the dividend payouts to shareholders. This is almost exactly the setting of the base model, save for different values of expected net earnings and initial reserves, as investment can only happen once. If we denote by $\overline{\mathbf{V}}$ the value function of the base model when the drift of the cumulative-earnings process is $\bar{\mu}$, then shareholder value after investment is

$$\overline{\mathbf{V}}(m) = \frac{e^{\bar{r}_2 m} - e^{\bar{r}_1 m}}{\bar{r}_2 e^{\bar{r}_2 \overline{m}^*} - \bar{r}_1 e^{\bar{r}_1 \overline{m}^*}}, \qquad (6.3.1)$$

where

$$\overline{m}^* = \frac{2}{\bar{r}_1 - \bar{r}_2} \log\left(-\frac{\bar{r}_2}{\bar{r}_1}\right)$$

is the target cash level after investment and $\bar{r}_1 < 0 < \bar{r}_2$ are the roots of the characteristic equation $\rho = (\sigma^2/2)r^2 + \bar{\mu}\rho$. Observe that $\overline{\mathbf{V}}(m - I)$ is the continuation value of the firm if the option to invest is taken when the liquid reserves are m. Using the Dynamic Programming Principle, we can write the shareholders' value function as

$$V(m) = \sup_{\pi=(L,\tau_i)} \mathbb{E}\left[\int_0^{\tau \wedge \tau_i} e^{-\rho t} dL_t + e^{-\rho \tau_i} \overline{\mathbf{V}}(M_{\tau_i} - I)\mathbb{1}_{\{\tau_i > \tau\}} \Big| M_0^\pi = m\right],$$
$$(6.3.2)$$

where $\tau \wedge \tau_i$ stands for "the minimum of τ and τ_i." There are two fundamentally different reasons why τ may be smaller than τ_i: i) the firm has a bad run and its cash reserves are depleted before investment is undertaken; ii) the investment option is deemed too costly; hence $\tau_i = \infty$, i.e. the firm operates as if there were no investment option and $V = \mathbf{V}$ (we revert to the base model). A natural condition for investment to be deemed too costly is

$$\frac{\bar{\mu}}{\rho} - \frac{\mu}{\rho} < \overline{m}^* + I - m^*. \qquad (6.3.3)$$

On the left-hand side we have the increment in value when the target level changes from m^* to $\overline{m}^*$, whereas the right-hand side is the

---

[8] A well-known optimal-stopping problem is exercising an American option (see, e.g. Musiela and Rutkowski (2005), Section 1.7).

investment cost. In the next section we focus on the case where investment is valuable. In particular, we assume that Condition (6.3.3) does not hold.

6.3.3 The optimal investment time

There are two alternative scenarios that may arise when searching for the optimal investment time. The simpler one is when earnings are retained and no dividends are distributed until liquid reserves reach a certain investment threshold m_i. At that point the investment is undertaken, the firm starts to operate under the new technology and dividends are distributed whenever the target $\overline{m}^*$ is reached. In this case the value function V coincides with U, the solution to the following optimal-stopping problem:

$$U(m) = \sup_{\tau_i \in \mathcal{T}} \mathbb{E}\left[e^{-\rho(\tau \wedge \tau_i)}\overline{\mathbf{V}}(M_{\tau_i} - \mathrm{I})\right] \qquad (6.3.4)$$

where $\mathcal{T}$ is the set of all $\mathbb{F}$-stopping times (see Appendix C.4). Observe that having $V = U$ requires that

$$U(m^*) > \mathbf{V}(m^*),$$

i.e. it must hold that the net present value of investing in the new project is larger than the value of the firm operated under the old technology. It is important to notice that, in this case, the manager ignores the old thresholds m^*, waits until m_i is reached to invest and then distributes dividends whenever the new target level $\overline{m}^*$ is reached. If the initial level of liquid reserves $m > m_i$, then an exceptional dividend $m - m_i$ is distributed at date $t = 0$ and the value function is

$$V(m) = m - m_i + \overline{\mathbf{V}}(m_i - \mathrm{I}).$$

The function U solves the following boundary-value problem:

$$\begin{cases} \rho U(m) = \mu U'(m) + \frac{\sigma^2}{2}U''(m), & m \in (0, m_i); \\ U(0) = 0 \text{ and } U(m_i) = \overline{\mathbf{V}}(m_i - \mathrm{I}). \end{cases} \qquad (6.3.5)$$

The optimal investment threshold m_i^* is determined by the smooth-pasting condition[9]

$$U'(m_i) = \overline{\mathbf{V}}'(m_i - \mathrm{I}).$$

---

[9]Determining threshold strategies in optimal control problems (as in Chapters 2–6) usually requires supercontact conditions. In optimal-stopping problems, on the other hand, smooth pasting is the equivalent condition.

If we let $r_1 < 0 < r_2$ be the roots of the characteristic equation $\rho = (\sigma^2/2)r^2 + \mu\rho$, then determining U reduces to finding A and m_i such that

$$A\left(e^{r_1 m_i} - e^{r_2 m_i}\right) = \overline{\mathbf{V}}(m_i - \mathrm{I}) \quad \text{and} \quad A\left(r_1 e^{r_1 m_i} - r_2 e^{r_2 m_i}\right) - \overline{\mathbf{V}}'(m_i - \mathrm{I}).$$

Figure 6.4 shows the value function and the investment threshold for the following parameters: expected profitabilities $\mu = 0.3$, $\overline{\mu} = 0.35$, discount rate $\rho = 0.15$, volatility $\sigma = 0.1$ and investment cost $I = 0.1$. The functions $\mathbf{V}$ and $\overline{\mathbf{V}}(\cdot - I)$ are also plotted.

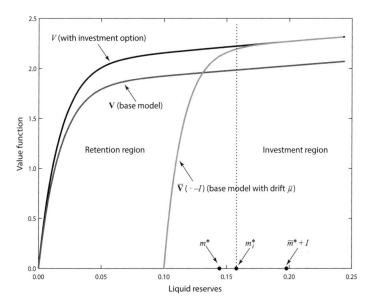

Figure 6.4: The value function and the investment threshold (first scenario)

A more complicated scenario arises when $U(m^*) \leq \mathbf{V}(m^*)$, in which case the optimal investment decision is no longer to retain earnings until the investment threshold has been reached. Instead, there are two thresholds $\underline{m}_i < \overline{m}_i$ on the interval $(m^*, \overline{m}^* + I)$ such that:

1. $V(m) = \mathbf{V}(m)$ for $m \in [0, \underline{m}_i]$. In particular, if the initial level of liquid reserves $m \leq \underline{m}_i$, then an exceptional dividend $\max\{m - m^*, 0\}$ is distributed at $t = 0$, investment is never undertaken and $M_t \leq m^*$ holds for all $t > 0$;

2. $V(m) = \overline{\mathbf{V}}(m - \mathrm{I})$ for $m \geq \overline{m}_i$, i.e $\overline{m}_i$ is the investment threshold;

3. If the initial reserves $m \in (\underline{m}_i, \overline{m}_i)$, then no dividends are distributed and the manager waits to see how cash reserves evolve. If they grow up to the point where $\overline{m}_i$ is reached, then investment is undertaken. On the contrary, if they decrease to $\underline{m}_i$, then the net present value of the investment option is dominated by the value $\mathbf{V}(\underline{m}_i)$ and investment will never occur.

Observe that the mechanism at work in point (3) above is similar to the case where the optimal investment decision is to retain earnings until the investment threshold has been reached (Problem (6.3.5)). However, the boundary conditions are different:

$$U(\underline{m}_i) = \mathbf{V}(\underline{m}_i) \quad \text{and} \quad U(\overline{m}_i) = \overline{\mathbf{V}}(\overline{m}_i - \mathrm{I}).$$

That is, if $m \in (\underline{m}_i, \overline{m}_i)$, earnings are retained until the investment threshold $\overline{m}_i$ is reached as long as cash reserves remain greater than $\underline{m}_i$. If instead $\underline{m}_i$ is reached before $\overline{m}_i$, then the firm reverts to the base-model setting. Therefore, the value function V has the following structure:

$$V(m) = \begin{cases} \mathbf{V}(m), & m \in [0, \underline{m}_i]; \\ Ae^{r_1 m_i} + Be^{r_2 m_i}, & m \in (\underline{m}_i, \overline{m}_i); \\ \overline{\mathbf{V}}(m - \mathrm{I}), & m \geq \overline{m}_i, \end{cases} \qquad (6.3.6)$$

where the constants A and B and the thresholds $\underline{m}_i$ and $\overline{m}_i$ have to be chosen so as to satisfy the smooth-pasting conditions at $\underline{m}_i$ and $\overline{m}_i$.

Observation. *By construction, we have $V'(\underline{m}_i) = 1$ and $V'(\overline{m}_i) > 1$. We show that V' is increasing on $(\underline{m}_i, \overline{m}_i)$ and V is then convex on this interval. The marginal value of cash in the firm becomes increasing due to the proximity to exercising the option to invest (which requires I in cash).*

6.4 Further reading

An alternative way to introduce frictions in Hayashi (1982) is to consider agency issues, as we do in Chapter 7. For instance, Ai and Li (2015) use a contract-theoretical framework with LIMITED COMMITMENT. The authors study the design of contracts between the financiers of a firm and its manager in three scenarios: i) the manager can always appropriate a fraction of the firm's capital stock and quit the contract, resulting in a dynamic participation constraint that is a function of the firm's capital stock; ii) shareholders cannot commit to negative NPV projects (something that happens, for instance, in the model we present in Section 7.2); iii) neither managers nor shareholders can commit. The authors show that small firms invest more, grow faster and have higher Tobin's q.

Hugonnier et al. (2015) incorporate the uncertain capital-supply assumption that we presented in Section 3.3 to the investment model of Décamps and Villeneuve (2006). What makes capital supply particularly interesting in this setting is that it may not only be used to recapitalize the firm when reserves become negative, but it can also be used to partially finance investment. This results in an additional (compared to Décamps and Villeneuve (2006)) region where the firm is not capitalized enough to finance its growth fully out of its reserves, but where (mixed) investment takes place if an arrival of external financiers takes place. Furthermore, when investment costs are high, it may happen that a firm with low enough levels of capital decides to completely abandon the investment opportunity and pays out a lumpy dividend so as to have its cash reserves land in a region $[0, \tilde{m}]$, where it reverts to the model presented in Section 3.3 with $\tilde{m}$ as its target level of reserves.

A classical reference is the book by Dixit and Pindyck (1994), where the treatment of investment as a real-option problem is thoroughly studied. The authors analyze issues of investment timing and the value of an investment option (similar to Section 6.3), as well as sequential investment. They also look into incremental investment and capacity issues and at dynamic equilibrium in a competitive industry (we look at equilibrium models in Chapter 8).

7 Agency Frictions

THE MODELS IN the previous chapters assume exogenous financial frictions (for instance, costly refinancing and bankruptcy costs). An alternative approach is to focus on endogenous frictions due to asymmetric information and conflicts of interest between managers, shareholders and debtholders. These frictions are called AGENCY FRICTIONS. In this chapter we present three agency models. First, we analyze a model where creditors are exposed to an ASSET-SUBSTITUTION problem. This means that shareholders may secretly alter the firm's risk structure after debt has been issued. Next, we study two models where the interests of the firm's manager and those of its shareholders are not fully aligned. More specifically, we look into CASH-DIVERSION and MORAL-HAZARD issues, where the firm's owners are unable to determine whether the manager is "diverting cash" or "exerting appropriate effort" (there are several equivalent ways to specify this). As a consequence, we must study the optimal-contracting problem between the firm's shareholders and its manager. The implementation of the optimal contract sheds light into the firm's capital structure. Very fittingly, the implementations that we present use the firm's current level of cash reserves as one of its instruments, which establishes a connection to the liquidity-management models of Chapters 2–6.

7.1 Asset substitution and capital structure

The first type of agency cost that we study in this chapter arises from a conflict of interests between the debtholders and the shareholders of a firm. We saw in Section 1.4 that the limited-liability option protects shareholders against downside risks, which are borne by debtholders. By contrast, shareholders benefit from upside risks, whereas debtholders do not, as soon as the firm is sufficiently far from bankruptcy. Following Leland (1998) and Décamps and Djembissi (2007), this section presents a model where the manager of a firm (acting on behalf of shareholders)[1] can secretly substitute the

---

[1] In the upcoming sections, the conflict of interests at the forefront is between managers and shareholders. Here the said conflict is between debtholders and shareholders.

assets in place by other, riskier ones. We characterize the situations
in which such an asset substitution occurs.

7.1.1 The model

We start with a setting similar to Section 1.4. However, we use the
cashflows X of the firm as the state variable (instead of its unlevered
value S). Earnings follow a Geometric Brownian Motion under the
risk-adjusted probability measure:

$$dX_t = X_t\big[(r - \beta)dt + \sigma dZ_t\big],$$

where $r > 0$ is the riskless rate, $\beta > 0$ is the payout rate of the assets
and $\sigma > 0$ is the volatility of earnings. The value of the unlevered
(that is, not indebted) firm at date $t = 0$ is[2]

$$V_0(x) = \mathbb{E}\left[\int_0^\infty e^{-rt}X_t dt\Big|X_0 = x\right] = \int_0^\infty e^{-rt}xe^{(r-\beta)t}dt = \frac{x}{\beta}.$$

Therefore, β can be interpreted as the payout rate.

Consider now the same firm with perpetual debt with coupon C
(i.e. a consol bond). For simplicity we set the tax rate to zero.[3]
The shareholders of this indebted firm benefit from limited liability:
assuming that they have "deep pockets," they can freely choose the
bankruptcy threshold x_B, below which the firm defaults. The value
of equity at date t is $E_t = E(X_t)$. We know from the valuation equation (1.3.1) that E satisfies the following boundary-value problem:

$$\begin{cases} rE(x) = x - C + (r - \beta)xE'(x) + \frac{\sigma^2 x^2}{2}E''(x), \\ E(x_B) = E'(x_B) = 0 & \text{(smooth pasting) and} \\ E(x) \sim \frac{x}{\beta} - \frac{C}{r} \text{ as } x \to \infty & \text{(default risk vanishes at infinity).} \end{cases}$$

Proceeding as in Section 1.4.2 we obtain the solution

$$E(x) = \frac{x}{\beta} - \frac{C}{r} + \left(\frac{C}{r} - \frac{x_B}{\beta}\right)\left(\frac{x}{x_B}\right)^\gamma, \tag{7.1.1}$$

where γ is the negative root of the characteristic equation

$$r = (r - \beta)\gamma + \frac{\sigma^2}{2}\gamma(\gamma - 1).$$

---

[2]Recall that the solution to the stochastic differential equation
$$dX_t = X_t\big[(r - \beta)dt + \sigma dZ_t\big], \quad X_0 = x$$
is
$$X_t = x\exp\big\{(r - \beta - \sigma^2/2)t + \sigma Z_t\big\}.$$

[3]In contrast to Section 1.4, here we do not determine the optimal value C^*.

The optimal bankruptcy threshold x_B^* is chosen to maximize

$$\left(\frac{C}{r} - \frac{x_B}{\beta}\right)x_B^{-\gamma},$$

so that[4]

$$x_B^* = \frac{\gamma}{\gamma - 1}\frac{\beta C}{r}. \tag{7.1.2}$$

7.1.2 The risk-shifting problem

Suppose now that the manager of the firm can secretly substitute the assets in place by riskier ones, generating different cashflow dynamics:

$$dX_t = X_t\big[(r - \overline{\beta})dt + \overline{\sigma}dZ_t\big].$$

We assume that $\overline{\beta} = \beta + \Delta\beta > \beta$ and $\overline{\sigma}^2 = \sigma^2 + \Delta\sigma^2 > \sigma^2$; thus, the riskier project delivers a higher payout rate but it has higher volatility. The value of equity $\widehat{E}$ when the manager has a risk-shifting option satisfies the following Bellman equation:

$$\begin{aligned}
r\widehat{E}(x) =&\, x - C + (r - \beta)x\widehat{E}'(x) + \frac{\sigma^2 x^2}{2}\widehat{E}''(x) \\
&+ \max\left\{0, -\Delta\beta x\widehat{E}'(x) + \frac{\Delta\sigma^2 x^2}{2}\widehat{E}''(x)\right\},
\end{aligned} \tag{7.1.3}$$

where the last term captures the asset-substitution option. It is easy to see that the value of this option is always positive when x is sufficiently close to x_B^*. If this were not the case, then E and $\widehat{E}$ would coincide in a right neighborhood of x_B^*. This would result in $\widehat{E}(x_B^*) = \widehat{E}'(x_B^*) = 0$; however, the Bellman equation (7.1.3) would yield[5]

$$\frac{\Delta\sigma^2 x_B^*}{2}\widehat{E}''(x_B^*) = C - x_B^* > 0,$$

which would imply that the option has a positive value, hence a contradiction. We conclude that the risk-shifting option is taken when x belongs to some interval $[\widehat{x}_B, \widehat{x}_S]$, where $\widehat{x}_B$ is the new bankruptcy threshold and $\widehat{x}_S$ is the risk-shifting threshold. In light of this, the Bellman equation (7.1.3) becomes

$$r\widehat{E}(x) = \begin{cases} x - C + (r - \overline{\beta})x\widehat{E}'(x) + \frac{\overline{\sigma}^2 x^2}{2}\widehat{E}''(x), & x \in (\widehat{x}_B, \widehat{x}_S); \\ x - C + (r - \beta)x\widehat{E}'(x) + \frac{\sigma^2 x^2}{2}\widehat{E}''(x), & x \geq \widehat{x}_S, \end{cases} \tag{7.1.4}$$

---

[4]Equivalently, x_B^* satisfies $E'(x_B^*) = 0$.
[5]The inequality $C - x_B^* > 0$ is a consequence of the convexity of E. It can also be established directly using Expression (7.1.2) and the characteristic equation $r = (r - \beta)\gamma + (\sigma^2/2)\gamma(\gamma - 1)$.

with the usual boundary conditions at $x = \widehat{x}_B$: $\widehat{E}(\widehat{x}_B) = \widehat{E}'(\widehat{x}_B) = 0$.
Proceeding as in the previous section we have that, for $x \in (\widehat{x}_B, \widehat{x}_S)$,

$$\widehat{E}(x) = \frac{x}{\overline{\beta}} - \frac{C}{r} + \left(\frac{C}{r} - \frac{\widehat{x}_B}{\overline{\beta}}\right)\left(\frac{x}{\widehat{x}_B}\right)^{\overline{\gamma}}. \tag{7.1.5}$$

Here $\overline{\gamma}$ is the negative root of the new characteristic equation

$$r = (r - \overline{\beta})\gamma + \frac{\overline{\sigma}^2}{2}\gamma(\gamma - 1),$$

and the optimal bankruptcy threshold becomes

$$\widehat{x}_B = \frac{\overline{\gamma}}{\overline{\gamma} - 1}\frac{\overline{\beta}C}{r}. \tag{7.1.6}$$

The asset-substitution threshold $\widehat{x}_S$ is characterized by the condition

$$\Delta\beta\widehat{x}_S\widehat{E}'(\widehat{x}_S) = \frac{\Delta\sigma^2}{2}\widehat{x}_S^2\widehat{E}''(\widehat{x}_S),$$

which is obtained by equating both forms of Equation (7.1.4) at
$x = \widehat{x}_S$. Finally, on the upper interval $[\widehat{x}_S, \infty)$, there is no asset
substitution and

$$\widehat{E}(x) = \frac{x}{\beta} - \frac{C}{r} + Kx^{\gamma},$$

where the constant K is such that $\widehat{E}$ is continuous at $x = \widehat{x}_S$.

7.1.3 The impact of risk shifting on firm value

The value of equity is increased by the option to substitute assets,
which, as we saw in the previous section, is exercised when x is small
enough. However, asset substitution reduces the total value of the
firm. Indeed, assuming for simplicity that the liquidation value of the
firm is zero, we have from Section 1.4.3 that, absent risk shifting, the
value of debt is

$$D(x) = \frac{C}{r} - \frac{C}{r}\left(\frac{x}{x_B}\right)^{\gamma}.$$

Adding the value of equity from Expression (7.1.1) to the value of
debt, we see that the total value of the firm, i.e. debt+equity, without
asset substitution is

$$TV(x) = \frac{x}{\beta} - \frac{x_B}{\beta}\left(\frac{x}{x_B}\right)^{\gamma}.$$

Observe that $TV(x_B) = 0$. The increment in shareholder value if asset
substitution occurs is

$$-\Delta\beta x TV'(x) + \frac{\Delta\sigma^2}{2}x^2 TV''(x). \tag{7.1.7}$$

It is easy to show that the mapping $x \mapsto TV(x)$ is increasing and **concave**. This implies that $TV'(x) > 0$ and $TV''(x) < 0$; thus, Expression (7.1.7) is **negative**. We conclude that the total value of the firm is decreased when shareholders substitute assets.

7.2 Dynamic capital structure

This section studies the consequences of a potential conflict of interest between an entrepreneur (the manager of a firm) and the investors who finance the firm. This conflict arises because the entrepreneur can secretly divert funds for personal consumption.[6] DeMarzo and Sannikov (2006) and Biais et al. (2007) were among the first to model this agency problem in a continuous-time framework. The material in this section is based on these articles.

7.2.1 The model

An entrepreneur has the expertise, but not the required funds $I \geq 0$, to start a project. In contrast, a group of financiers have the required funds but lack the necessary skills to steer the project. In the contract-theoretical terminology, the entrepreneur is referred to as the AGENT, whereas the group of financiers represent the PRINCIPAL. As before, these economic actors are all risk neutral, yet they have different preferences vis-à-vis time: the entrepreneur's discount rate ρ is higher than the financiers' discount rate r. In other words, the agent is more impatient than the principal. In the sequel we study the structure of the possible contracts between the principal and the agent that allow them to establish a firm to run the project, as well as the interaction between the two parties once the firm is running.

Once the firm has been established, it produces cashflows that follow the diffusion process

$$dY_t = \mu dt + \sigma dZ_t, \quad Y_0 = 0, \qquad (7.2.1)$$

just like the net earnings of the base liquidity-management model of Chapter 2. However, in the current setting cashflows are not accumulated and the financiers are assumed to have DEEP POCKETS, with which they can finance any shortfall.

---

[6] As in Section 7.2, we could assume that the entrepreneur may "work" or "shirk," which investors cannot verify, and that shirking carries some private benefits. The optimal contract would be quite similar to the one presented in this section.

At the core of the agency problem is the fact that the process Y is only observed by the agent, who plays the role of the firm's manager. He may report a different process

$$\widehat{Y} = \{\widehat{Y}_t, t \geq 0\}$$

and appropriate the difference $Y - \widehat{Y}$. This diversion of cash may entail deadweight costs, which we capture by assuming that for each dollar diverted only $\alpha \leq 1$ can be consumed by the agent. When $\alpha < 1$, there are DIVERSION COSTS. The principal offers a contract $\Theta = (\tau, L)$ to the agent specifying at each date t, contingent on the history of reports $\{\widehat{Y}_s, t \geq s \geq 0\}$, a TERMINATION TIME τ and an adapted process $L = \{L_t, t \geq 0\}$ of CUMULATED TRANSFERS to the manager, which is nondecreasing (because the agent has limited liability). Note that Θ can depend only on the reports $\widehat{Y}$ and not on the true cashflows Y, which the principal does not observe. In technical terms, Θ is $\sigma(\widehat{Y})$ adapted. In the case of termination, the agent's CONTINUATION PAYOFF is 0, whereas the principal collects the proceeds of liquidating the firm $v_0 \geq 0$. Throughout this section we work under the assumption that both parties can commit to the long-term contract and that they cannot renegotiate it.

If the manager owned the firm but did not have "deep pockets", then we would be back to the base liquidity-management model. Then τ would coincide with the first moment the firm would run out of funds, no diversion would take place, and L would represent cumulative dividends paid to the owner-manager. When the manager does not own the firm, τ is decided by the financiers, much as in the termination problem of the trade-off model in Section 1.4. The agent's consumption is given by the process $\widehat{C} = \{C_t, t \geq 0\}$, whose dynamics are

$$d\widehat{C}_t = dL_t + \alpha(dY_t - d\widehat{Y}_t).$$

Given a contract Θ, the agent's TOTAL UTILITY is the sum of the expected, discounted stream of consumption until termination

$$W_0(\widehat{Y}, \Theta) := \mathbb{E}\left[\int_0^\tau e^{-\rho t} d\widehat{C}_t\right].$$

If the agent chooses the report strategy $\widehat{Y}$, corresponding to the consumption strategy $\widehat{C}$, the value of the firm to the financiers is[7]

$$V_0(\widehat{Y}, \Theta) := \mathbb{E}\left[\int_0^\tau e^{-rt}(d\widehat{Y}_t - dL_t)\right],$$

---

[7]In DeMarzo and Sannikov (2006), the agent may also privately save part of the diverted cashflows; hence, she must choose how much to consume and how much to save from any diverted cashflows.

which they want to maximize. Given that the principal cannot observe Y, the maximization of the firm's value has to take into account that the agent may divert cash.

A central notion when analyzing contracts under asymmetric information is that of INCENTIVE COMPATIBILITY. A contract Θ is incentive compatible if $W_0(\widehat{Y}, \Theta)$ is maximal when $\widehat{C} = L$: in such case, it is optimal for the manager not to divert any cash. The OPTIMAL CONTRACTING PROBLEM of the principal is to find the contract that maximizes the principal's valuation among all incentive-compatible contracts that give the agent at least his reservation utility.

7.2.2 The manager's continuation utility

Thus far we have described a fairly complicated, constrained optimization problem for the financiers. Fortunately, we may appeal to the dynamic-programming techniques used in the previous chapters by showing the recursivity of this problem. To this end we define

$$W_t(\widehat{Y}, \Theta) := \mathbb{E}\left[\int_t^\tau e^{-\rho(s-t)} d\widehat{C}_s \middle| \mathcal{F}_t^{\widehat{Y}}\right]. \qquad (7.2.2)$$

The quantity $W(\widehat{Y}, \Theta)$ is the agent's CONTINUATION UTILITY provided by contract Θ. Observe that the sum of

$$e^{-\rho t} W_t(\widehat{Y}, \Theta) \quad \text{and} \quad \int_0^t e^{-\rho s} d\widehat{C}_s$$

is a martingale. Indeed,

$$e^{-\rho t} W_t(\widehat{Y}, \Theta) + \int_0^t e^{-\rho s} d\widehat{C}_s = \mathbb{E}\left[W_0(\widehat{Y}, \Theta) \middle| \mathcal{F}_t^{\widehat{Y}}\right].$$

Using the Martingale Representation Theorem (See Appendix C.3) we obtain the following result:

Proposition 7.2.1. *The process* $W(\widehat{Y}, \Theta)$ *corresponds to the agent's continuation utility for the contract* Θ *(Formula (7.2.2)) if and only if there exists an adapted process* $\beta = \{\beta_t, 0 \le t \le \tau\}$, *such that*

$$dW_t(\widehat{Y}, \Theta) = \rho W_t(\widehat{Y}, \Theta) dt - d\widehat{C}_t + \beta_t[d\widehat{Y}_t - \mu dt]. \qquad (7.2.3)$$

Proof. See Appendix A.6.

Just as the cash-reserves process serves as the (controlled) state variable in the liquidity-management models studied in Chapters 2–6,[8] here we use the agent's continuation utility as the state variable.

---

[8] In Section 4.2 we used the value of equity as a state variable, but by means of the balance-sheet equation we could have also used the liquidity level.

The main difference is that the contract Θ must be incentive compatible. The following result characterizes such contracts:

Lemma 7.2.2. *The contract Θ is incentive compatible, i.e. $d\widehat{C}_t \equiv dL_t$, if and only if the condition $\beta_t \geq \alpha$ holds for all $t \leq \tau$ almost surely.*

Proof. See Appendix A.6.

The intuition behind this condition is simple: β_t is the sensitivity of the agent's continuation utility to the reported cashflows at date t, whereas α is the sensitivity of his current payoff to his report. Hence, if $\beta_t \geq \alpha$, the agent has no interest in underreporting the cashflows.

7.2.3 The principal's value function and the optimal contract

Thanks to Proposition 7.2.1, the contract can be fully characterized by the triple (β, L, τ). It is incentive compatible if and only if $\beta_t \geq \alpha$ for all $t \geq 0$. Note that for any incentive-compatible contract we have

$$W_t = \mathbb{E}\left[\int_t^\tau e^{-\rho(s-t)}dL_s \Big| \mathcal{F}_t\right].$$

Given that $dL_s \geq 0$ for all $s \geq 0$ (limited liability), the contract must be terminated when W reaches zero:

$$W_t = 0 \Rightarrow dL_s = 0 \quad \text{for all} \quad s \geq t.$$

Obviously, a contract that never promises any future payments cannot be incentive compatible; therefore, $\tau \leq \inf\{t|W_t = 0\}$. On the other hand, the project is on average profitable (as $\mu > 0$); thus, it would be inefficient to terminate it before W reaches zero. Hence,

$$\tau = \inf\{t|W_t = 0\}.$$

Now we can apply the dynamic-programming principle. For any given continuation utility W for the agent, the best contract for the princi-pal is obtained by solving the following stochastic-control problem:

$$V(W) = \max_{\beta_t \geq \alpha, dL_t \geq 0} \mathbb{E}\left[\int_0^\tau e^{-rt}(dY_t - dL_t) \Big| W_0 = W\right]$$

where the dynamics of the state equation are

$$dW_t = \rho W_t dt + \beta_t \sigma dZ_t - dL_t$$

and the termination time is

$$\tau = \inf \{ t \,|\, W_t = 0 \}.$$

There are many similarities between the properties of the principal's value function and those of the shareholder value function in the liquidity-management models. Indeed, the mapping $W \mapsto V(W)$ is concave and the optimal payout strategy to the manager consists in compensating the manager only when W reaches a PAYOUT BARRIER W^* (the manager's continuation utility is reflected downward at W^*, as we see below). However, the current value function has very distinctive properties that arise, for instance, from the fact that the dynamics of the agent's continuation utility do not follow a controlled, Arithmetic Brownian Motion. We delve into these issues below, but first we state the main result:

Proposition 7.2.3. *The value function V is concave and it satisfies the following Hamilton-Jacobi-Bellman variational inequality for $W > 0$:*

$$\max \left\{ \mu + \rho W \, V'(W) + \frac{\alpha^2 \sigma^2}{2} V''(W) - rV(W), -V'(W) - 1 \right\} = 0,$$

together with the boundary condition $V(0) = v_0$.

The concavity of V (i.e. $V'' \leq 0$) implies that the principal never has any interest to choose $\beta_t > \alpha$. Therefore, the optimal contract is such that $\beta_t \equiv \alpha$. Some analogies notwithstanding, the interpretation of function V is different from the total value function of the firm as in Chapters 2–5. Here, the total value of the firm is $V(w) + w$: the sum of the continuation payoffs of both the financiers and the manager. In particular, V is not always increasing in the state variable W. It is in general hump-shaped. One should keep in mind that W does not belong to the principal, but to the agent. When W is low the incentives of the manager are also low; hence, it is value increasing to offer a higher W. At some point, though, increases in cashflows to be consumed by the principal no longer outweigh the required level of W; thus, for large enough values of W the value function becomes decreasing. Another point of contrast between the current model and the dividend-distribution ones is that the complementarity condition is now $V'(W) \geq -1$. In other words, payouts to the manager take place at the payout barrier W^*, which is characterized by the condition $V'(W^*) = -1$. The explanation is simple: both W and dL_t are transfers (future and current, respectively) from the financiers to the manager, hence payouts are made when the marginal cost of an immediate payment equals that of an increased continuation utility. The super-contact condition $V''(W^*) = 0$ is again used to characterize the payout barrier.

Termination takes place when the continuation utility promised to the manager reaches zero. At this point the manager simply quits. Observe that termination is here a matter of incentives and not of illiquidity. In fact, it could very well be the case that $V(W) < v_0$ for a proper subinterval of $[0, W^*]$. In such a situation the financiers would prefer to liquidate the firm, but they have committed to the long-term contract, which prevents them from stopping the project. However, if $V(W) \leq v_0$ for all $W \geq 0$, then the financiers have no incentives to start the firm in the first place. This can happen, for instance, when μ is small relative to v_0. Furthermore, the project is implemented only if the set $\{W \geq 0 \mid V(W) \geq I\}$ is not empty. If the financial markets are competitive, the optimal contract promises the manager a continuation payoff

$$W_0^* := \max \{W \geq 0 \mid V(W) \geq I\}.$$

In Figure 7.1 we have used the following parameter values: $r = 0.25, \rho = 0.3, \alpha = 0.8, v_0 = 1.3$ and $\sigma = 1$. With these parameters and for $I = 1.4$ and $\mu = 0.75$ the project is financed, even though $V(W) < v_0$ for W large enough. We observe that $W_0^* \approx 0.7$ and that the project would not be started if I were larger than ~ 1.45.

Summarizing, the optimal contract has the following structure:

1. The contract initially promises the continuation payoff W_0^* to the manager.

2. The sensitivity of the agent's continuation payoff to his reports is $\beta_t \equiv \alpha$, which yields the following dynamics for the manager's continuation utility:

$$dW_t = \rho W_t dt + \alpha \sigma dZ_t - dL_t.$$

3. When $W \in (0, W^*)$ no payments are made to the manager ($dL_t = 0$) and the value function satisfies the differential equation

$$rV(W) = \mu + \rho W V'(W) + \frac{\alpha^2 \sigma^2}{2} V''(W).$$

4. Payouts to the manager are made when $W \geq W^*$. In this region the value function is affine:

$$V(W) = V(W^*) - (W - W^*).$$

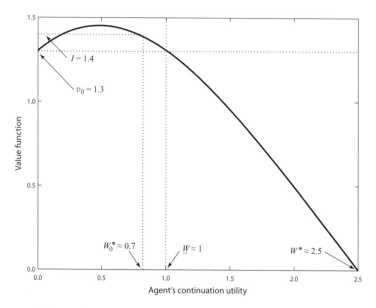

Figure 7.1: A firm that operates ($I = 1.4$ and $\mu = 0.75$)

The optimal payout strategy L^* instantaneously reflects the manager's continuation utility downward at the level W^*. An exceptional payment $W_0^* - W^*$ is made at $t = 0$ if $W_0^* > W^*$.

5. The project is terminated whenever the manager's continuation utility is zero.

7.2.4 Implementing the optimal contract through the firm's capital structure

The characterization of the optimal contract in Section 7.2.3 uses the agent's continuation utility as a state variable. We now discuss a more concrete implementation[9] of the optimal contract based on Biais et al. (2007), which uses a combination of debt, equity and cash reserves. The state variable is the level M_t of cash reserves at date t, as in the models in Chapters 2–6. The key assumption that we make concerning the implementation of the optimal contract is that the firm only issues limited-liability securities (say, stocks and bonds) that can be held by a diffuse investor base. In this implementation, all managerial decisions are contingent on the level of cash reserves.

---

[9]It should be noted that the implementation is not unique.

Put differently, the reserves level plays the role of a record-keeping device, just as the manager's continuation utility does in the abstract characterization of the optimal contract. A remarkable consequence is that, despite a very different nature of the financial frictions, the resulting firm structure is quite similar to that of the base liquidity-management model of Chapter 2, except that some debt financing becomes optimal, even in the absence of tax exemptions. In the implementation of the optimal contract proposed by Biais et al. (2007), the firm's capital structure consists of

- **debt** that pays a flow of coupons until the firm is liquidated,
- **equity** that pays dividends each time a target cash level is reached and
- **liquid reserves** that are used to meet any necessary cash outlays.

The implementation is designed in such a way that the level of cash reserves and the agent's continuation utility remain always proportional:

$$M_t := \frac{W_t}{\alpha}. \qquad (7.2.4)$$

We assume that these reserves are kept in a special account that pays the interest rate ρ and whose balance is observable. The change in the level of cash reserves in each period is equal to the net operating cashflows, plus the interest on cash reserves, minus the payments to the entrepreneur and the financiers. As no further investments are made after date 0, these additional cash reserves are accounted for as retained earnings in the firm's financial statements. From Equation (7.2.3) and the structure of the optimal contract we have

$$dM_t = \frac{1}{\alpha}\left(\rho W_t dt - dL_t + \alpha\sigma dZ_t\right) = \rho M_t dt + \sigma dZ_t - \frac{dL_t}{\alpha}. \qquad (7.2.5)$$

For this to be consistent with the assumption that interest accrues at rate ρ on retained earnings[10] we write

$$dM_t = \left(\rho M_t + \mu\right)dt + \sigma dZ_t - \frac{dL_t}{\alpha} - dC_t, \qquad (7.2.6)$$

where the process $C = \{C_t, t \geq 0\}$ represents the cumulative coupons paid out to bondholders up to date t. Equation (7.2.6) tells us that cash reserves grow with the interest earned ($\rho M_t dt$), grow (or decrease) with net earnings ($\mu dt + \sigma dZ_t$) and decrease with the payouts

---

[10] In Biais et al. (2007), the interest rate on reserves is assumed to be r. Implementation of the optimal contract then has to use a more complex bond, with a coupon $\mu - (\rho - r)M_t$ that decreases with the volume of reserves M_t.

$(dL_t/\alpha + dC_t)$. By identification, the flow of coupons is given by

$$dC_t = \mu dt. \qquad (7.2.7)$$

Therefore, we obtain the simple result that the optimal coupon equals the expected profitability of the firm.

Finally, the agent receives a (nontradeable) fraction α of the stocks, whereas the remaining $(1 - \alpha)$ go to a diffuse investor base. This is consistent with our assumption that both contracting sides can commit to a long-term agreement, as the agent cannot sell her shares and diffuse (outside) shareholders cannot coordinate so as to renegotiate the contract. Whenever the firm's cash reserves reach the threshold $M^* = W^*/\alpha$ dividends to the amount dL_t/α are paid out. A fraction α goes to the agent, who then receives dL_t. The remaining fraction $(1-\alpha)$ goes to the financiers, who also hold all the debt. The coupon is constant and equal to μ. To wrap up, the optimal contract is implemented with a combination of debt, equity and liquid reserves:

1. The coupon on debt equals μ, the expected profitability of the firm.

2. The manager receives a fraction α of the firm's equity (inside equity).

3. The firm's cash reserves evolve as

$$dM_t = \rho M_t dt + dY_t - \frac{dL_t}{\alpha} - \mu dt.$$

4. Dividends are paid out when cash reserves reach the target level $M^* = W^*/\alpha$.

5. A fraction α of these dividends goes to the manager.

6. The firm is liquidated the first time its cash reserves reach zero.

This last feature is similar to what we observe in the base liquidity-management model. However, the reason for liquidating is **not** that injecting cash is costly to financiers, but rather to threaten the manager if he diverts cash: he is fired, and the company liquidated, if reserves are depleted. If renegotiation of the contract were possible, the firm would never be liquidated. However, this would be severely impair the manager's incentives.

7.3 Preventing large risks

Firms may sometimes be subject to large risks (disasters), i.e. events of small probability that generate large costs, typically modeled using Poisson processes. This feature is absent in the model presented in Section 7.2, as risk is only modeled via a continuous (diffusion) process. The probability of disasters can be reduced if the manager exerts appropriate preventive efforts. In this section, based on Biais et al. (2010), we characterize the optimal remuneration contract for the manager among those that give him the incentives to exert these preventive efforts.

7.3.1 The model

We keep the principal-agent setting of Section 7.2 unaltered, but now consider a firm whose size at date t, denoted by X_t, can be scaled down after bad performances.[11] At any point in time any fraction of the assets may be instantaneously liquidated. We assume that assets have a zero liquidation value. What is then the purpose of downsizing? We show in Section 7.3.3 that it is a useful device to provide incentives. The predictable process $X = \{X_t, t \geq 0\}$ is a second state variable, besides the agent's continuation utility.

The size of the firm directly affects the operating profits per unit of time, which are

$$X_t \mu dt,$$

with $\mu > 0$. In order to introduce the possibility of disasters, let us consider the Poisson process $N^\Lambda = \{N_t^\Lambda, t \geq 0\}$. The intensity of N_t^Λ, i.e. the likelihood that a loss occurs over an infinitesimal time interval $[t, t + dt]$, is denoted by $\Lambda_t dt$. The firm's total output flow is given by

$$dS_t = X_t(\mu dt - \kappa dN_t^\Lambda), \quad S_0 = 0, \tag{7.3.1}$$

where $X_t \kappa$ is the cost incurred if a disaster takes place at date t. It is here that the moral-hazard component of the model comes into play. Indeed, the manager decides at each date whether or not to exert preventive effort . Whenever he chooses to exert preventive effort, the intensity of disasters is only $\Lambda_t = \lambda > 0$. This choice, though, yields no private benefits. On the other hand, not exerting effort increases the probability of large losses: under such choice $\Lambda_t = \lambda + \Delta\lambda > 0$, where $\Delta\lambda > 0$. In this case, however, the manager's private benefit per unit of time is $X_t B dt$, where $B > 0$. We denote by $\mathcal{F}^\Lambda = \{\mathcal{F}_t^\Lambda, t \geq 0\}$ the

---

[11]In Biais et al. (2010) the size can also be scaled up but, for the sake of simplicity, we do not consider this feature here.

filtration generated by N^Λ. Unlike the setting in Section 7.2, where the principal could not observe the cashflows, here the firm's output is public knowledge. What the principal does not observe, though, is the manager's effort level and, since $\lambda > 0$, large losses could happen even if he never shirked. We refer to $\Lambda = \{\Lambda_t, t \geq 0\}$ as the EFFORT PROCESS. The key parameters of the moral-hazard problem are $\Delta\lambda$ and B. If the former is very small, detecting shirking is very difficult, whereas a large B makes it very enticing for the agent to shirk. In the sequel we assume that

$$\kappa > \frac{B}{\Delta\lambda} =: b,$$

where the parameter b represents the intensity of the moral-hazard problem.

7.3.2 The contracting problem

A contract Γ between the financiers and the manager specifies, contingent on the agent's performance history, a nonnegative process $L = \{L_t, t \geq 0\}$ of flow transfers[12] to the agent and a nonincreasing process $X = \{X_t, t \geq 0\}$ that specifies the size of the project.[13] Upon observing Γ, the manager decides on an effort process Λ, and we assume that both parties can commit to the contract: renegotiation is not possible.

The manager's continuation utility and the principal's value have now to be modified to account for the private benefits of shirking and the large losses that the principal may incur. These two quantities are, for a given contract Γ

$$W_0(\Lambda, \Gamma) := \mathbb{E}^\Lambda \left[\int_0^\infty e^{-\rho t} \left(L_t + \mathbb{1}_{\{\Lambda_t = \lambda + \Delta\lambda\}} X_t B \right) dt \right] \qquad \text{(manager)}$$

and

$$V_0(\Lambda, \Gamma) := \mathbb{E}^\Lambda \left[\int_0^\tau e^{-rt} \left(X_t [\mu dt - \kappa dN_t^\Lambda] - L_t dt \right) \right] \qquad \text{(financiers)},$$

where the expectation operator $\mathbb{E}^\Lambda[\cdot]$ accounts for the fact that the arrival of large losses is governed by Λ. A contract Γ is incentive

---

[12] In this section, L_t represents the transfer to the agent per unit of time (flow) as in Section 2.2. In other words, transfers are uniformly continuous. We show below that this is without loss of generality, as the optimal choice of transfers to the agent is absolutely continuous even if this is not assumed ex-ante.

[13] The Poisson nature of underlying risk implies that the optimal payment to the agent is of the form $L_t dt$, as in Section 2.2. Another simplification is that, due to the possibility of downsizing the project, a complete liquidation never occurs ($\tau = \infty$).

compatible if exerting effort (i.e. $\Lambda_t \equiv \lambda$) is always optimal for the manager.[14] The principal strives to find an incentive-compatible contract (Λ, Γ) so as to maximize her value while delivering the manager the required level of utility.

7.3.3 Addressing incentive compatibility

When solving the model presented in Section 7.2, we saw that the agent's continuation utility could be used as the sole state variable. Although here the continuation utility is still used as a state variable, now we also have to keep track of the firm's size X. This fact notwithstanding, having an equivalent formulation to Equation (7.2.3) for the dynamics of the manager's continuation utility

$$W_t(\Lambda, \Gamma) = \mathbb{E}^\Lambda \left[\int_t^\tau e^{-\rho(s-t)} \left(L_s + \mathbb{1}_{\{\Lambda_s = \lambda + \Delta\lambda\}} X_s B \right) ds \Big| \mathcal{F}_t^\Lambda \right]$$

is still crucial so as to characterize incentive-compatible contracts. As in section 7.2.2, the sum of the agent's discounted continuation utility and past discounted payoffs is a martingale:

$$e^{-\rho t} W_t(\Lambda, \Gamma) + \int_0^t e^{-\rho s} \left(L_s + \mathbb{1}_{\{\Lambda_s = \lambda + \Delta\lambda\}} X_s B \right) ds = \mathbb{E}^\Lambda \left[W_0(\Lambda, \Gamma) \,|\, \mathcal{F}_t^\Lambda \right].$$

In Proposition 7.2.1 we made use of the Martingale Representation Theorem to show the existence of a process β, corresponding to the sensitivity of the manager's continuation utility $W(\widehat{C}, \Theta)$ to his report, such that we could write $W(\widehat{C}, \Theta)$ as an Itô process. We can do something similar here, now making use of the Martingale Representation Theorem for jump-diffusion processes:

Proposition 7.3.1. *The process $W(\Lambda, \Gamma)$ corresponds to the agent's continuation utility under contract Γ if and only if there exists an $\mathcal{F}^\Lambda$-adapted process $H = \{H_t, t \geq 0\}$, such that*

$$dW_t(\Lambda, \Gamma) = \left[\rho W_t(\Lambda, \Gamma) - L_t - \mathbb{1}_{\{\Lambda_t = \lambda + \Delta\lambda\}} X_t B \right] dt + H_t \left[\Lambda_t dt - dN_t^\Lambda \right]. \tag{7.3.2}$$

H_t is the contractual penalty inflicted upon the agent if a disaster occurs at date t.

Proof. See Appendix A.6.

The link between incentive compatibility and H is provided in the next result:

---

[14] We assume that the losses generated by a disaster are so large that the optimal contract always involves maximal risk prevention, i.e. $\Lambda_t \equiv \lambda$.

Lemma 7.3.2. *A necessary and sufficient condition for a contract Γ to be incentive compatible is that*

$$H_t \geq b\, X_t \qquad\qquad (7.3.3)$$

holds for all $t \leq \tau$ almost surely.

Proof. See Appendix A.6.

The presence of the term $H_t \left[\Lambda_t dt - dN_t^\Lambda \right]$ in the evolution of $W_t(\Lambda, \Gamma)$ indicates that, if a loss occurs at date t, then the agent's continuation utility is instantaneously reduced by the amount H_t. This is analogous to exposing the agent to some fraction of the volatility of his report in the Brownian setting of Section 7.2. Lemma 7.3.2 shows that, in order to preserve incentive compatibility, the manager's continuation utility must be reduced by $b\, X_t$ whenever a disaster occurs, which is precisely the ratio of the benefits he enjoys from shirking and the increase $\Delta\lambda$ in the probability of disasters if he shirks.

7.3.4 The financiers' value function

Our study of the financiers' value function in Section 7.2.3 was very much in line with that of the liquidity-management models in Chapters 2–6, with the dynamics of a single state variable driving the results. Now we must also account for the firm's size X_t, which implies that the value function of financiers is now a function of the pair (X, W). This yields, in principle, a considerable increase in complexity. However, the way in which the model is set up allows for the study of the problem in SIZE-ADJUSTED terms. To streamline the notation, from this point on we use the size-adjusted control variables

$$h_t := H_t/X_t; \quad l_t := L_t/X_t; \quad w_t := W_{t-}/X_t \quad \text{and} \quad x_t := X_{t+}/X_t.$$

When a disaster happens, the size-adjusted continuation utility of the agent and the size of the firm drop from w_t to $w_t - h_t$ and from X_t to $x_t X_t$, respectively. Notice that the incentive-compatibility condition that guarantees maximal risk prevention is $h_t \geq b$. We are now in the position to present the Hamilton-Jacobi-Bellman equation that we use to find the structure of the optimal contract.[15] The financiers' value function is the expected, discounted sum of the net payoffs they will receive in the future:

$$F(X, W) = \mathbb{E}\left[\int_0^\infty e^{-rt} \left([X_t - L_t]dt - \kappa dN_t \right) \Big| X_0 = X, W_0 = W \right].$$

---

[15]To follow the notation in Biais et al. (2010), here we use F instead of the previously employed V to denote the financiers' value function.

The dynamics of the state variables under an incentive-compatible contract (i.e. inducing the agent to always exert effort: $\Lambda_t \equiv \lambda$) are

$$dX_t = (1 - x_t)X_t dN_t;$$
$$dW_t = (\rho W_t - L_t)dt + H_t(\lambda dt - dN_t).$$

Proposition 7.3.3. *The financiers' value function satisfies the following Hamilton-Jacobi-Bellman equation:*

$$rF(X,W) = X(\mu - \lambda\kappa) + \max_{(h,l,x)} \left\{ -lX + [\rho W + (\lambda h - l)X]\frac{\partial F}{\partial W}(X,W) \right.$$
$$\left. - \lambda[F(X,W) - F(Xx, W - Xh)] \right\},$$
$$(7.3.4)$$

where the maximization is subject to

$$b \le h; \quad 0 \le l \quad and \quad x \le \frac{w - h}{b}.$$

Let us break down the components of Equation (7.3.4) and the corresponding constraints. As usual, the financiers' discounted flow value at each date is $rF(X,W)$. The expected net cashflows from the project of size X is $X(\mu - \lambda\kappa)$. Concerning the terms within the maximization, paying the manager decreases the financiers' flow value; hence the term $-lX$. In the absence of a disaster, variations in the manager's continuation utility induce a flow variation $[\rho W + (\lambda h - l)X](\partial F/\partial W)(X,W)$. Finally, the expected change in the financiers' value brought about by possibility of a disaster, which happens with frequency λ, is $-\lambda[F(X,W) - F(Xx, W - Xh)]$. The first two constraints have been already discussed and correspond to incentive compatibility and limited liability of the manager in terms of nonnegative transfers. The "downsizing constraint" $x \le (w - h)/b$ requires an additional explanation: A loss implies that the manager's continuation utility decreases from W to $W - Xh$. We have from Lemma 7.3.2 that if another loss were to happen arbitrarily close to the first one, then a reduction of at least Xb of the manager's continuation utility would be required for incentive compatibility. Doing so, however, would only be compatible with the manager's limited liability if $W - Xh \ge Xb$, which, in size-adjusted terms, is precisely the constraint in question. Observe that this tells us that downsizing, i.e. $x < 1$, is necessary after a loss whenever the manager's size-adjusted continuation utility is low enough that the expression $w < h + b$ is satisfied.

7.3.5 The size-adjusted problem and the optimal contract

A common assumption in the contract theory literature that deals with scalable projects (e.g. Biais et al. (2010), He (2009) and Moreno-Bromberg and Roger (2016)) is that the firm's productive technology exhibits constant returns to scale, like that in our Equation (7.3.1). This, together with a liquidation value that is linear in the firm's size, implies that the financiers' value function is homogeneous of degree 1 in (X, W):

$$F(X, W) = XF\left(1, \frac{W}{X}\right). \qquad (7.3.5)$$

The advantage of doing this is that, if we define the manager's size-adjusted continuation utility $w := W/X$ and set $f(w) := F(1, w)$, then we can separately study the behavior of the firm's scale and that of the financiers' size-adjusted flow value $f(w)$. In particular, we can rewrite Expression (7.3.4) as

$$rf(w) = (\mu - \lambda\kappa) + \max_{(h,l,x)} \left\{ -l + [\rho w + (\lambda h - l)] f'(w) \right.$$
$$\left. - \lambda\left[f(w) - xf\left(\frac{w-h}{x}\right)\right]\right\}, \qquad (7.3.6)$$

where we have used the fact that, from Equation (7.3.5),

$$\frac{\partial F}{\partial W}(X, W) = f'\left(\frac{W}{X}\right).$$

As in Section 7.2, we assume (and verify ex-post) that the mapping $w \mapsto f(w)$ is concave. Maximization with respect to $l \geq 0$ is only possible if $f'(w) \geq -1$. Transfers to the manager take place when the marginal cost of increasing his continuation utility is larger than or equal to that of an immediate transfer, i.e. when $f'(w) \leq -1$. The transfer threshold w^* is then defined via the equation $f(w^*) = -1$. An important comment is in order here. Unlike the model in Section 7.2, here there is no Brownian motion driving the changes in the manager's continuation utility. As a consequence, maintaining $w_t \leq w^*$ does not involve an instantaneous reflection as we have had hitherto. This is precisely the reason why the size-adjusted payments to the manager are absolutely continuous: we may write $dl_t = l_t dt$.

Whenever the manager's size-adjusted continuation w is smaller than b, incentive compatibility can no longer be guaranteed and the firm must be liquidated. Given that $f(0) = 0$ and f is concave, we have that

$$x \mapsto xf\left(\frac{w-h}{x}\right)$$

is increasing. This is the only place where x appears in Equation (7.3.6); therefore, it is optimal to choose it as large as possible, which captures the fact that downsizing is per se undesirable and only used to provide incentives to the agent. In other words, if there is a loss at date t the optimal downsizing policy is given by

$$x_t = \min\left\{\frac{w_t - h_t}{b}, 1\right\}.$$

Similarly, the penalty inflicted upon the agent in case of a Poisson shock never exceeds the minimum required to preserve incentive compatibility: $h_t \equiv b$. In other words, as long as there is no downsizing and $w < w^*$ we have that Equation (7.3.6) can be written as

$$rf(w) = \mu - \lambda\kappa + [\rho w + \lambda b] f'(w) - \lambda[f(w) - f(w-b)].$$

Note that downsizing is necessary after a loss if $w_t < 2b$. When it comes to the optimal choice of l_t, observe that if we set $h_t \equiv b$, which implies $\Lambda_t \equiv \lambda$, then the dynamics of the manager's continuation utility (7.3.2) can be written as

$$dW_t = (\rho W_t - X_t l_t)dt + bX_t[\lambda dt - dN_t^\lambda]. \qquad (7.3.7)$$

As long as there is no loss at date t, the continuation utility of the agent remains constant: $W_t = w^* X_t$. Then, Equation (7.3.7) can be rearranged so as to obtain the value of l_t:

$$X_t l_t = X_t[\rho w^* + \lambda b].$$

We conclude that, in size-adjusted terms, the transfer flow to the agent is

$$l_t = l^* := [\rho w^* + \lambda b]\mathbb{1}_{\{w=w^*\}}. \qquad (7.3.8)$$

The size-adjusted payments to the agent are made to keep $w_t = w^*$ until there is a loss. The payout threshold is STICKY instead of reflective. Summarizing, the optimal contract stipulates, as a function of the agent's continuation utility W:

1. Payments to the agent are made when $w_t = w^*$ and they are of magnitude $l^* X_t$. At that point, the agent's size-adjusted continuation utility then remains constant ($w_t = w^*$) as long as no further loss materializes.

2. Following a loss at date t, the agent's continuation utility is adjusted downward. If $W_t \geq 2bX_t$, then $W_{t+} = W_t - bX_t$; otherwise the firm is downsized:

$$X_{t+} = \frac{1}{b}\left(W_t - bX_t\right),$$

and $W_{t+} = bX_{t+}$. In size-adjusted terms, $w_{t+} = \max\{w_t - b, b\}$.

7.4 Further reading

The use of discrete-time models to address questions of corporate capital structure precedes the continuous-time results in this chapter. In particular, DeMarzo and Fishman (2007) develop an infinite-horizon model with cash diversion and show that the resulting optimal contract can be implemented using equity, long-term debt and a credit line. Biais et al. (2007) study the convergence of the discrete-time model when the time increment goes to zero and show that it converges to the continuous-time model presented in Section 7.2. Discrete-time models require an additional component in the optimal contract; namely, a probability of liquidation/downsizing. This feature vanishes in the continuous-time limit. It should be said that both DeMarzo and Sannikov (2006) and Biais et al. (2007) explore many more angles than what we have presented. For instance, they look at the pricing of securities and provide comparative statics. Biais et al. (2007) also present empirical implications of their model, such as the prediction that the volatility of stock prices and leverage ratio of firms should increase after bad performances. For further developments in Contract Theory, see Bolton and Dewatripont (2004) for discrete-time models and Cvitanić and Zhang (2013) for continuous-time ones.

He (2009) studies the Geometric Brownian Motion version of the model presented in Section 7.2. The scale component introduced by the use of a Geometric Brownian Motion is interpreted as firm size, which generates incentives that are analogous to the allocation of equity to the agent presented in Section 7.2.4. When the agent is as patient as investors, performance-based stock grants can be used to implement the optimal contract. An important implication of this work is that agency issues should be more severe for small firms.

Sannikov (2008) also looks into a model where the agent, while exerting costly effort, controls the drift of the output process. Unlike He (2009), however, this scaling does not affect the volatility of cashflows. A distinctive feature of this work is that, although the principal remains risk neutral, the agent is risk averse and receives consumption continuously. As a consequence, payouts no longer have the localized feature of those presented in this chapter. Nevertheless, the optimal contract still uses the agent's continuation value. The agent's "career path" is determined by several thresholds. Once her continuation utility reaches a certain point, retirement, replacement or promotion is triggered.

As we mentioned in Section 1.4, one of the major drawbacks of the trade-off theory is that it predicts a too-high leverage. In order to address this issue, He (2011) adds an agency-frictions component to the classical trade-off model. He assumes that exerting effort is costly for the manager. As a consequence, besides costs associated with bankruptcy, a debt-overhang problem arises. This is the channel through which the agency problem impacts the firm's capital structure; thus, its leverage. Even though the model does not allow for closed-form solutions to the values of debt and equity, it lends itself to calibration and predicts considerably lower leverages than the standard trade-off model.

DeMarzo et al. (2013) extend DeMarzo and Fishman (2007) and DeMarzo and Sannikov (2006) to introduce speculative behavior, both in discrete- and continuous-time settings. By this we mean the possibility of an increase in short-term profits that exposes the firm to a low-probability disaster event. In continuous time this is commonly modeled using a Poisson process. In contrast to Section 7.3, it is possible that by exerting high effort the manager fully eliminates the risk of a disaster. Moreover, an arrival of the Poisson process immediately results in termination. Naturally, lacking any other means, if the financiers want to avoid large risk taking, they must cede additional rents to the manager. In analogous fashion to what we observed in Section 7.3.5, the manager must be punished following poor performance in order to prevent shirking. Without a downsizing option, however, this must ensue through reduced rents, which implies that it might be optimal to let poorly performing managers shirk.

Moreno-Bromberg and Roger (2016) combine a downsizing feature as in Section 7.3 with the diversion+risk-taking setting of DeMarzo et al. (2013). The fact that contracts may include downsizing, which in certain cases is necessary so as to preserve incentive compatibility, allows the financiers to fully eliminate large risks. This comes at the cost of a reduced operating scale and the need to control size is interpreted as leverage management. The authors conclude that, consistent with empirical observations, firms for which risk taking is less attractive can afford a higher leverage.

DeMarzo and He (2016) develop a dynamic trade-off model with limited commitment, in terms of the shareholders' ex-ante choice of leverage, much in the spirit of Leland (1998). They characterize the equilibrium prices of equity and debt in a jump-diffusion framework, where the firm's liability structure evolves dynamically. They find that, without commitment, shareholders increase debt levels gradually over time and never voluntarily reduce them. However, the effects of asset growth and debt maturity counterweigh each other and, as a consequence, leverage converges to a long-run steady state. Then, given that creditors anticipate future increases of leverage, they demand high risk premia even when default is not a pressing concern. Hence, the tax benefits of future debt dissipate and the equilibrium value of equity coincides with that of the case where shareholders can commit to no future debt issuances.

8 Equilibrium Models

OUR UNDERSTANDING OF the macroeconomic consequences of financial frictions has recently improved thanks to continuous-time, general equilibrium models such as Brunnermeier and Sannikov (2014) and He and Krishnamurthy (2012, 2013). This chapter shows how the methods presented earlier in this book can be used to solve such models. Section 8.1 presents the model of Brunnermeier and Sannikov (2014), which, in its original form, is technically challenging. Sections 8.2 and 8.3 are devoted to simpler models that can be solved explicitly. The former contains an equilibrium version of the base liquidity-management model, whereas the latter provides an explanation for the UNDERWRITING CYCLES phenomenon that can be observed in insurance markets.

8.1 The Brunnermeier-Sannikov model

We follow the simplified presentation of Brunnermeier and Sannikov (2014) given by Isohätälä et al. (2016), which uses the methods developed in this book.

8.1.1 The model

There are two types of agents in the economy: HOUSEHOLDS and EXPERTS (who can be interpreted as financial intermediaries). Experts may borrow from households in order to finance their investments in a risky asset called CAPITAL. However, households only agree to lend if there is no risk of default. Therefore, the net wealth of financial intermediaries must remain positive at all times.

Capital is used to produce a consumption good. The productivity of capital is constant within the two classes of agents: each unit of capital operated by a financial intermediary yields a units of the consumption good per unit of time, whereas the same unit operated by households yields $\underline{a}$. Experts are more productive than households ($a > \underline{a}$) and they are also more impatient: their discount rate ρ is larger than r, the discount rate of the households. Both financial intermediaries and households are risk neutral. Note that the disparity in productivity and impatience between financial intermediaries and households generates a motive for lending.

Capital depreciates at a stochastic rate

$$\delta dt + \sigma_0 dZ_t,$$

where $\delta, \sigma_0 > 0$.[1] The standard Brownian motion Z is the only source of uncertainty in the model and it is the same for all agents: it represents the aggregate shocks faced by the economy as a whole. Capital can also be created by investing the consumption good but, as in Chapter 6, doing so is subject to adjustment costs: an investment rate i requires $\Psi(i)$ units of the good per unit of capital, where Ψ is a convex, increasing function such that $\Psi(i) > i$ for all $i \geq 0$. The difference $\Psi(i) - i$ represents the adjustment costs.

At each date t, capital can be traded at price q_t. Our aim is to determine the equilibrium dynamics of $q = \{q_t, t \geq 0\}$, as well as the agents' decisions in terms of investment, consumption and output. To this end, let us denote by D_t and k_t the debt and capital stock of a financial intermediary at date t. Given that debt is risk free and households are risk neutral, the interest rate they demand on debt must equal their discount rate r. Then, the debt and capital-stock dynamics are

$$dD_t = \left[-ak_t + rD_t + \Psi(i_t)k_t + q_t x_t \right] dt + dL_t, \tag{8.1.1}$$

$$dk_t = \left[(i_t - \delta)k_t + x_t \right] dt + \sigma_0 k_t dZ_t, \tag{8.1.2}$$

where x_t denotes the CAPITAL PURCHASES (if $x_t > 0$) or CAPITAL SALES (if $x_t < 0$) of the financial intermediary at date t. The nondecreasing process $L = \{L_t, t \geq 0\}$ denotes the cumulative dividends paid to the shareholders of financial intermediaries. As capital may be bought and sold without restrictions, the relevant state variable for the decisions of a financial intermediary is its net wealth at each date t:

$$n_t = q_t k_t - D_t.$$

We assume that the price of capital q follows a Markov diffusion process

$$dq_t = \mu(q_t)dt + \sigma(q_t)dZ_t, \tag{8.1.3}$$

which we characterize later. Making use of the stochastic product rule (see Appendix C.2) we may write

$$dn_t = q_t dk_t + k_t dq_t + dq_t dk_t - dD_t.$$

---

[1] In contrast, the models in Sections 6.1 and 6.2 assumed a deterministic depreciation rate and a stochastic productivity of capital. As we see below, both approaches are very similar.

From Expressions (8.1.2) and (8.1.3), we obtain

$$q_t dk_t = q_t \big[(i_t - \delta) k_t + x_t \big] dt + \sigma_0 q_t k_t dZ_t,$$
$$k_t dq_t = k_t \mu(q_t) dt + k_t \sigma(q_t) dZ_t,$$
$$dq_t dk_t = \sigma_0 \sigma(q_t) k_t dt.$$

Expression (8.1.1) then yields, after simplifications,

$$dn_t = \big\{ rn_t + k_t \big[a - rq_t - \Psi(i_t) + \mu(q_t) + q_t(i_t - \delta) + \sigma_0 \sigma(q_t) \big] \big\} dt$$
$$+ \sigma_0 q_t k_t dZ_t - dL_t.$$

$$(8.1.4)$$

8.1.2 The value function of a financial intermediary

Financial intermediaries maximize the expected present value of the (nonnegative) stream of dividends paid out to their shareholders:

$$V(n, q, k) = \max_{x, (i, L) \geq 0} \mathbb{E} \left[\int_0^\infty e^{-\rho t} dL_t \,\big|\, n_0 = n, q_0 = q, k_0 = k \right], \quad (8.1.5)$$

with the dynamics of the state variables given by Expressions (8.1.2), (8.1.3) and (8.1.4). Observe that, as the model is stationary, the value of a financial intermediary at any date is a function of the current values of its net worth n, of the rental price of capital q and of its capital stock k. The value function (8.1.5) satisfies the Bellman equation

$$\rho V(n, q, k) = \max_{x, (i, dL) \geq 0} \left\{ \left[rn + k(a - \Psi(i) + \mu(q) + q(i - \delta) + \sigma_0 \sigma(q) \right. \right.$$
$$\left. - rq) \right] \frac{\partial V}{\partial n}(n, q, k) + \big[(i - \delta) k + x \big] \frac{\partial V}{\partial k}(n, q, k)$$
$$+ \mu(q) \frac{\partial V}{\partial q}(n, q, k) + dL \left(1 - \frac{\partial V}{\partial n}(n, q, k) \right)$$
$$+ \frac{\sigma^2(q)}{2} \frac{\partial^2 V}{\partial q^2}(n, q, k) + \frac{\sigma_0^2 k^2}{2} \frac{\partial^2 V}{\partial k^2}(n, q, k)$$
$$+ qk \sigma_0 \sigma(q) \frac{\partial^2 V}{\partial n \partial q}(n, q, k) + k^2 q \sigma_0^2 \frac{\partial^2 V}{\partial n \partial k}(n, q, k)$$
$$+ k \sigma_0 \frac{\partial^2 V}{\partial q \partial k}(n, q, k) \right\}.$$

$$(8.1.6)$$

Several observations allow us to simplify Expression (8.1.6):

1. The only term where the control x appears is $x(\partial V/\partial k)(n, q, k)$. The maximization with respect to x (which can be positive or negative) is only possible if $\partial V/\partial k \equiv 0$. This implies $V(n, q, k)$ is in fact $V(n, q)$ and the terms $\partial V/\partial k, \partial^2 V/\partial k^2, \partial^2 V/\partial n \partial k$ and $\partial^2 V/\partial q \partial k$ are all identically zero.

2. Given that Expression (8.1.5) and the evolution equations for the state equations are homogeneous in (k, n, dL), the value function is linear in n; thus, there exists a function W such that $V(n, q) = nW(q)$. Hence,

$$\frac{\partial V}{\partial n}(n, q) = W(q), \quad \frac{\partial^2 V}{\partial n^2}(n, q) \equiv 0,$$

$$\frac{\partial V}{\partial q}(n, q) = nW'(q) \quad \text{and} \quad \frac{\partial^2 V}{\partial q^2}(n, q) = nW''(q).$$

If we interpret n as the book value of the equity of the financial intermediary, then $W(q)$ can be viewed as the market-to-book ratio of the firm's equity. In analogous fashion to the liquidity-management models in previous chapters, W determines the dividend-distribution strategy. Indeed, the maximization problem

$$\max_{dL \geq 0} dL\big(1 - W(q)\big)$$

only has a solution when $W(q) \geq 1$ for all q. We assume (and verify ex-post) that W is decreasing; therefore, there exists $q^* \geq 0$ such that dividends are distributed (i.e. $dL > 0$) when $q = q^*$ and q^* is determined via the relation $W(q^*) = 1$. In other words, dividend payouts only occur when the market-to-book ratio of equity equals one. Note that, contrary to the base model, here dividend distribution is not triggered by an excess of cash reserves. Instead, it is when the price of capital q reaches the upper boundary q^* that payouts take place. This is due to the fact that the financial intermediaries' value function is not strictly concave in n but simply linear. Using this linearity property, when $q < q^*$ the Bellman equation (8.1.6) can be simplified as follows:

$$\rho n W(q) = \max_{i \geq 0}\Big\{ W(q)\big[rn + k(a - \Psi(i) + \mu(q) + q(i - \delta) + \sigma_0 \sigma(q) - rq)\big]$$

$$+ \mu(q)nW'(q) + \frac{\sigma^2(q)}{2}nW''(q) + \sigma_0\sigma(q)qkW'(q)\Big\}.$$

$$(8.1.7)$$

The left-hand term of Expression (8.1.7) is independent of k, but on its right-hand side we have the term

$$W(q)kA(q) + \sigma_0\sigma(q)qkW'(q),$$

where

$$\Phi(q) := \max_{i \geq 0}\big\{qi - \Psi(i)\big\} \quad \text{and} \quad A(q) := a + \Phi(q) + \mu(q) - q\delta + \sigma_0\sigma(q) - rq.$$

This is only possible if

$$W(q)A(q) + \sigma_0\sigma(q)qW'(q) = 0. \tag{8.1.8}$$

This allows us to rewrite Expression (8.1.7), after dividing it by n, as

$$(\rho - r)W(q) = \mu(q)W'(q) + \frac{\sigma^2(q)}{2}W''(q). \tag{8.1.9}$$

Observe that we can rewrite Condition (8.1.8) as

$$\frac{W'(q)}{W(q)} = B(q), \quad \text{with} \quad B(q) := -\frac{A(q)}{\sigma_0\sigma(q)q}. \tag{8.1.10}$$

Moreover, $W''(q)/W(q) = B'(q) + B^2(q)$. Inserting these two expressions into Equation (8.1.9) yields a second equation for the market-to-book ratio of the firm's equity:

$$\rho - r = \mu(q)B(q) + \frac{\sigma^2(q)}{2}\left[B'(q) + B^2(q)\right]. \tag{8.1.11}$$

For a given q^* (still to be determined), B can be found by solving Equation (8.1.11) with the boundary condition $B(q^*) = 0$ (implied by the super-contact condition $W'(q^*) = 0$). Then W can be obtained by a simple integration:

$$W(q) = \exp\left\{\int_{q^*}^q B(s)ds\right\}.$$

8.1.3 The value function of households and the competitive equilibrium

We can address the households' problem in a similar way, but we must take into account that their discount rate is $r < \rho$, their productivity is $\underline{a} < a$ and, importantly, their consumption is allowed to be negative. Their value function is denoted $n\underline{W}(q)$ and satisfies the Bellman equation

$$rn\underline{W}(q) = \max_{i\geq 0, dL}\left\{\underline{W}(q)\left[rn + k(\underline{a} - \Psi(i) + \mu(q) + q(i - \delta) + \sigma_0\sigma(q) - rq)\right]\right.$$
$$+ dL\left(1 - \underline{W}(q)\right) + \mu(q)n\underline{W}'(q) + \frac{\sigma^2(q)}{2}n\underline{W}''(q)$$
$$\left. + \sigma_0\sigma(q)qk\underline{W}'(q)\right\}.$$
$$\tag{8.1.12}$$

Given that $dL < 0$ is now possible, a solution to this equation only exists if $\underline{W}(q) \equiv 1$, which leads to the simplified equation

$$0 = k(\underline{a} + \Phi(q) + \mu(q) - q\delta + \sigma_0\sigma(q) - rq).$$

There are two possible solutions to this maximization problem:

1. either some capital is in the hands of households ($k > 0$) and

$$\mu(q) = q\delta + rq - \sigma_0\sigma(q) - \underline{a} - \Phi(q), \qquad (8.1.13)$$

2. or no capital is in the hands of households ($k = 0$) and

$$\mu(q) \leq q\delta + rq - \sigma_0\sigma(q) - \underline{a} - \Phi(q). \qquad (8.1.14)$$

In the first case, the equilibrium can be readily determined: there are three unknown functions (B, μ and σ) and the system of Equations (8.1.7), (8.1.11) and (8.1.13). Using standard (but complex) numerical methods, Brunnermeier and Sannikov (2014) are able to determine the shape of these three functions in the region where some capital is in the hands of households. However, the efficient allocation of capital only occurs when financial intermediaries manage all capital (recall they are more productive than households). In that case, Equation (8.1.13) is replaced by Inequality (8.1.14) and the equilibrium is found using the conditions that guarantee that all capital is held by financial intermediaries.

Brunnermeier and Sannikov (2014) show that there is a one-to-one (increasing) mapping between the fraction η of total wealth held by financial intermediaries and the price q of capital. When this fraction is high enough, financial intermediaries have sufficient net wealth to manage all the productive capital in the economy, which is the efficient allocation. However, after a long series of negative shocks, the net wealth of financial intermediaries may become too low. As a consequence, the economy may be stuck for some time in an inefficient situation. One of the merits of the methodology in Brunnermeier and Sannikov (2014) is that it uncovers the global dynamics of the economy and shows that it exhibits nonlinearities. In contrast, the traditional way to proceed is to compute the reaction (impulse response) of a deterministic economy to a single, unexpected shock by linearizing the economy around the deterministic steady state. Using Brunnermeier and Sannikov's methodology, one can incorporate repeated shocks (modeled by the Brownian motion Z) and determine their long-term impact on the economy. The deterministic steady state is replaced by the stationary (and ergodic) distribution of the state variable, which can either be the fraction η of aggregate wealth held by financial intermediaries or the price q of capital itself.

The next two sections present simpler equilibrium models where this stationary distribution and the global dynamics of the economy are easier to determine. Section 8.2 studies a farming economy where farmers cannot pledge any collateral; thus, they have to self-finance their activities. Section 8.3 studies cycles in the insurance industry.

8.2 An equilibrium version of the base model

In this section, based on Klimenko et al. (2017), we extend the base liquidity-management model to an equilibrium setting. This leads to a simple model in the spirit of Brunnermeier and Sannikov (2014). The probabilistic setup is identical to that of Chapter 2.

8.2.1 The model

There are two goods (land and corn) and two types of agents: LAND-LORDS and FARMERS. The stock of land in the economy is fixed and, for simplicity, it is normalized to 1. The land belongs to the landlords, who may either rent it out to farmers or cultivate it on their own. The RENTAL PRICE of land at date t, denoted by q_t, is determined in equilibrium. Farmers are more efficient in cultivating land than landlords; thus, absent financial frictions it would be optimal for all the land to be cultivated by farmers.

The PRODUCTION TECHNOLOGIES of landlords and farmers (analogous to the net-earnings process of Section 2.1) are now heterogeneous. All farmers are equally productive; one unit of land cultivated by a farmer yields a net flow

$$dy_t = a\,dt + \sigma_0 dZ_t$$

of corn. Here a is the expected productivity of farmers, dZ_t represents an aggregate productivity shock (say, weather) and σ_0 is the fundamental volatility (measuring the impact of weather shocks on productivity). By contrast, landlords are heterogeneous. The corn yield of each unit of land cultivated by a landlord of TYPE $\tilde{\alpha}$ is

$$d\tilde{y}_t = \tilde{\alpha}\,dt + \sigma_0 dZ_t,$$

where $\tilde{\alpha}$ is distributed according to some cumulative distribution $F : [0, a] \mapsto [0, 1]$. Observe that, regardless of his type, a landlord is almost surely less productive than any farmer.

Financial frictions in this model are captured by the fact that farmers have limited liability and cannot borrow to buy land. They have to rent it from the landlords. For each unit of land they cultivate, farmers have to pay a flow of q units of corn to their landlords (q is the RENTAL PRICE of land). Without frictions, all the land would be cultivated by the farmers and the rental rate would match expected productivity: $q_t \equiv a$. With frictions, however, we show that $q_t \in [0, a]$.

In this section we focus on MARKOV EQUILIBRIA, where the price q_t satisfies

$$dq_t = \mu(q_t)dt + \sigma(q_t)dZ_t. \qquad (8.2.1)$$

The rental rate $q = (q_t, t \geq 0)$ is the sole aggregate state variable in this model. The mappings $q \mapsto \mu(q)$ and $q \mapsto \sigma(q)$ are determined below.

The agents' decision problems.   All agents discount the future at rate $r > 0$. Landlords are risk neutral and immediately consume their earnings (recall they cannot lend to the farmers, because the latter have no collateral). Farmers are risk averse and choose their CONSUMPTION FLOW $\{c_t, t \geq 0\}$ so as to maximize

$$\mathbb{E}\left[\int_0^\infty e^{-rt}\log(c_t)dt\right].$$

At each date t, farmers hold precautionary savings $m_t \geq 0$. They choose the scale of their activity k_t (the size of the plot that they cultivate) and consumption as functions of their savings m_t and the rental price of land q_t. The value function of each farmer is

$$V(m, q) = \sup_{(c,k)\geq 0} \mathbb{E}\left[\int_0^\infty e^{-rt}\log(c_t)dt \Big| m_0 = m, q_0 = q\right] \qquad (8.2.2)$$

under the state equations

$$dm_t = k_t\big[(a - q_t)dt + \sigma_0 dZ_t\big] - c_t dt,$$
$$dq_t = \mu(q_t)dt + \sigma(q_t)dZ_t.$$

The first equation, concerning the evolution of a farmer's savings, is controlled by the farmer through the choice of c_t and k_t. The second equation is taken as given because individual farmers are too small to influence land prices: each farmer is a price taker. Note that farmers have rational expectations regarding the dynamics of the rental price q.

The optimal decisions of a farmer.   In similar fashion to the valuation equations that we saw in the previous chapters, the value function of an individual farmer satisfies the Bellman equation

$$rV(m,q) = \max_{(c,k)\geq 0} \Big\{ \underbrace{(k(a-q)-c)\frac{\partial V}{\partial m}(m,q) + \frac{k^2\sigma_0^2}{2}\frac{\partial^2 V}{\partial m^2}(m,q)}_{\text{impact of changes in the level of savings}}$$

$$+ \log(c) + k\sigma_0\sigma(q)q\frac{\partial^2 V}{\partial m\partial q}(m,q)$$

$$+ \underbrace{\mu(q)q\frac{\partial V}{\partial q}(m,q) + \frac{\sigma^2(q)q^2}{2}\frac{\partial^2 V}{\partial q^2}(m,q)}_{\text{impact of rental rate changes}} \Big\}$$

$$(8.2.3)$$

The feasible set of trajectories $(c,k) = \{(c_t, k_t), t \geq 0\}$ for a farmer is homogeneous of degree one with respect to his initial savings m_0. In other words, if (c,k) is feasible when $m_0 = 1$, then (mc, mk) is feasible when $m_0 = m$. Given that $\log(m \cdot c) = \log(m) + \log(c)$, it is easy to show[2] that the optimal trajectory when $m_0 = m$ is just a homothetic transformation of that when $m_0 = 1$:

$$c^*(m,q) = m\, c^*(1,q) \quad \text{and} \quad k^*(m,q) = m\, k^*(1,q).$$

This implies that the value function is separable:

$$V(m,q) = \mathbb{E}\left[\int_0^\infty e^{-rt}\log\big(m\, c_t^*(1,q_t)\big)dt \right] = \frac{\log(m)}{r} + V(1,q).$$

This separability property considerably simplifies the maximization problem in Expression (8.2.3), given that $(\partial^2 V/\partial m\partial q)(m,q) = 0$. Then, the first-order condition for c in Equation (8.2.3) yields:

$$\frac{1}{c} = \frac{\partial V}{\partial m}(m,q) = \frac{1}{r\,m}. \qquad (8.2.4)$$

When it comes to the maximization with respect to k, we obtain from the first-order condition that

$$k = -\frac{(a-q)\frac{\partial V}{\partial m}(m,q)}{\sigma_0^2\frac{\partial^2 V}{\partial m^2}(m,q)} = \frac{a-q}{\sigma_0^2}m. \qquad (8.2.5)$$

From Equations (8.2.4) and (8.2.5) we readily obtain the following result:

---

[2]Indeed, by definition $V(1,q)$ is larger than the value obtained from any trajectory (c,k) that starts at $m_0 = 1$. Then

$$V(m,q) = \frac{\log(m)}{r} + V(1,q)$$

is larger than any trajectory (mc, mk) that starts at $m_0 = m$.

Proposition 8.2.1. *The optimal consumption and demand for land (c^*, k^*) of individual farmers are characterized by*

$$c^*(m, q) = r\, m \quad and \quad k^*(m, q) = \frac{(a - q)}{\sigma_0^2} m.$$

8.2.2 Equilibrium

In order to solve for the equilibrium, we proceed with the aggregation of individual behaviors and find the dynamics of q that equate supply and demand for corn and land. From Proposition 8.2.1 we have that the overall demand for land K_D at time t is given by:

$$K_D(q_t) = \frac{a - q_t}{\sigma_0^2} M_t, \tag{8.2.6}$$

where M_t denotes the aggregate savings of farmers, which evolve according to

$$dM_t = K_D(q_t)\big[(a - q_t)dt + \sigma_0 dZ_t\big] - r M_t dt. \tag{8.2.7}$$

Here $r M_t$ is the aggregate consumption flow of farmers (recall Proposition 8.2.1). A landlord of type $\tilde{\alpha}$ rents his land whenever $\tilde{\alpha} \le q$. Thus, the overall supply of land K_S at time t is

$$K_S(q_t) = \int_0^{q_t} dF(\tilde{\alpha}) = F(q_t). \tag{8.2.8}$$

Definition 8.2.2. *A Markov equilibrium consists of a Markov price process $q = \{q_t, t \ge 0\}$ and an aggregate savings function M such that markets for land and corn clear when $M_t = M(q_t)$.*

Equality of demand and supply for corn results in

$$F(q_t) = \frac{a - q_t}{\sigma_0^2} M_t,$$

which determines aggregate savings as a function of q :

$$M_t = \sigma_0^2 \left[\frac{F(q_t)}{a - q_t}\right] =: M(q_t).$$

Using Itô's lemma, we obtain

$$d\big[M(q_t)\big] = \big[\mu(q_t)M'(q_t) + \frac{1}{2}\sigma^2(q_t)M''(q_t)\big]dt + \sigma(q_t)M(q_t)dZ_t.$$

Equilibrium of the market for corn also yields

$$dM_t = F(q_t)\big[(a - q_t)dt + \sigma_0 dZ_t\big] - rM_t dt.$$

Matching the drift and volatility terms of dM_t and $d\big[M(q_t)\big]$ yields explicit expressions for $\mu(q)$ and $\sigma(q)$, which we present in the following result:

Proposition 8.2.3. *There exists a unique Markov equilibrium. The dynamics of the rental rate are:*

$$dq_t = \mu(q_t)dt + \sigma(q_t)dZ_t, \tag{8.2.9}$$

with

$$\mu(q) = \sigma(q)H(q), \quad \sigma(q) = \frac{(a-q)^2 q}{\sigma_0[q + (a-q)\epsilon_1(q)]}, \tag{8.2.10}$$

where

$$\epsilon_1(q) = q\frac{K_S'(q)}{K_S(q)}$$

is the elasticity of land supply and $H(q)$ has an unsightly (but explicit) expression[3]. Aggregate savings equal

$$M(q) = \frac{\sigma_0^2}{a-q}K_S(q).$$

8.2.3 The long-term behavior of the economy

In this section we characterize the long-term behavior of the economy. To simplify computations, we assume that $\tilde{\alpha}$ is uniformly distributed on $[0, a]$, so that the supply of land satisfies

$$K_S(q) = \frac{q}{a}.$$

In this case, $\epsilon_1(q) \equiv 1$ and Expression (8.2.10) results in the law of motion of q being determined by

$$\mu(q) = \frac{a-q}{a}\left[\frac{(a-q)^3}{a\sigma_0^2} - r\right]q \quad \text{and} \quad \sigma(q) = \frac{(a-q)^2}{a\sigma_0}q. \tag{8.2.11}$$

Aggregate savings are given by

$$M(q) = \frac{\sigma_0^2}{a-q}\frac{q}{a}.$$

---

[3] $H(q) := \left[\frac{\epsilon_1(q)(a-q)^2[(2\epsilon_1(q)-\epsilon_2(q))(a-q)+2q]}{2\sigma_0[\epsilon_1(q)(a-q)+q]^2} - \frac{r\sigma_0}{a-q}\right]$, $\epsilon_1(q) = \frac{qK_S'(q)}{K_S(q)}$ and $\epsilon_2(q) = \frac{qK_S''(q)}{K_S'(q)}$.

Observe that μ is negative when q is close to a and positive when q is close to zero. More precisely,

$$\lim_{q \searrow 0} \frac{\mu(q)}{q} = \frac{a^2}{\sigma_0^2} > 0 \quad \text{and} \quad \lim_{q \nearrow a} \frac{\mu(q)}{a - q} = -r < 0.$$

Moreover,

$$\lim_{q \searrow 0} \frac{\sigma(q)}{q} = \frac{a}{\sigma_0} > 0 \quad \text{and} \quad \lim_{q \nearrow a} \frac{\sigma(q)}{a - q} = 0.$$

Therefore, the process q **never** reaches the boundaries 0 and a. This is because, close to zero, q behaves like a Geometric Brownian Motion, whereas $(a-q)$ behaves like a deterministic, decreasing process around $q = a$. We present in Figure 8.1 the equilibrium drift and volatility of the rental price of land q for the following parameters: productivity of farmers $a = 0.1$, discount rate $r = 5\%$, and unitary volatility of corn yield $\sigma_0 = 0.1$. We observe that $\mu(q) < 0$ for $q > 0.062$.

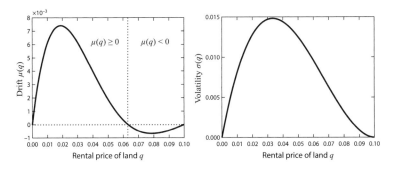

Figure 8.1: Equilibrium drift and volatility of q.

The process q determined by μ and σ in Expression (8.2.11) has a unique stationary distribution that satisfies the ERGODIC PROPERTY. Roughly speaking, this means that when $t \to \infty$, the average time that the process q spends on any interval (q_1, q_2) is equal to

$$\int_{q_1}^{q_2} f(q) dq,$$

where f is the density of the ergodic distribution.[4] In our case, the shape of the ergodic distribution depends uniquely on the risk-adjusted profitability of farming:

$$\theta := \frac{a}{\sigma_0}.$$

[4]An introduction to ergodicity from an economic perspective can be found in Horst (2008). A more technical reference is Bellet (2006).

In order to show this, consider the scaled process $\hat{q} := q/a$. The law of motion of $\hat{q}$ is

$$d\hat{q}_t = \hat{\mu}(\hat{q})dt + \hat{\sigma}(\hat{q})dZ_t,$$

where

$$\hat{\mu}(\hat{q}) = (1 - \hat{q})\Big[(1 - \hat{q})^3\theta^2 - r\Big]\hat{q} \quad \text{and} \quad \hat{\sigma}(\hat{q}) = (1 - \hat{q})^2\hat{q}\theta.$$

Proposition 8.2.4. *For any $\theta > 0$, the ergodic distribution of the scaled process $\hat{q}$ has the density function*

$$f(\hat{q}) = \frac{g(\hat{q})}{\hat{\sigma}^2(\hat{q})} \quad on \ [0,1],$$

where

$$g(\hat{q}) = \exp\Big\{\frac{(2\hat{q} - 3)}{(1 - \hat{q})^2}\frac{r}{\theta^2}\Big\}\Big(\frac{1 - \hat{q}}{\hat{q}}\Big)^{\frac{2r}{\theta^2}}\frac{1}{\theta^2(1 - \hat{q})^4}.$$

Proof. See Appendix A.7.

Figure 8.2 shows that the density of the ergodic distribution may have different shapes according to the value of θ. In Figure 8.2(b), where $\theta = 1.5$, the distribution is concentrated around a high value of $\hat{q}$. The economy stays most of the time in a situation that is not too far from "full employment of farmers" ($\hat{q} = 1$). By contrast, when θ is low (e.g. $\theta = 1$ as in Figure 8.2(a)) the distribution of $\hat{q}$ is not single peaked and it carries more mass around the "low-employment" states (where $\hat{q}$ is small) and even exhibits what can be called a POVERTY TRAP. Consider, indeed, the region where q (or $\hat{q}$) is close to zero: the farmers' savings are almost depleted ($M(q) = (\sigma_0^2 F(q))/(a - q) \sim 0$), which makes the farmers very risk averse, as

$$-\frac{\partial^2 V}{\partial m^2}\Big/\frac{\partial V}{\partial m} = 1/m.$$

They operate on a small scale ($K(q) = F(q) \sim 0$). Hence, even if productivity shocks are positive, the farmers do not make large profits and, therefore, their savings do not increase rapidly. As a result, the economy may spend a large amount of time in this poverty trap.

8.3 Insurance cycles

Insurance markets are said to be SOFT when prices and profits are low and insurance capacity is high. On the other hand, they are HARD when prices and profits are high, insurance capacity is restricted and policy cancellations or nonrenewals are frequent. Akin to the better

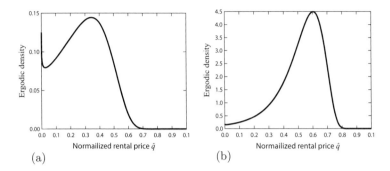

Figure 8.2: Scaled ergodic density for $r = 5\%$ and different values of θ. (a) Risk-adjusted profitability $\theta = 1$. (b) Risk-adjusted profitability $\theta = 1.5$.

known BUSINESS CYCLE, the insurance industry is exposed to UNDER-WRITING CYCLES. Insurance premia and profits rise (in hard-markets phases) and fall (in soft-markets phases) with some regularity over time.[5] A simple narrative for this phenomenon is depicted in Figure 8.3. From a theoretical perspective, cycles are hard to justify if we stick to the view that markets are efficient, implying that insurance premia should equal the expected present value of policy claims. The model we present below follows Klimenko et al. (2017). It is a continuous-time version of Winter (1994). Both works show that real frictions on capital markets may cause underwriting cycles by making the industry's capacity dependent on past profits and losses.

8.3.1 The model

The insurance market consists of a continuum of insurance firms that offer coverage to individuals, all of which face perfectly correlated risks (say, the weather). All agents use the same discount rate $r > 0$. In order to have a stationary model, we assume that losses are incurred continuously. Namely, the losses incurred by an individual at date t are of the form

$$l\,dt + \sigma_0 dZ_t,$$

where l denotes expected losses per unit of time, σ_0 is an exposure parameter and Z is a standard Brownian motion. As all risks are perfectly correlated, Z is the same for all individuals. Insurance contracts are also continuously rolled over and their market premium at

---

[5]A detailed review of the literature on underwriting cycles can be found in Harrington et al. (2013).

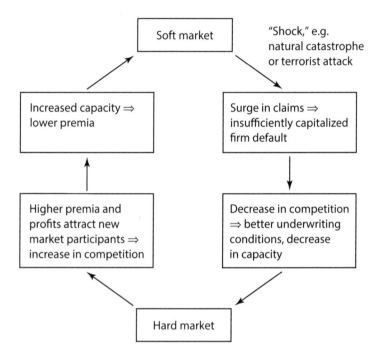

Figure 8.3: An underwriting cycle.

date t is

$$\pi_t = l + \sigma_0 p_t.$$

The LOADING FACTOR $\sigma_0 p_t$ is the margin that the underwriter collects on top of the FAIR PREMIUM (in this case the expected loss). In a slight abuse of the language, in the following we refer to p as to the PRICE OF INSURANCE. The demand for insurance is a decreasing and differentiable function D of p.

Due to the fact that insurance contracts have an infinitesimal length, in this model insurers have no long-term liabilities. As a consequence, at each date t the balance sheet of an insurance firm has only one item per side: equity e_t on the liability side and liquid reserves on the asset side. By the balance-sheet equation $e_t = m_t$; thus, m_t can be viewed simultaneously as the volume of reserves and as the book value of equity of an insurance firm.

The cumulative earnings from date 0 to t of an individual insurer are denoted by Y_t and evolve according to

$$dY_t = x_t\big[\pi_t dt - (ldt + \sigma_0 dZ_t)\big], \quad Y_0 = 0,$$

where x_t is the INSURANCE SUPPLY at date t (the control is continuously chosen by the insurer). As in Section 3.2, net earnings may
be distributed as dividends or retained as liquid reserves.[6] The level
of liquid reserves also may be increased by raising new equity, which
entails a proportional cost β. Liquid reserves have the following dynamics:

$$dm_t = \sigma_0 x_t \left(p_t dt - dZ_t \right) + dj_t - dl_t, \quad m_0 = m, \qquad (8.3.1)$$

where the nondecreasing, predictable processes $j = \{j_t, t \geq 0\}$ and
$l = \{l_t, t \geq 0\}$ denote cumulative equity issues and dividends, respectively.[7] Provided that, in equilibrium, the supply of insurance
contracts equals the demand for them, the aggregate reserves (the
capacity) of the entire insurance sector satisfy

$$dM_t = \sigma_0 D(p_t) \left(p_t dt - dW_t \right) + dJ_t - dL_t, \quad M_0 = M, \qquad (8.3.2)$$

where L and J are the aggregate counterparts of the cumulative dividend and recapitalization processes l and j introduced above.

As in the previous section, a Markov equilibrium is characterized by
a price-reserves couple of processes (p, M). However, in the current
case it is more convenient to take the aggregate reserves M as the state
variable and look for the insurance price p as a deterministic function
of M. In other words, a Markov equilibrium is a couple (p, M) such
that the aggregate liquid reserves M follow a Markov diffusion and
there exists a deterministic function p such that if at each date the
insurance price satisfies $p_t = p(M_t)$, then the market for insurance
clears. In the following section, we establish the existence of a unique
stationary Markov equilibrium and study its main properties.

8.3.2 Equilibrium

We assume that insurance firms are price takers: at each date t they
take the aggregate reserves M_t and the corresponding insurance price
$p(M_t)$ as given and choose their supply $x_t \geq 0$ and their dividend
(dl_t) and recapitalization (dj_t) policies so as to maximize shareholder
value:

$$V(m, M) = \max_{(x,l,j)} \mathbb{E} \left[\int_0^\infty e^{-rt} \{dl_t - (1 + \beta)dj_t\} \,\middle|\, m_0 = m, M_0 = M \right],$$

---

[6] Again, for simplicity, we assume no interest accrues on retained earnings.

[7] This model may be viewed as an equilibrium version of the classical ruin theory
model (in its Brownian version, as in Gerber and Shiu (2004)), where reserves
dynamics are
$$dm_t = \mu dt - \sigma_0 dZ_t - dl_t.$$
Besides the fact that here prices and quantities are endogenous, companies
also have the recapitalization option.

where the individual and cumulative reserves evolve according to Expressions (8.3.1) and (8.3.2), respectively.

We assume that the issuing cost β is small, so that there is no default ($\tau = \infty$) as insurance companies issue capital when they run out of reserves. Therefore, defaulting is suboptimal for insurance shareholders. The value function satisfies the following Bellman equation:

$$
\begin{aligned}
rV(m, M) = \max_{(x, dj, dl) \geq 0} \Big\{ & dl - (1 + \beta)dj + \frac{\partial V}{\partial m}(m, M)\big[\sigma_0 x p(M) + dj - dl\big] \\
& + \frac{\partial V}{\partial M}(m, M)\big[\sigma_0 D\big(p(M)\big)p(M)\big] + \frac{(\sigma_0 x)^2}{2}\frac{\partial^2 V}{\partial m^2} \\
& + \frac{\partial^2 V}{\partial m \partial M}(m, M)\big[\sigma_0^2 x D\big(p(M)\big)\big] + \frac{\sigma_0^2 D^2\big(p(M)\big)}{2}\frac{\partial^2 V}{\partial M^2}\Big\}.
\end{aligned}
$$
$$(8.3.3)$$

Note that the objective function and the state equation (8.3.1) are homogeneous in (m, x, dl, dj). As in Section 8.2, this property implies that optimal strategies are linear in m. Due to risk neutrality, the value function is then linear in the individual level of reserves, i.e. there exists a function $U : \mathbb{R} \to \mathbb{R}$ such that

$$V(m, M) = mU(M).$$

The linearity of V in m allows us to simplify the Bellman equation (8.3.3):

$$
rmU(M) = \max_{(x, dj, dl) \geq 0} \Big\{ \underbrace{x\sigma_0\big[p(M)U(M) + \sigma_0 D\big(p(M)\big)U'(M)\big]}_{\text{impact of individual risk exposure}}
$$

$$
+ \underbrace{\sigma_0 D\big(p(M)\big)p(M)mU'(M) + \frac{\sigma_0^2 D^2\big(p(M)\big)}{2}mU''(M)}_{\text{impact of changes in aggregate capacity}}
$$

$$
+ \underbrace{dl\big(1 - U(M)\big) - dj\big(1 + \beta - U(M)\big)}_{\text{impact of payout and recapitalization policies}} \Big\}.
$$
$$(8.3.4)$$

Observe that $U(M) = V(m, M)/m$ is the market-to-book ratio of equity for the insurance company, which is the same for the entire insurance sector.[8] As in Section 8.2, dividend and recapitalization decisions are entirely driven by $U(M)$. They do not depend on individual liquid reserves, as is the case in the base model (which is

---

[8] Given that $U(M)$ is the market value of one dollar of net worth (book value) in the insurance sector when total capacity is M, it can be interpreted as the insurance analogue of Tobin's q (see Chapter 6).

not an equilibrium model!). Analogous to Section 3.2, we have, on the one hand, that $U(M) \geq 1$ (with equality when dividends are distributed). On the other hand, $U(M) \leq 1 + \beta$ (with equality in case of recapitalization).

We show below that $U' \leq 0$: the market-to-book ratio of the insurance sector is a decreasing function of its aggregate capacity. As a result, aggregate capacity varies between two (reflecting) barriers $\underline{M} < \overline{M}$ (just like the liquid-reserves process in Section 3.2). Dividends are distributed when the insurance sector is sufficiently capitalized so that the market-to-book value of the insurers' equity falls to 1, i.e. $U(\overline{M}) = 1$. On the other side of the spectrum, recapitalization takes place when the insurance sector is so undercapitalized that the marginal value of holding one share in the firm equals the marginal cost of issuing a new one, i.e. $U(\underline{M}) = 1 + \beta$.

We turn now to the optimal choice of the scale of operation of an insurer. Maximization with respect to x implies that an interior solution exists if and only if the market-to-book value $u(M)$ and the price $p(M)$ satisfy

$$p(M) = -\frac{U'(M)}{U(M)}\sigma_0 D\big(p(M)\big). \tag{8.3.5}$$

The above equality implies that the term in x vanishes from the Bellman equation (8.3.4). On the interval $(\underline{M}, \overline{M})$ where aggregate capacity evolves solely due to retained earnings, the latter transforms into

$$rU(M) = \sigma_0 D\big(p(M)\big)p(M)U'(M) + \frac{\sigma_0^2 D^2\big(p(M)\big)}{2}U''(M),\ M \in (\underline{M}, \overline{M}).$$

Dividing the above equation by $U(M)$ and using Equation (8.3.5) to replace the term $U'(M)/U(M)$ by $-p(M)/(\sigma_0 D\big(p(M)\big))$, we obtain:

$$r + p^2(M) = \frac{\sigma_0^2 D^2\big(p(M)\big)}{2}\frac{U''(M)}{U(M)}. \tag{8.3.6}$$

The shareholders of an insurance company are indifferent about the scale of operation as long as the insurance price $p(M)$ satisfies Equations (8.3.5) and (8.3.6). The size of the insurance sector is, therefore, entirely determined by the demand side.

In order to determine the equilibrium insurance price, we use once more the fact that Equation (8.3.5) can be rewritten as

$$\frac{U'(M)}{U(M)} = -\frac{p(M)}{\sigma_0 D\big(p(M)\big)}.$$

By differentiating this equation and rearranging terms we obtain

$$\frac{U''(M)}{U(M)} = \left[\frac{U'(M)}{U(M)}\right]^2 - p'(M)\left[\frac{1}{\sigma_0 D(p(M))} - \frac{p(M)D'(p(M))}{\sigma_0 D^2(p(M))}\right]. \quad (8.3.7)$$

Combining Expressions (8.3.7) and (8.3.6) yields

$$2(r + p^2(M)) = p^2(M) - \sigma_0 p'(M)\Big(D(p(M)) - pD'(p(M))\Big),$$

which ultimately leads to the first-order differential equation determining the equilibrium price:

$$p'(M) = -\frac{1}{\sigma_0}\frac{2r + p^2(M)}{D(p(M)) - p(M)D'(p(M))}. \quad (8.3.8)$$

Given that $D' < 0$, we observe from Equation (8.3.8) that the price of insurance is decreasing in the aggregate capacity of the insurance sector. Moreover, applying Itô's lemma to $p_t = p(M_t)$, we can obtain an explicit characterization of the insurance price process. Indeed,

$$dp_t = \underbrace{\sigma_0 D(p(M_t))\Big(p_t(M_t)p'(M_t) + \frac{\sigma_0 D(p(M_t))}{2}p'(M_t)\Big) dt}_{\mu(p_t)}$$
$$\underbrace{- \sigma_0 D(p(M_t))p'(M_t) dZ_t.}_{\sigma(p_t)} \quad (8.3.9)$$

A simple computation yields the expression of the insurance price volatility:

$$\sigma(p) = -\sigma_0 D(p(M_t))p'(M_t) = \frac{2r + p^2}{1 + \varepsilon_1(p)}, \quad (8.3.10)$$

where $\varepsilon_1(p)$ is the elasticity of the demand for insurance:

$$\varepsilon_1(p) := -\frac{pD'(p)}{D(p)}.$$

Therefore, Equation (8.3.8) can be rewritten as

$$p'(M) = -\frac{\sigma[p(M)]}{\sigma_0 D(p(M))}. \quad (8.3.11)$$

Furthermore, simplifying the expression of the drift of the insurance price yields

$$\mu(p) = \sigma(p) \left[\frac{(2r + p^2)\varepsilon_1(p)\varepsilon_2(p)}{2p(1 + \varepsilon_1(p))^2} - \frac{p\varepsilon_1(p)}{1 + \varepsilon_1(p)} \right], \qquad (8.3.12)$$

where

$$\varepsilon_2(p) := -\frac{pD''(p)}{D'(p)}.$$

In order to complete the characterization of the competitive equilibrium, we define $V(M) := MU(M)$, which is the market value of the entire insurance industry. The absence of arbitrage opportunities at the (reflecting) boundaries $\underline{M}$ and $\overline{M}$ implies that

$$V'(\overline{M}) = U(\overline{M}) + \overline{M}U'(\overline{M}) = 1$$

and

$$V'(\underline{M}) = U(\underline{M}) + \underline{M}U'(\underline{M}) = 1 + \beta.$$

These expressions, together with the fact that $U(\overline{M}) = 1$ and $U(\underline{M}) = 1 + \beta$, yield

$$U'(\overline{M}) = 0 \quad \text{and} \quad \underline{M} = 0.$$

Observe that $U'(\overline{M}) = 0$ is a form of super-contact condition at $M = \overline{M}$, which, together with Expression (8.3.5), implies that the loading factor vanishes when the insurance industry operates at the maximum level of reserves:

$$\underline{p} := p(\overline{M}) = 0.$$

Given that $p'(M) < 0$, this implies that $p(M) > 0$[9] for all $M > 0$ and, therefore, $U'(M) < 0$ as we conjectured before. Thus, in the competitive equilibrium, insurance companies recapitalize only when running out of reserves. The target level of aggregate reserves in the insurance industry is obtained by integrating Expression (8.3.11):[10]

$$\overline{M} = \int_0^{\overline{p}} \frac{\sigma_0 D(p)}{\sigma(p)} dp. \qquad (8.3.13)$$

---

[9] In practice, however, loading factors can be negative, as insurers can hedge their losses via complementary financial market activities.

[10] This is because

$$\frac{dp}{dM} = -\frac{\sigma(p)}{\sigma_0 D(p)}.$$

Hence,

$$dM = -\frac{\sigma_0 D(p)}{\sigma(p)} dp$$

and, by integration, we obtain

$$\int_0^{\overline{p}} \frac{\sigma_0 D(p)}{\sigma(p)} dp = M(0) - M(\overline{p}) = \overline{M}.$$

The following proposition summarizes our results.

Proposition 8.3.1. *There exists a unique stationary Markov equilibrium, in which aggregate reserves in the insurance sector evolve according to:*

$$dM_t = \sigma_0 D\big(p(M_t)\big)\,(p(M_t)dt - dZ_t)\,, \quad M_t \in (0, \overline{M})$$

The volatility of insurance prices is

$$\sigma(p) = \frac{2r + p^2}{1 + \varepsilon_1(p)}.$$

The insurance price function $p(M)$ satisfies the differential equation

$$p'(M) = -\frac{\sigma\big(p(M)\big)}{\sigma_0 D\big(p(M)\big)}, \tag{8.3.14}$$

with the boundary condition $p(0) = \overline{p}$, where $\overline{p}$ solves

$$\int_0^{\overline{p}} \frac{p}{\sigma(p)}\,dp = \ln(1 + \beta). \tag{8.3.15}$$

Finally

$$\overline{M} = \int_0^{\overline{p}} \frac{\sigma_0 D(p)}{\sigma(p)}\,dp.$$

Proof. See Appendix A.7.

It follows directly from Expressions (8.3.15) and (8.3.13) that both the maximum level of insurance price $\overline{p}$ and the target level of reserves $\overline{M}$ increase with the financing cost β.

8.3.3 Dynamics of insurance prices

In this section we study the dynamics of the equilibrium price of insurance as predicted by the model. For convenience, we use the following specification of the demand for insurance:

$$D(p) = (\alpha - p)^2,$$

with $\alpha > 0$. The parameter α can be interpreted as the price above which demand for insurance vanishes. It affects the elasticity of demand for insurance. More precisely, we have

$$\varepsilon_1(p) = \frac{2p}{\alpha - p} \quad \text{and} \quad \varepsilon_2(p) = \frac{p}{\alpha - p}.$$

Inserting $\varepsilon_1(p)$ and $\varepsilon_2(p)$ into the general formulas for $\mu(p)$ and $\sigma(p)$, we obtain

$$\mu(p) = 2p\sigma(p) \left[\frac{(\beta - 1)(2r - p^2) - 2\alpha p}{2(\alpha + (\beta - 1)p)^2} \right] \quad \text{and}$$
$$\sigma(p) = \frac{(\alpha - p)\left(p^2 + 2r\right)}{p(\alpha + p)}. \tag{8.3.16}$$

Mean reversion. It is easy to see from Expression (8.3.16) that the sign of the insurance-price drift $\mu(p)$ is determined by the sign of the polynomial

$$h(p) := 2r - p^2 - 2\alpha p.$$

When $\alpha > \sqrt{2r}$, the equation $h(p) = 0$ has a unique root p^* on the interval $(0, \alpha)$. Moreover, $\mu(p) > 0$ on $(0, p^*)$ and $\mu(p) < 0$ on (p^*, α). This implies that the price process p exhibits mean reversion. However, this mean-reversion property is not very strong. Indeed, for α large enough, $|\mu(p)|$ turns out to be small compared to $\sigma(p)$. The main feature of the dynamics of the price process p is its reflection at the boundaries of the interval $(0, \bar{p})$, which induces what we call PRICE REVERSALS.

Price reversals. The reflection property of the aggregate reserve process in the model induces reversals of the price of insurance. Empirical work has indeed shown that the insurance market alternates "soft-market" phases characterized by falling premiums together with an expansion of insurers' capacities and "hard-market" phases characterized by rising premiums together with a contraction of insurers' capacities. What has been called "underwriting cycles" appears to be more adequately described as "price reversals."

8.4 Further reading

Kiyotaki and Moore (1997) is the seminal article on credit cycles. In their model, debts are collateralized by land, which is also used for production. The value of land exceeds its marginal productivity due to its value as collateral. This results in an interaction between the prices of land and the limits on borrowing that, when performing a steady-state analysis, serves to amplify macroeconomic shocks as well as generating persistent variations in output and asset prices.

Overlapping-generations (OLG) models are another (discrete-time) approach to model economic dynamics. An example within the financial business cycles literature is Suárez and Sussman (1997), who study a dynamic model of lending under moral hazard. Their model results in a pure reversion mechanism: the economy may converge to a two-period equilibrium boom-bust credit cycle.

Meh and Moran (2010) develop a dynamic stochastic general equilibrium (DSGE) model in which bank capital mitigates moral hazard between banks and investors (supplying funds for loans). As a result, the capital position of banks influences macroeconomic fluctuations (it affects the banking sector's ability to attract funds). This transmission channel amplifies and propagates the effects of supply shocks on output and investment. The authors show that adverse financial shocks that cause sudden decreases in bank capital lead to considerable declines in bank lending and economic activity.

He and Krishnamurthy (2012, 2013) emphasize the role of capital constraints. They model the impact of financial constraints on the agents whose productivity is high (like the financial intermediaries in Section 8.1 or the farmers in Section 8.2). This form of financial friction generates ENDOGENOUS RISK that impact the risk premia on risky assets, at times driving it up. This, however, happens for short enough periods of time that the economy's long-run behavior is similar to what a steady-state (static) approach would predict.

Isohätälä et al. (2016) provide a comprehensive review of continuous-time, macroeconomic modeling. Their Section 3.1 focuses on capital constraints and asset pricing, like the model in Section 8.1 of this chapter.

A Proofs of Main Results and Technical Complements

A.1 Chapter 1

Proof of Proposition 1.3.1. The valuation equation is a classic formula whose proof can be found in most (if not all) texts on mathematical finance. Observe that the value of the security at date t equals the NPV of coupon payments until maturity or default, plus the payout to the security holders at either maturity or default, given the current value S_t of the firm asset. To formalize this statement, define the stopping time

$$\eta := \min\{\tau, T\}, \quad \text{where} \quad \tau := \inf\{t \geq 0 | S_t = K_t\}$$

and let

$$p(\eta) := \begin{cases} B_\eta, & \text{if } \eta < T; \\ F(S_T), & \text{if } \eta = T. \end{cases}$$

Then, we may write

$$P(t, S) = \mathbb{E}\left[\int_t^\eta e^{-r(l-t)} C(l, S_l) dl + e^{-r(\eta-t)} p(\eta) \Big| S_t = S\right].$$

That P is a solution to the boundary-value problem

$$\begin{cases} rP(t, S) = \frac{\partial P}{\partial t}(t, S) + (r - \beta)S \frac{\partial P}{\partial S}(t, S) + \frac{\sigma^2}{2} S^2 \frac{\partial^2 P}{\partial S^2}(t, S) + C(t, S), \\ \qquad\qquad 0 \leq t \leq T, 0 \leq S \leq K_t; \\ P(t, K_t) = B_t \quad \text{and} \quad P(T, S) = F(S) \end{cases}$$

is a direct consequence of the Feyman-Kac formula for boundary-value problems (see, e.g. Oeksendal (2003), Chap. 8–9. See also the proof of Proposition 2.3.2 below).

Q.E.D.

A.2 Chapter 2

Proof of Proposition 2.2.1. Let $L \in \mathscr{A}$, $0 < s < \tau_L$ and define for $l \geq s$ the auxiliary process

$$H_l := M_s^L + \mu(l - s) + \sigma Z_{l-s}.$$

Given that L is nondecreasing, we have that for all $l \geq s$ it holds that $M_l^L \leq H_l$. If we define

$$\tau_H := \inf \{l > s \mid H_l \leq 0\}$$

and choose $t > s$, then $\mathbb{Q}\{\tau_H < t\} \leq \mathbb{Q}\{\tau_L < t \mid M_s^L\}$. A simple translation argument yields

$$\mathbb{Q}\{\tau_H < t\} = \mathbb{Q}\{\tau_{\widetilde{H}} < t - s\},$$

where $\widetilde{H}_l := M_s^L + \mu l + \sigma Z_l$ and $\tau_{\widetilde{H}}$ is defined accordingly. Let $T = t - s$ and notice that

$$\mathbb{Q}\{\tau_{\widetilde{H}} < t - s\} = \mathbb{Q}\{\widetilde{\tau} < T\},$$

where $\widetilde{\tau}$ is the first crossing time of the standard Brownian motion Z of the linear boundary defined by $k_t = \sigma^{-1}(M_s^L + \mu t)$. From Pötzelberger and Wang (1997), we have that

$$\mathbb{Q}\{\widetilde{\tau} < T\} = 1 - N\left(\frac{M_s^L + \mu T}{\sigma\sqrt{T}}\right) + e^{-2\mu M_s^L/\sigma^2} N\left(\frac{\mu T - M_s^L}{\sigma\sqrt{T}}\right) > 0,$$

where N denotes the standard normal cumulative distribution function.

Q.E.D.

Proof of Proposition 2.3.1.

Consider the reserves levels $m_1, m_2 > 0$ and let L_1 and L_2 be two corresponding admissible strategies. Let $\lambda \in (0, 1)$ and define

$$\widetilde{m} := \lambda m_1 + (1 - \lambda)m_2 \quad \text{and} \quad \widetilde{L} := \lambda L_1 + (1 - \lambda)L_2.$$

Clearly $\widetilde{L}$ is admissible and $dM^{\widetilde{L}} = \lambda dM^{L_1} + (1 - \lambda)dM^{L_2}$. Define $\widetilde{\tau} := \max\{\tau_{L_1}, \tau_{L_2}\}$, then, using the fact that the conditional-expectation operator is linear, we have

$$V(\widetilde{m}) \geq V^{\widetilde{L}}(\widetilde{m}) = \lambda V^{L_1}(m_1) + (1 - \lambda)V^{L_2}(m_2).$$

By definition, for all $\epsilon > 0$ the strategy L_1 can be chosen such that $V^{L_1}(m_1) \geq V(m_1) - \epsilon/2$, and analogously for $V(m_2)$. In other words, the expression

$$V(\tilde{m}) \geq \lambda V(m_1) + (1 - \lambda)V(m_2) - \epsilon$$

holds for any positive ϵ, thus the mapping $m \mapsto V(m)$ is concave.

Q.E.D.

Proof of Proposition 2.3.2. We first consider the condition on V'. By definition, for any $h, y > 0$ there exists a strategy L^y such that $V^{L^y}(m) \geq V(m) - h^2$. Let $0 < h < m$ and construct a strategy $\tilde{L}$ by setting $\tilde{L}_t = h + L_t^{x-h}$, then

$$V(m) \geq V^{\tilde{L}}(m) = h + V^{L^{m-h}}(m - h) \geq h + V(m - h) - h^2,$$

which is equivalent to

$$\frac{V(m) - V(m - h)}{h} \geq 1 - h.$$

By the differentiability of V, we may let h go to zero and conclude that $V'(m) \geq 1$.

Next, fix a strategy $L \in \mathscr{A}$ with corresponding cash-reserves process M^L ($M_0^L = m$) and apply the generalized Itô formula to $f(t, m) = e^{-\rho t}V(m)$:

$$\begin{aligned}
e^{-\rho t}V(M_t^L) = V(m) &+ \int_0^t e^{-\rho s}\left(\mu V'(M_s^L) - \rho V(M_s^L)\right)ds \\
&+ \frac{1}{2}\int_0^t e^{-\rho s}V''(M_s^L)d\langle M^L, M^L\rangle_s \\
&+ \int_0^t e^{-\rho s}\sigma V'(M_s^L)dZ_s - \int_0^t e^{-\rho s}V'(M_s^L)dL_s \\
&+ \sum_{s \in \Gamma} e^{-\rho s}\left(\Delta V(M^L(s)) - V'(M_s^L)\Delta M_s^L\right),
\end{aligned}$$

(A.2.1)

where Γ is the set of discontinuities of L and

$$\Delta V(M^L(s)) := V(M^L(s_+)) - V(M_s^L) \quad \text{and} \quad \Delta M_s^L := M^L(s_+) - M_s^L.$$

As L is of bounded variation (it is an increasing process) we have that

$$d\langle M^L, M^L\rangle_s = \sigma^2 ds.$$

Thus, Equation (A.2.1) becomes

$$e^{-\rho t}V(R_t^L) = V(m) + \int_0^t e^{-\rho s}\mathcal{L}(V(M_s^L))ds$$

$$+ \int_0^t e^{-\rho s}\sigma V'(M_s^L)dZ_s - \int_0^t e^{-\rho s}V'(M_s^L)dL_s$$

$$+ \sum_{s\in\Gamma} e^{-\rho s}\left(\Delta V(M_s^L) - V'(R_s^L)\Delta M_s^L\right),$$

(A.2.2)

where $\mathcal{L}$ is the infinitesimal generator of the diffusion part of M^L. We now take expectations on both sides and the Itô integral vanishes. On the other hand, by the Dynamic Programming Principle we have

$$\mathbb{E}\left[e^{-\rho t}V(M_t^L)\big|M_0^L = m\right] \leq V(m) - \mathbb{E}\left[\int_0^t e^{-\rho s}V'(M_s^L)dL_s\big|M_0^L = m\right].$$

(A.2.3)

Combining Expressions (A.2.2) and (A.2.3) yields

$$0 \geq \mathbb{E}\left[\int_0^t e^{-\rho s}\left(-\rho V(M_s^L) + \mu V'(M_s^L) + \frac{1}{2}\sigma^2 V''(M_s^L)\right)ds\big|M_0^L = m\right]$$

$$+ \mathbb{E}\left[\sum_{s\in\Gamma} e^{-\rho s}\left(\Delta V(M_s^L) - V'(M_s^L)\Delta M_s^L\right)\big|M_0^L = m\right].$$

(A.2.4)

For the set Γ, using the Mean Value Theorem we know there exists $n \in (M^L(s_+), M_s^L)$ such that

$$\Delta V(M_s^L) = V'(n)\Delta M_s^L.$$

Therefore

$$\Delta V(M_s^L) - V'(M_s^L)\Delta M_s^L = \left(V'(n) - V'(M_s^L)\right)\Delta M_s^L$$

and by concavity of V we have $V'(n) - V'(M_s^L) < 0$; thus, the right hand side is positive. We have that the second summand of the right-hand side of Expression (A.2.4) is positive, which implies

$$0 \geq \mathbb{E}\left[\int_0^t e^{-\rho s}\left(-\rho V(M_s^L) + \mu V'(M_s^L) + \frac{1}{2}\sigma^2 V''(M_s^L)\right)ds\big|M_0^L = m\right].$$

Next we multiply both sides of the equation above by $1/t$. As

$$\frac{1}{t}\int_0^t e^{-\rho s}\left(-\rho V(M_s^L) + \mu V'(M_s^L) + \frac{1}{2}\sigma^2 V''(M_s^L)\right)ds \leq$$

$$\max_{s\in[0,t]} e^{-\rho s}\left|-\rho V(M_s^L) + \mu V'(M_s^L) + \frac{1}{2}\sigma^2 V''(M_s^L)\right|,$$

we may apply Lebesgue's Dominated Convergence Theorem, and take the limit as $t \to 0$ inside the expectation operator, which results in

$$0 \geq \left\{ \frac{1}{2}\sigma^2 V''(m) + \mu V'(m) - \rho V(m) \right\}.$$

To prove that one of the inequalities (the above one or $V' \geq 1$) is always tight, we resort again to the dynamic programming principle and write for $t > 0$

$$V(m) = \max_{L \in \mathscr{A}} \mathbb{E}\left[\int_0^t e^{-\rho s} dL_s + e^{-\rho t} V(M_t^L) \big| M_0^L = m \right].$$

Inserting Equation (A.2.2) in the equation above we obtain

$$
0 = \max_{L \in \mathscr{A}} \left\{ \mathbb{E}\left[\int_0^t e^{-\rho s} \mathcal{L}(V(M_s^L)) ds \big| M_0^L = m \right] \right.
$$

$$
+ \mathbb{E}\left[\int_0^t e^{-\rho s}(1 - V'(M_s^L)) dL_s \big| M_0^L = m \right] \tag{A.2.5}
$$

$$
\left. + \mathbb{E}\left[\sum_{s \in \Gamma} e^{-\rho s}(\Delta V(M_s^L) - V'(M_s^L)\Delta M_s^L) \big| M_0^L = m \right] \right\}.
$$

If we write $\widetilde{L}$ for the continuous parts of L, then Equation (A.2.5) may be rewritten as

$$
0 = \max_{L \in \mathscr{A}} \left\{ \mathbb{E}\left[\int_0^t e^{-\rho s} \mathcal{L}(V(M_s^L)) ds \big| M_0^L = m \right] \right.
$$

$$
+ \mathbb{E}\left[\int_0^t e^{-\rho s}(1 - V'(M_s^L)) d\widetilde{L}_s \big| M_0^L = m \right]
$$

$$
\left. + \mathbb{E}\left[\sum_{s \in \Gamma_1} e^{-\rho s}(\Delta V(M_s^L) + \Delta L_s) \big| M_0^L = m \right] \right\}.
$$

Notice that for all $s \in (0, t)$ it holds that, for all $s \in \Gamma$,

$$\Delta V(M_s^L) + \Delta L_s = \int_{M_s^L - \Delta L_s}^{M_s^L} (1 - V'(m)) dm \leq 0.$$

This implies all summands on the right-hand side of Equation (A.2.5) are nonpositive, which concludes the proof.

Q.E.D.

Proof of Theorem 1. Consider an arbitrary strategy $L \in \mathscr{A}$, and an initial level of cash reserves $m \geq 0$. Recall that the corresponding cash-reserves process evolves according to the SDE

$$dM_t^L = \mu dt + \sigma dZ_t - dL_t, \ M_0^L = m.$$

Proceeding as in the proof of Proposition 2.3.2 we use (the generalized) Itô formula applied to $f(t, m) = e^{-\rho t}V(m)$ and obtain, after simplifications (recall that $\mathcal{L}V(R_t^L) \leq 0$)

$$e^{-\rho t}\mathbb{E}\left[V(M_t^L)\big|M_0^L = m\right] \leq V(m) - \mathbb{E}\left[\int_0^t e^{-\rho s}V'(M_s^L)d\widetilde{L}_s\big|M_0^L = m\right]$$

$$+ \mathbb{E}\left[\sum_{s \in \Gamma} e^{-\rho s}\Delta V(M_s^L)\big|M_0^L = m\right],$$
(A.2.6)

where $\widetilde{L}_s := L_s - \Delta L_s$ is the continuous parts of L. Let $s \in \Gamma$, then by the Mean Value Theorem and the fact that $1 \leq V'(M_s^L)$, there exists $n \in (M^L(s_+), M_s^L)$ such that

$$\Delta V(M_s^L) = V'(n)\Delta M_s^L \leq L_{s+} - L_s = -\Delta L_s.$$

Inserting the above expressions into Expression (A.2.6) we get

$$e^{-\rho t}\mathbb{E}\left[V(M_t^L)\big|M_0^L = m\right] \leq V(m) - \mathbb{E}\left[\int_0^t e^{-\rho s}dL_s\big|M_0^L = m\right].$$

By continuity, $V(m)$ is bounded for $m \in [0, m^*]$ and it grows linearly as m tends to infinity; therefore

$$\lim_{t \to \infty} e^{-\rho t}\mathbb{E}\left[V(M_t^L)\big|M_0^L = m\right] = 0.$$

This implies that

$$V(m) \geq \mathbb{E}\left[\int_0^\infty e^{-\rho s}dL_s\big|M_0^L = m\right]. \qquad (A.2.7)$$

Next consider the strategy L^*. Since L^* is the local time of M^* at level m^*, we may assume that $m \in [0, m^*]$. Furthermore, L^* is a continuous process, and on $[0, m^*]$ it holds that $\mathcal{L}(V(M_s^*)) = 0$. Hence, for the strategy L^*, Itô's Lemma yields

$$e^{-\rho t}V(M_t^*) = V(m) + \int_0^t e^{-\rho s}\sigma V'(M_s^*)dZ_s$$

$$- \int_0^t e^{-\rho s}V'(M_s^*)dL_s^*. \qquad (A.2.8)$$

The measure dL_s^* is supported on the set $\{M_s^* = m^*\}$ and $V'(m^*) = 1$, therefore, taking expectations, Equation (A.2.8) may be rewritten as

$$e^{-\rho t}\mathbb{E}\left[V(M_t^*)\big|M_0^* = m\right] = V(m) - \mathbb{E}\left[\int_0^t e^{-\rho s}dL_s^*\big|M_0^* = m\right].$$

Letting $t \to \infty$ we have

$$V(m) = \mathbb{E}\left[\int_0^\infty e^{-\rho s}dL_s^*\big|M_0^* = m\right], \qquad (A.2.9)$$

which is equivalent to $V(m) = V^{L^*}(m)$. From Equation (A.2.7) we have that for any $L \in \mathscr{A}$, $V(m) \geq V^L(m)$. Given that $L^* \in \mathscr{A}$, Equation (A.2.9) yields

$$V(m) = \sup_{L \in \mathscr{A}} V^L(m),$$

which concludes the proof.

Q.E.D.

A.3 Chapter 3

Computing the value function from Section 3.3

In order to compute V numerically we proceed as follows:

1. Start with an arbitrary pair of upper refinancing limit and target cash level $(\widetilde{m}_\eta, m_\eta)$. The candidate value function is constructed piecewise to the left and right of $\widetilde{m}_\eta$ and we denote these "pieces" by V_l and V_r, respectively. The solution on $(\widetilde{m}_\eta, m_\eta)$ to Equation (3.3.3b) that satisfies $V'(m_\eta) = 1$ and $V''(m_\eta) = 0$ has the same expression as the solution to the Hamilton-Jacobi-Bellman equation of the base model:

$$V_r(m) = \frac{1}{r_1 r_2}\left(\frac{r_2^2}{r_2 - r_1}e^{r_1(m - m_\eta)} - \frac{r_1^2}{r_2 - r_1}e^{r_2(m - m_\eta)}\right).$$

2. Given that for any choice of $m_\eta > 0$ it holds that

$$V_r(m_\eta) = \frac{r_2^2 - r_1^2}{r_1 r_2 (r_2 - r_1)} = \frac{\mu}{\rho},$$

Equation (3.3.3a) can be written as

$$(\rho + \lambda)V(m) = \frac{\sigma^2}{2}V''(m) + \mu V'(m) + \lambda m + M_\eta,$$

where $M_\eta := \lambda[\mu/\rho - m_\eta - \kappa]$. It is easy to see that a particular solution to this equation is

$$V_p(m) = \frac{\lambda}{\rho + \lambda}m + \frac{1}{\rho + \lambda}\left[M_\eta + \frac{\lambda\mu}{\rho + \lambda}\right].$$

The solution to Equation (3.3.3a) can then be written as the sum of the general solution to its homogeneous part plus V_p :

$$V_l(m) = A\,e^{\beta_1 m} + B\,e^{\beta_2 m} + V_p(m),$$

where $\beta_1 < 0 < \beta_2$ are the solutions to the characteristic equation $(\sigma^2/2)\beta^2 + \mu\beta = \rho + \lambda$ and A and B are chosen so as to satisfy the boundary and value-matching conditions

$$V_l(0) = 0 \quad \text{and} \quad V_l(\tilde{m}_\eta) = V_r(\tilde{m}_\eta).$$

Up to this point V_l and V_r can be found in closed form, but in general neither the smooth-pasting condition at $\tilde{m}_\eta$ nor the (feasibility) condition $SV(\tilde{m}_\eta) = 0$ is satisfied. This is exemplified in Figure A.1, which shows the candidate value function with parameters: $\kappa = 0.5$, $\lambda = 1$, $\mu = 0.7$, $\rho = 0.2$, $\sigma = 0.5$ and thresholds $\tilde{m}_\eta = 0.3$ and $m_\eta = 0.5$. The surplus on $[0, \tilde{m}_\eta]$ is also presented. We clearly observe $SV(\tilde{m}_\eta) < 0$.

3.   The last step is to determine $\overline{m}_\eta$ and m_η^* jointly so as to have

$$V_l'(\overline{m}_\eta) = V_r'(\overline{m}_\eta) \quad \text{and} \quad SV(\overline{m}_\eta) = 0.$$

In order to do this we define the following functions:
  a) $U_l(m, \tilde{m}_\eta, m_\eta)$ is the left-hand candidate value function V_l found in Step (2) with the possible upper-refinancing limit and dividend barrier incorporated as arguments.
  b) $U_r(m, m_\eta)$ is the right-hand candidate value function V_r found in Step (1) with the possible dividend barrier incorporated as an argument. Notice that in this case, $\tilde{m}_\eta$ is not an argument.
  c) $SV(m, \tilde{m}_\eta, m_\eta)$ is the surplus from raising equity when liquid reserves are m given $\tilde{m}_\eta$ and m_η. This function is defined for $m \in [0, m_\eta]$, i.e. at this point we do not impose the restriction $m \le \tilde{m}_\eta$ because, as we saw in Point (2), it need not be the case that $SV(\tilde{m}_\eta, \tilde{m}_\eta, m_\eta) = 0$. We have

$$SV(m, \tilde{m}_\eta, m_\eta) := \mu/\rho - U_l(m, \tilde{m}_\eta, m_\eta) - (m_\eta - m) - \kappa$$

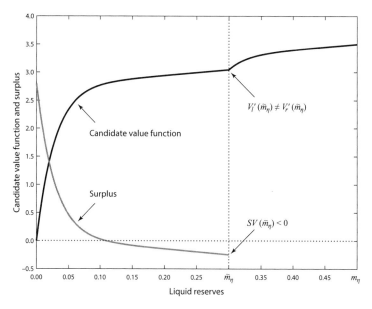

Figure A.1: A candidate value function and the corresponding surplus

if $m \leq \tilde{m}_\eta$ and

$$\mathbf{SV}\left(m, \tilde{m}_\eta, m_\eta\right) := \mu/\rho - U_r\left(m, \tilde{m}_\eta, m_\eta\right) - \left(m_\eta - m\right) - \kappa$$

if $m > \tilde{m}_\eta$.

d) The final step is to numerically solve the following nonlinear system of equations with $\tilde{m}_\eta$ and m_η as the unknowns:

$$\begin{cases} \frac{\partial}{\partial m} U_l\left(\tilde{m}_\eta, \tilde{m}_\eta, m_\eta\right) - \frac{\partial}{\partial m} U_r\left(\tilde{m}_\eta, m_\eta\right) = 0; \\ \mathbf{SV}\left(\tilde{m}_\eta, \tilde{m}_\eta, m_\eta\right) = 0, \end{cases} \quad \text{(A.3.1)}$$

where the first equation yields smooth pasting and the second one guarantees that the choice of $\tilde{m}_\eta$ is feasible (unlike $\tilde{m}_\eta = 0.3$ in Figure A.1). Computing such numerical solutions can be done, for instance using the functions "fsolve" in Matlab[1] or "NSolve" in Mathematica.[2]

The estimation of solutions to System (A.3.1) deserves some additional comments: first, we have hitherto worked under the assumption that the issuance cost κ is "small" in the sense that $\mu/\rho - m_\eta^* - \kappa > 0$.

---

[1]Matlab is a registered trademark of The MathWorks Inc., Natick, MA.
[2]Mathematica is a registered trademark of Wolfram Research, Champaign, IL.

Clearly, whether this condition holds for a given set of parameters cannot be verified ex-ante because m_η^* is itself part of the solution to System (A.3.1). In other words, we could be unable to find solutions to this system of equations due to a too large choice of κ. Second, dedicated solvers for nonlinear systems of equations generally require initial guesses of the solutions and, depending on the problem, the efficacy of the solver depends critically on the initial guess.[3] That is to say that the first step to be taken when failing to estimate the solution to a particular instance of System (A.3.1) is to pass a different guess for the solution. Finally, *ceteris paribus* System (A.3.1) does not have a solution when λ becomes too large. This is due to the fact that the solutions to the current model do not converge, as $\lambda \to \infty$ to the solution of the certain-refinancing model in Section 3.1 (where $\lambda = \infty$). The reason for this nonconvergence is that, due to the independence of the processes P and Z, we have $V(0) = 0$ for any $\lambda < \infty$. However, we saw in Section 3.1 that whenever equity issuance is desirable in the certain-refinancing case, then $V(0) = \mu/\rho - m_\kappa^* - \kappa > 0$ (see Figure 3.1).

Proofs

In order to describe in full generality the possible times and levels of equity issuance we introduce the following definition.

Definition A.3.1. *Let $\{\tau_i\}_{i=1}^\infty$ be a sequence of strictly increasing $\mathcal{F}$-stopping times. Let $\{m_i\}_{i=1}^\infty$ be a sequence of nonnegative random variables such that $m_i \in \mathcal{F}_{\tau_i}$. Define*

$$J_t := \sum_{i=1}^\infty m_i \mathbb{1}_{\{t \geq \tau_i\}} \quad and \quad J_{\kappa,t} := \sum_{i=1}^\infty (m_i + \kappa) \mathbb{1}_{\{t \geq \tau_i\}},$$

J will be referred to in the sequel as a CUMULATIVE ISSUANCE PROCESS.

When we say that τ_i is a $\mathcal{F}$-stopping time we mean that at any date t we know whether $\tau_i \leq t$. On the other hand, stating that $m_i \in \mathcal{F}_{\tau_i}$ simply means that the choice of the magnitude of the ith equity injection, which takes place at date $t = \tau_i$, is made contingent on the information available to the manager at that date. In other

---

[3]Volumes have been written about solving nonlinear systems of equations. The corresponding intricacies are beyond the scope of this book. We refer the interested reader to Press et al. (2007), Chapters 9 and 15, and the references therein.

words, at date $t = 0$ the manager chooses when equity will be issued as a function of the evolution of the firm's cash reserves, which will also determine the size of the issuances.

Proof of Proposition 3.1.1. Consider an initial level of cash reserves m, an admissible strategy $\pi = (L, J)$ and the corresponding value $V^\pi(m)$. Let us assume that $M^\pi_{\tau_1} > 0$ and define the auxiliary processes

$$\widehat{J}_t := \sum_{i=2}^{\infty} m_i \mathbf{1}_{\{t \geq \tau_i\}},$$

the strategy $\widehat{\pi} = (\widehat{J}, L)$, the corresponding cash-reserves process $M^{\widehat{\pi}}$ and the stopping time

$$\widehat{\tau} := \inf\{t > 0 \,|\, M^{\widehat{\pi}}_t \leq 0\}.$$

By construction $\widehat{\tau} > \tau_1$. If we define $\widetilde{J}_t := \widehat{J}_t + x_1 \mathbf{1}_{\{t \geq \tau\}}$ we have that the strategy $\widetilde{\pi} := (L, \widetilde{J})$ is admissible and the corresponding value $V^{\widetilde{\pi}}(m)$ satisfies

$$V^{\widetilde{\pi}}(m) > V^\pi(m).$$

This last assertion follows from the facts that $-e^{-\rho\widehat{\tau}}(m_1 + \kappa) < e^{-\rho\tau_1}(m_1 + \kappa)$, and that for any $t \geq \tau_2$ it holds that $M^\pi_t = M^{\widetilde{\pi}}_t$. It is then optimal to postpone the first time of issuance to the first time the cash–reserves process hits zero. An inductive argument implies that such is the case for all re-injection times.

Q.E.D.

A.4 Chapter 4

Proof of Lemma 4.2.1. Let V be a solution to

$$-\rho V(\epsilon) + r\epsilon V'(\epsilon) - \frac{1}{2}\left(\frac{\mu - r}{\sigma}\right)^2 \frac{(V'(\epsilon))^2}{V''(\epsilon)} = 0, \quad V(0) = 0 \quad \text{(A.4.1)}$$

and define

$$u(\epsilon) := \epsilon \frac{V'(\epsilon)}{V(\epsilon)}.$$

We have that

$$V'(\epsilon) = \frac{u(\epsilon)\, V(\epsilon)}{\epsilon},$$

therefore

$$V''(\epsilon) = \frac{\epsilon\, u'(\epsilon) - u(\epsilon)}{\epsilon^2} V(\epsilon) + \frac{u(\epsilon)\, V'(\epsilon)}{\epsilon} = \frac{\epsilon\, u'(\epsilon) - u(\epsilon) + u^2(\epsilon)}{\epsilon^2} V(\epsilon).$$

From the above expression we get

$$\frac{\left(V'(\epsilon)\right)^2}{V''(\epsilon)} = \frac{u(\epsilon)^2}{\epsilon u'(\epsilon) - u(\epsilon) + u^2(\epsilon)} V(\epsilon) \qquad \text{(A.4.2)}$$

If we divide Equation (A.4.1) by $V(\epsilon)$, we obtain

$$\rho = r u(\epsilon) - \frac{\varsigma u^2(\epsilon)}{\epsilon u'(\epsilon) + u^2(\epsilon) - u(\epsilon)}, \qquad \text{(A.4.3)}$$

where $\varsigma := \frac{1}{2}\left((\mu - r)/\sigma\right)^2$. This is equivalent to

$$\epsilon u'(\epsilon)(r u(\epsilon) - \rho) = -r u(\epsilon)(u(\epsilon) - \alpha)(u(\epsilon) - \tilde{\alpha}),$$

where $0 < \alpha < 1 < \rho/r < \tilde{\alpha}$ are the roots of

$$f(\epsilon) := r \epsilon^2 - (r + \rho + \varsigma)\epsilon + \rho.$$

By separating variables and integrating, we can see that the solutions to Equation (A.4.2) are all such that

$$|u(\epsilon) - \alpha|^{r_1} |u(\epsilon) - \tilde{\alpha}|^{r_2} = \lambda \frac{u(\epsilon)}{\epsilon}, \qquad \text{(A.4.4)}$$

where $r_1 := (\tilde{\alpha}-1)/(\tilde{\alpha}-\alpha)$, $r_2 := (1-\alpha)/(\tilde{\alpha}-\alpha)$ and λ is determined by the initial condition $V(0) = 0$. The latter implies that

$$\lim_{\epsilon \to 0} \frac{u(\epsilon)}{\epsilon} = \lim_{\epsilon \to 0} \frac{V'(\epsilon)}{V(\epsilon)} = \infty.$$

Equations (A.4.2) and (A.4.3), together with the concavity of V, imply that $u(\epsilon) \leq \rho/r$. Notice that, as a consequence, the left-hand side of Equation (A.4.4) is then bounded (as $r_1, r_2 > 0$). Therefore it must hold that $\lambda = 0$, which yields $u(\epsilon) \equiv \alpha$ or $\tilde{\alpha}$. The latter is ruled out, as $\tilde{\alpha} > \rho/r$, which would violate the concavity of V. Thus $u(\epsilon) \equiv \alpha$ is the only possibility and we have

$$V(\epsilon) = K \epsilon^\alpha,$$

where K is a positive constant.

Q.E.D.

Proof of Lemma 4.2.2. Let us define $\varsigma := \frac{1}{2}\left((\mu - r)/\sigma\right)^2$ and recall that α is the smallest root of

$$f(\epsilon) := r \epsilon^2 - (r + \rho + \varsigma)\epsilon + \rho.$$

Let β be the largest root of $f(\epsilon) = 0$. Proving that $k < 1$ is equivalent to showing that $\alpha > 1 - (\mu - r)/\sigma^2$. As $f(\epsilon) > 0$ for $a \in (-\infty, \alpha) \cup (\beta, \infty)$, if we showed that $\beta > 1 - (\mu - r)/\sigma^2$, then the desired result would follow from showing that

$$f\left(1 - \frac{\mu - r}{\sigma^2}\right) > 0.$$

Indeed, we have that the condition $\beta > 1 - (\mu - r)/\sigma^2$ is equivalent to

$$\sqrt{(r + \rho + \varsigma)^2 - 4r\rho} > r - \rho - \varsigma\left(1 + \frac{4r}{\mu - r}\right),$$

which trivially holds because the right-hand side of the expression above is negative from the assumption that $\rho > r$. Next we compute

$$f\left(1 - \frac{\mu - r}{\sigma^2}\right) = \frac{\mu - r}{2\sigma^2}\left(2\rho - \mu - r + 2\varsigma + \frac{2r}{\sigma^2}(\mu - r)\right),$$

which is greater than zero, given the assumption that $\rho > \mu > r$.

Q.E.D.

Proof of Lemma 4.2.3. Observe that the boundary-value problem in hand can be rewritten, for $\mathbf{e} > 0$, as

$$\frac{2\rho}{\sigma^2(\epsilon + D)^2}V(\epsilon; \mathbf{e}) = \frac{2(\mu\epsilon + (\mu - r)D)}{\sigma^2(\epsilon + D)^2}V'(\epsilon; \mathbf{e}) + V''(\epsilon; \mathbf{e}),$$

with boundary conditions $V'(\mathbf{e}; \mathbf{e}) = 1, V''(\mathbf{e}; \mathbf{e}) = 0$. The mappings

$$\epsilon \mapsto \frac{2\rho}{\sigma^2(\epsilon + D)^2} \quad \text{and} \quad \epsilon \mapsto \frac{2(\mu\epsilon + (\mu - r)D)}{\sigma^2(\epsilon + D)^2}$$

are continuous on $[0, \infty)$. Furthermore, their derivatives on $(0, \infty)$ are bounded, hence they are Lipschitz. The existence and uniqueness of a solution to the boundary-value problem follows then directly from the Cauchy-Lipschitz Theorem.

Q.E.D.

Proof of Proposition 4.2.4. Observe that from Lemma 4.2.3 we immediately get that, for any $\mathbf{e} > \epsilon_0^*$, the linear extension of the function $V(\cdot; \mathbf{e}) : (\epsilon_0^*, \mathbf{e}) \to \mathbb{R}$ to $[\mathbf{e}, \infty)$ via the mapping $\epsilon \mapsto (\epsilon - \mathbf{e}) + V(\mathbf{e}; \mathbf{e})$ yields a $\mathcal{C}^2$ function on $[\epsilon_0^*, \infty)$. We are left with the task of showing that the pair $(K, \mathbf{e})$ may be chosen so as to satisfy the smooth-pasting condition

$$K(\epsilon_0^*)^\alpha = V(\epsilon_0^*; \mathbf{e}) \quad \text{and} \quad \alpha K(\epsilon_0^*)^{\alpha-1} = V'(\epsilon_0^*; \mathbf{e}).$$

We obtain immediately that $K = V(\epsilon_0^*; \mathbf{e}) \cdot (\epsilon_0^*)^{-\alpha}$, which leaves us with the equation

$$V'(\epsilon_0^*; \mathbf{e}) = \alpha \frac{V(\epsilon_0^*; \mathbf{e})}{\epsilon_0^*}. \tag{A.4.5}$$

To finalize the proof we must show that Equation (A.4.5) admits a unique solution $\mathbf{e} = \epsilon_1^* > \epsilon_0^*$. To this end we require the following auxiliary result: For all $\epsilon \le \mathbf{e}$, the mapping $\mathbf{e} \mapsto V(\epsilon; \mathbf{e})$ is decreasing, and the mapping $\mathbf{e} \mapsto V'(\epsilon; \mathbf{e})$ is increasing. Consider $\mathbf{e} < \mathfrak{f}$ and for $\epsilon \le \mathbf{e}$ Let us define $g(\epsilon) := V(\epsilon; \mathbf{e}) - V(\epsilon; \mathfrak{f})$. It follows from the facts that $V(\mathfrak{f}; \mathfrak{f}) < (\mathfrak{f} - \mathbf{e}) + V(\mathbf{e}; \mathbf{e})$ and $V'(\cdot; \mathfrak{f} \ge 1$ that $g(\mathbf{e}) > 0$ and $g'(\mathbf{e}) < 0$. By concavity of $V(\cdot; \mathfrak{f})$ we also have $g''(\mathbf{e}) \ge 0$. Next we wish to show that $g'(\epsilon) < 0$ for all $\epsilon < \mathbf{e}$. Assume this is not the case and let $y < \mathbf{e}$ be the largest solution to $g'(y) = 0$. Then for $\epsilon \in (y, \mathbf{e})$ we have $g'(\epsilon) < 0$, which implies $g(y) > g(\mathbf{e}) > 0$ and $g''(y) < 0$. However, from the differential equation

$$\rho V(\epsilon) = \big(\mu\epsilon + (\mu - r)D\big)V'(\epsilon) + \frac{\sigma^2}{2}(\epsilon + D)^2 V''(\epsilon)$$

we obtain that $g(y) = \frac{\sigma^2}{2}(y + D)^2 g''(y) < 0$. This is a contradiction, which implies that that $g'(\epsilon) < 0$ for all $\epsilon < \mathbf{e}$, thus $\mathbf{e} \mapsto V'(\epsilon; \mathbf{e})$ is increasing. Since $g(\mathbf{e}) > 0$ we conclude that $g(\epsilon) > 0$ for all $\epsilon < \mathbf{e}$, thus $\mathbf{e} \mapsto V(\epsilon; \mathbf{e})$ is decreasing. Furthermore, given that $V(\cdot; \mathbf{e})' \ge 1$, we have from the Mean Value Theorem for $\mathbf{e} > \epsilon_0^*$

$$V(\epsilon_0^*; \mathbf{e}) \le V(\mathbf{e}; \mathbf{e}) - (\mathbf{e} - \epsilon_0^*) = \frac{\mu\mathbf{e} + (\mu - r)D}{\rho} - (\mathbf{e} - \epsilon_0^*).$$

Given the assumption $\mu < \rho$, we have that $\lim_{\mathbf{e} \to \infty} V(\epsilon_0^*; \mathbf{e}) = -\infty$. As $\mathbf{e} \mapsto V'(\epsilon; \mathbf{e})$ is an increasing mapping, all we have left to prove is that

$$V'(\epsilon_0^*; \epsilon_0^*) < \alpha \frac{V(\epsilon_0^*; \epsilon_0^*)}{\epsilon_0^*}.$$

Using the fact that $V'(\epsilon_0^*; \epsilon_0^*) = 1$, this condition may be rewritten as

$$0 < \alpha\big(\mu\mathbf{e} + (\mu - r)\frac{D}{\epsilon_0^*}\big) - \rho.$$

from the expression $\epsilon_0^* = \frac{kD}{1-k}$ and the fact that $\frac{1}{k} = \frac{\sigma^2(1-\alpha)}{\mu - r}$ we have the above expression is equivalent, after simplifications, to

$$0 < \frac{1}{1 - \alpha}\big(2\alpha\varsigma + \alpha(1 - \alpha)r - \rho + \alpha\rho\big).$$

Recall, however, that by definition α satisfies $r\alpha^2 + \rho = (r + \rho + \varsigma)\alpha$, thus we are required to show that

$$0 < \frac{1}{1 - \alpha}\left(2\alpha\varsigma + \alpha(1 - \alpha)r - \rho + \alpha\rho\right) = \frac{1}{1 - \alpha}\frac{\alpha\varsigma}{1 - \alpha},$$

which trivially holds, as $\alpha \in (0, 1)$ and $\varsigma > 0$. This finalizes the proof.

Q.E.D.

Proof of Propositions 4.2.5 and 4.2.6. Recall that $k = (\sigma^2/(\mu - r))(1 - \alpha)$. As $(r + \rho + \varsigma)^2 - 4r\rho = (\rho - r + \varsigma)^2 + 4r\varsigma$, we may write

$$1 - \alpha = \frac{r - \rho - t + \sqrt{(\rho - r + \varsigma)^2 + 4r\varsigma}}{2r},$$

where ς is as in the proof of Lemma 4.2.2. Multiplying both numerator and denominator of $1 - \alpha$ by $-(r - \rho - \varsigma) + \sqrt{(\rho - r + \varsigma)^2 + 4r\varsigma}$ and simplifying we obtain

$$1 - \alpha = \frac{2}{\frac{\rho - r}{\varsigma} + 1 + \sqrt{(\frac{\rho - r}{\varsigma} + 1)^2 + 4\frac{r}{\varsigma}}}. \qquad (A.4.6)$$

From Equation (A.4.6) we conclude that $1 - \alpha$ and therefore, k is decreasing in $\rho - r$ and increasing in ς. Given that the latter is decreasing in σ and increasing in $\mu - r$, Proposition 4.2.6 is proved. Using Equation A.4.6 we have that

$$k = \frac{\mu - r}{\rho - r + \varsigma + \sqrt{(\rho - r + \varsigma)^2 + 4r\varsigma}}.$$

We immediately observe that k is decreasing in $\rho - r$. Furthermore, given that ς is decreasing in σ, then k is increasing in the volatility of assets. To show that k is single-peaked in $\mu - r$, observe that

$$\frac{1}{k} = \frac{\rho - r}{\mu - r} + \frac{\mu - r}{2\sigma^2} + \sqrt{\frac{2r}{\sigma^2} + \left(\frac{\rho - r}{\mu - r} + \frac{\mu - r}{2\sigma^2}\right)^2}$$

is an increasing function of

$$v(\mu - r) := \frac{\rho - r}{\mu - r} + \frac{\mu - r}{2\sigma^2}.$$

Notice that $\lim_{\epsilon \to 0} v(\epsilon) = \lim_{\epsilon \to \infty} v(\epsilon) = \infty$ and $v'(\epsilon) = 0$ has a unique positive solution $\epsilon = \sigma\sqrt{2}\sqrt{\rho - r}$. In other words, v is itself a U-shaped function of $\mu - r$, which implies that k is single peaked in $\mu - r$. This concludes the proof.

Q.E.D.

A.5 Chapter 5

The closed-form expressions for $B(A, m_l^*)$ and $C(A, m_l^*)$

We define

$$\alpha_1 := \frac{\lambda A e^{-\beta_1 l}}{\beta_1 \sigma^2 + \mu} \quad \text{and} \quad \alpha_2 := \frac{\lambda A e^{-\beta_2 l}}{\beta_2 \sigma^2 + \mu}.$$

Then, the closed-form expressions are:

$$B(A, m_l^*) = \frac{e^{-\beta_1 m_l^*}}{\beta_1} \left(1 + \alpha_1 (1 + \beta_1 m_l^*) e^{\beta_1 m_l^*} - \alpha_2 (1 + \beta_2 m_l^*) e^{\beta_2 m_l^*} \right)$$

$$- C(A, m_l^*) \frac{\beta_2}{\beta_1} e^{m_l^* (\beta_2 - \beta_1)}$$

and

$$C(A, m_l^*) = \frac{e^{-\beta_1 m_l^*}}{\beta_2 (\beta_2 - \beta_1)} \left(\alpha_1 \beta_1 e^{\beta_1 m_l^*} - (\beta_2 (2 + \beta_2 m_l^*) \right.$$

$$\left. - \beta_1 * (1 + \beta_2 m_l^*)) \alpha_2 e^{\beta_2 m_l^*} - \beta_1 \right).$$

Proofs

Proof of Proposition 5.2.4. We have from Expression (5.2.7) that, for any $c, m_1 > 0$,

$$V(m_{0-}) = c \left(\frac{\mu}{2} \right)^\gamma$$

and

$$V(m_{0+}) = \frac{1}{r_1 r_2} \left(\frac{r_2^2}{r_2 - r_1} e^{r_1 m_0^*} e^{-r_1 m_1} - \frac{r_1^2}{r_2 - r_1} e^{r_2 m_0^*} e^{-r_2 m_1} \right).$$

Let us define

$$A_1 := \left(\frac{\mu}{2} \right)^\gamma, \quad A_2 := \frac{r_2}{r_1 (r_2 - r_1)} e^{r_1 m_0^*} \quad \text{and} \quad A_3 := \frac{r_1}{r_2 (r_2 - r_1)} e^{r_2 m_0^*}.$$

$$\tag{A.5.1}$$

Then the expression

$$F_1(c, m_1) := A_1 c - A_2 e^{-r_1 m_1} + A_3 e^{-r_2 m_1} = 0$$

corresponds to the pasting condition $V(m_{0-}) = V(m_{0+})$. Notice that $A_3 < A_2 < 0$, which implies that $F_1(0,0) = A_3 - A_2 < 0$. Next we have

$$V'(m_{0-}) = c\rho \left(\frac{\mu}{2} \right)^{\gamma - 1}$$

and

$$V'(m_{0+}) = r_1 A_2 e^{-r_1 c m_1} - r_2 A_3 e^{-r_2 m_1}.$$

If we define

$$A_1' := \rho \left(\frac{\mu}{2} \right)^{\gamma - 1}, \tag{A.5.2}$$

then smooth pasting requires

$$F_2(c, m_1) := A_1' c - r_1 A_2 e^{-r_1 m_1} + r_2 A_3 e^{-r_2 m_1} = 0.$$

To solve the system of equations, we compute

$$F_2(c, m_1) - r_1 F_1(c, m_1) = (A_1' - r_1 A_1) c + (r_2 - r_1) A_3 e^{-r_2 m_1} = 0.$$

Solving for m_1 in the expression above yields

$$m_1 = -\frac{1}{r_2} \log (Bc), \quad \text{where} \quad B := \frac{A_1' - r_1 A_1}{(r_1 - r_2) A_3}. \tag{A.5.3}$$

It is easy to show from Expressions (A.5.1) and (A.5.2) that $B > 0$. Inserting Equation (A.5.3) into $F_1(c, m_1)$ gives

$$A_1 c - A_2 (Bc)^{\frac{r_1}{r_2}} + A_3 (Bc) = 0;$$

therefore

$$c_1^* = \left(\frac{A_1 + B A_3}{A_2 B^{r_1/r_2}} \right)^{r_2/(r_1 - r_2)}. \tag{A.5.4}$$

In order to prove that $c_1^* > 0$, we must show, as $A_2 B^{r_1/r_2} < 0$, that $A_1 + B A_3 < 0$. Observe that

$$A_1 + B A_3 = A_1 + \frac{A_1' - r_1 A_1}{r_1 - r_2} = \frac{A_1' - r_2 A_1}{r_1 - r_2}.$$

Given that $r_1 - r_2 < 0$, $c_1^* > 0$ whenever $A_1' - r_2 A_1 > 0$. After simplification, the latter is equivalent to $2\rho > r_2 \mu$, which in turn may be rewritten as

$$\frac{2\sigma^2 \rho}{\mu} > -\mu + \sqrt{\mu^2 + 2\sigma^2 \rho}. \tag{A.5.5}$$

Simple arithmetic is required to show that Expression (A.5.5) is equivalent to

$$0 < \mu^2 + 2\sigma^2 \rho,$$

which clearly holds for all $\mu, \sigma, \rho > 0$. Inserting Expression (A.5.4) into Expression (A.5.3) we get, after manipulations,

$$m_1^* = -\frac{1}{r_2}\log(B) - \frac{1}{r_2}\log(c_1^*)$$

$$= m_0^* - \frac{1}{r_2}\log\left(\frac{r_1 r_2 A_1 - r_2 A_1'}{r_1}\right) - \frac{1}{r_2}\log\left(\frac{A_1 + BA_3}{A_2 B^{r_1/r_2}}\right)^{r_2/(r_1-r_2)}$$

$$= m_0^* + \frac{1}{r_2 - r_1}\log\left(-\frac{r_1}{r_2}\right) > m_0^*.$$

Q.E.D.

Proof of Lemma 5.3.1 To prove that $m_0^* < l$ we must show that $R(0;l) < R(1;l)$. This however, is equivalent to

$$(\mu - \lambda l)V'(l) + \lambda V(l) > \mu V'(l) \Leftrightarrow V(l) > lV'(l).$$

Observe that, as $V(0) = 0$, the desired condition is equivalent to

$$\frac{V(l) - V(0)}{l} > V'(l),$$

which holds due to the concavity of V.

Q.E.D.

A.6 Chapter 7

Proof of Proposition 7.2.1. Given an incentive-compatible contract $(\Theta, \widehat{Y})$, we define the agent's total utility at date t as

$$\widehat{\psi}_t(\Theta, \widehat{Y}) := \mathbb{E}\left[\int_0^\tau e^{-\rho s}d\widehat{C}_s \,\Big|\, \mathcal{F}_t^{\widehat{Y}}\right],$$

which is an $\mathcal{F}_t^{\widehat{Y}}$-martingale by virtue of being a conditional expectation. From this point on we omit $(\Theta, \widehat{Y})$ as an argument to streamline the notation. Applying the Martingale Representation Theorem, there exist an $\mathcal{F}^{\widehat{Y}}$-adapted process $\beta^{\widehat{Y}} = \{\beta_t^{\widehat{Y}}, \tau \geq t \geq 0\}$ such that $\widehat{\psi}$ may be written as

$$\widehat{\psi}_t = \widehat{\psi}_0 + \int_0^t e^{-\rho s}\sigma\beta_s^{\widehat{Y}}dZ_s, \tag{A.7.1}$$

where $\sigma e^{-\rho s} > 0$ is a scaling factor. Moreover, given that $\int_0^t e^{-\rho s} d\widehat{C}_s$ is $\mathcal{F}_t^{\widehat{Y}}$-measurable, $\widehat{\psi}_t$ can be rewritten as

$$\widehat{\psi}_t = \int_0^t e^{-\rho s} d\widehat{C}_s + e^{-\rho t} W_t. \qquad (A.7.2)$$

Equations (A.7.1) and (A.7.2) then imply

$$\widehat{\psi}_0 + \int_0^t e^{-\rho s} \sigma \beta_s^{\widehat{Y}} dZ_s = e^{-\rho t} W_t + \int_0^t e^{-\rho s} d\widehat{C}_s. \qquad (A.7.3)$$

In differential form, Equation (A.7.3) becomes

$$dW_t = \rho W_t dt - d\widehat{C}_t + \sigma \beta_t^{\widehat{Y}} dZ_t.$$

Q.E.D.

Proof of Lemma 7.2.2. The intuition behind this proof is that diversion brings the agent the instantaneous amount $\alpha |dY_t - d\widehat{Y}_t|$ but it reduces his continuation utility by $\beta_t^{\widehat{Y}} |dY_t - d\widehat{Y}_t|$. If the sensitivity coefficient $\beta^{\widehat{Y}}$ is large enough, then the instantaneous gains from diverting are offset by the losses in continuation value. Using Expression (7.2.1), we may rewrite the dynamics of the agent's continuation utility W as

$$dW_t = \rho W_t dt + \beta_t^{\widehat{Y}} \left(dY_t - \mu dt \right) - d\widehat{C}_t$$

Furthermore, we have

$$\beta_t^{\widehat{Y}} \left(dY_t - \mu dt \right) - d\widehat{C}_t = \left[\beta_t^{\widehat{Y}} - \alpha \right] \left[dY_t - d\widehat{Y}_t \right] + \beta_t^{\widehat{Y}} \left[d\widehat{Y}_t - \mu dt \right].$$

As the agent cannot overreport, it holds that

$$\mathbb{E}\left[\widehat{Y}_t - \mu dt \right] \leq 0.$$

This implies that the agent's expected net gains

$$\mathbb{E}\left[dW_t - \rho W_t dt \right] \geq 0 \Leftrightarrow \left[\beta_t^{\widehat{Y}} - \alpha \right] \left[dY_t - d\widehat{Y}_t \right] \geq 0$$

and because $dY_t - d\widehat{Y}_t \geq 0$, the latter inequality requires $\beta_t^{\widehat{Y}} - \alpha \geq 0$.

Q.E.D.

Proof of Proposition 7.3.1. The proof of this result mimics that of Proposition 7.2.1. In this case, however, instead of using the "diffusion" version of the Martingale Representation Theorem, we only employ the "jump" version: The agent's total utility

$$\widehat{\psi}_t(\Gamma, \Lambda) := \mathbb{E}^\Lambda \left[\int_0^\tau e^{-\rho s} \left(dL_s + \mathbb{1}_{\{\Lambda_s = \lambda + \Delta\lambda\}} X_s B ds \right) \Big| \mathcal{F}_t^\Lambda \right]$$

is an $\mathcal{F}^\Lambda$-martingale. We again abstain from writing (Γ, Λ) for ease of reading. The Martingale Representation Theorem then guarantees the existence of an $\mathcal{F}^\Lambda$-adapted process $H = \{H_t, \tau \geq t \geq 0\}$ such that

$$\widehat{\psi}_t = \widehat{\psi}_0 - \int_0^t e^{-\rho s} H_s \left[\Lambda_s dt - dN_s^\Lambda \right], \tag{A.7.4}$$

where, once more, $e^{-\rho s}$ is a scaling factor. We can also write

$$\widehat{\psi}_t = \int_0^t e^{-\rho s} \left(dL_s + \mathbb{1}_{\{\Lambda_s = \lambda + \Delta\lambda\}} X_s B ds \right) + e^{-\rho t} W_t, \tag{A.7.5}$$

which is possible thanks to the $\mathcal{F}_t^\Lambda$-measurability of the integral on the right-hand side. Equating the right-hand sides of Equation (A.7.4) and (A.7.5) and expressing the result in differential form as in Proposition 7.2.1 we obtain the desired result.

Q.E.D.

Proof of Lemma 7.3.2. Let us denote the agents lifetime expected payoff, given the information available at date $t \leq \tau$, when she acts according to $\Lambda' = \{\Lambda_t', t \geq 0\}$ until date t and then reverts to $\Lambda = \{\Lambda_t, t \geq 0\}$ by

$$\Psi_t' := \int_0^t e^{-\rho s} \left(dL_s + \mathbb{1}_{\{\Lambda_s' = \lambda + \Delta\lambda\}} X_s B ds \right) + e^{-\rho t} W_t(\Gamma, \Lambda). \tag{A.7.6}$$

The first step is to show that if $\Psi' = \{\Psi_t', t \geq 0\}$ is a strict $\mathcal{F}^{\Lambda'}$-submartingale, then the strategy Λ is suboptimal. Indeed, if that were the case, then there would exist $t > 0$ such that

$$W_0(\Gamma, \Lambda) = \Psi_0' < \mathbb{E}^{\Lambda'} [\Psi_t'].$$

By Expression (A.7.6), the agent is then strictly better off acting according to Λ' until date t and then reverting to strategy Λ. The claim follows. Next, we show that if Ψ' is a strict $\mathcal{F}^{\Lambda'}$-supermartingale, then the agent finds strategy Λ at least as good as Λ'. By definition

$$\Psi_t' = W_t(\Gamma, \Lambda) + \int_0^t e^{-\rho s} \left(\mathbb{1}_{\{\Lambda_s' = \lambda + \Delta\lambda\}} - \mathbb{1}_{\{\Lambda_s = \lambda + \Delta\lambda\}} \right) X_s B. \tag{A.7.7}$$

Given that W is right continuous with left limits (its discontinuities are only isolated jumps) and nonnegative, then so is Ψ'. Therefore, we may make use of the Optimal Sampling Theorem (see Appendix C.4) to get

$$\Psi'_0 \geq \mathbb{E}^{\Lambda'}[\Psi'(\tau)] = W_0(\Gamma, \Lambda').$$

However, $\Psi'_0 = W_0(\Gamma, \Lambda')$ so the claim follows. To finalize the proof, notice that Proposition 7.3.1 and Equation (A.7.7) allow us to write

$$\Psi'_t = W_0(\Gamma, \Lambda) - \int_0^t e^{-\rho s} H_s(\Gamma, \Lambda)\left[\Lambda_s dt - dN_s^\Lambda\right]$$

$$+ \int_0^t e^{-\rho s}\left(\mathbb{1}_{\{\Lambda'_s = \lambda + \Delta\lambda\}} - \mathbb{1}_{\{\Lambda'_s = \lambda + \Delta\lambda\}}\right) X_s B.$$

This expression can be simplified to obtain

$$\Psi'_t = W_0(\Gamma, \Lambda) - \int_0^t e^{-\rho s} H_s(\Gamma, \Lambda)\left[\Lambda'_s dt - dN_s^{\Lambda'}\right]$$

$$+ \int_0^t e^{-\rho s} \Delta\lambda\left(\mathbb{1}_{\{\Lambda'_s = \lambda + \Delta\lambda\}} - \mathbb{1}_{\{\Lambda'_s = \lambda + \Delta\lambda\}}\right)\left[X_s b - H_s(\Gamma, \Lambda)\right] ds.$$

As $H(\Gamma, \Lambda)$ is $\mathcal{F}^{\Lambda'}$-predictable and and $\Lambda' - N^{\Lambda'}$ is $\mathcal{F}^{\Lambda'}$-martingale, the drift of Ψ' has the same sign as that of

$$\left(\mathbb{1}_{\{\Lambda'_t = \lambda + \Delta\lambda\}} - \mathbb{1}_{\{\Lambda'_t = \lambda + \Delta\lambda\}}\right)\left[X_t b - H_t(\Gamma, \Lambda)\right]$$

for all $t \in [0, \tau)$. If Condition (7.3.3) holds for the effort process Λ, then this drift remains nonpositive for all $t \in [0, \tau)$ and all choices of $\Lambda'_t \in \{\lambda, \lambda + \Delta\lambda\}$. Hence, for any effort process Λ' we have that Ψ' is an $\mathcal{F}^{\Lambda'}$-supermartingale; thus, Λ is at least as good as Λ' for the agent. If instead Condition (7.3.3) does not hold for the effort process Λ, then we may choose Λ' such that for each $t \in [0, \tau)$, it holds that $\Lambda'_t = \lambda$ if and only if $H_t(\Gamma, \Lambda) \geq X_t b$. The drift of Ψ' is then everywhere nonnegative and strictly positive over a set of $\mathbb{Q}^{\Lambda'}$-strictly positive measure. As a result of this, Ψ' is a strict $\mathcal{F}^{\Lambda'}$-submartingale; thus, Λ is suboptimal for the agent.

Q.E.D.

A.7 Chapter 8

Proof of Proposition 8.2.4. The density of the ergodic distribution of q can be found by solving the Fokker-Planck equation

$$[\mu(q)f(q)]' = \left[\frac{\sigma^2(q)}{2}f(q)\right]''$$

with an appropriate boundary condition (see the Appendix in Brunnermeier and Sannikov (2014) for details). This yields

$$f(q) = \frac{c_0}{\sigma^2(q)} \exp \int_0^{\hat{q}} \frac{2\mu(s)}{\sigma^2(s)} ds,$$

where the normalizing constant c_0 is such that

$$\int_0^a f(q) dq = 1.$$

Q.E.D.

Proof of Proposition 8.3.1. We have already established that any equilibrium price function $p(M)$ must satisfy the first-order differential Equation (8.3.11). Uniqueness of the equilibrium will result from the Cauchy-Lipschitz Theorem, once the boundary value $p(0) = \bar{p}$ is determined. Once $p(M)$ is known, the function U can be computed by solving

$$\frac{U'(M)}{U(M)} = -\frac{p(M)}{\sigma_0 D[p(M)]},$$

which yields

$$U(M) = U(\overline{M}) \exp \left\{ \int_M^{\overline{M}} \frac{p(s)}{\sigma_0 D[p(s)]} ds \right\}.$$

Given that $U(\overline{M}) = 1$ and $U(0) = 1 + \beta$, this implies

$$\int_0^{\overline{M}} \frac{p(s)}{\sigma_0 D[p(s)]} ds = \log(1 + \beta).$$

Finally, changing the integration variable in the above equation to $p(s) = p$ yields Equation (8.3.15).

Q.E.D.

B The Modigliani-Miller Theorem

In this appendix we use the setup of Chapter 1. In particular we assume the value of firm assets evolves according to the following stochastic differential equation:

$$dS_t = S_t\big[(r - \beta)dt + \sigma dZ_t\big], \quad S_0 = S,$$

When a firm is set up at $t = 0$, several financial decisions have to be made by its owners:

- the nominal debt B to be repaid at date T and the flow of coupons C_t, for $t \leq T$, promised to debtholders;

- the initial amount m_0 of reserves to be injected in the firm, and more generally the volume of cash M_t to be targeted for $t > 0$;

- the dividend policy, represented by the cashflow process dL_t paid to shareholders.

In a nutshell, the Modigliani-Miller paradox (often called "theorem") states that, in the absence of any frictions, all these financial decisions are irrelevant: initial shareholder value does not depend on nominal debt B, on possible coupon payments C_t, on the level of cash reserves M_t or on the volatility σ of assets. It only depends on the economic value added by the firm $S_0 - I$, where I is the initial amount invested to acquire the assets. Most people call this the Modigliani-Miller "theorem" because it is a logical consequence of the model's assumptions. We could call it the Modigliani-Miller "paradox" because it shows that if these assumptions were maintained, the whole field of corporate finance would be useless. Let us establish this result logically. Consider, for $t \leq T$, the firm's cash reserves M_t, which are remunerated at the riskless rate r, the coupons C_t and the dividend process dL_t. Then, the cash reserves evolve as follows:

$$dM_t = (rM_t - C_t)dt - dL_t. \tag{B1}$$

At date $t = 0$, when the firm is established, its shareholders also determine the initial levels of liquid reserves M_0 and nominal debt B to be repaid at date T. Their net initial investment in the company is $I + M_0 - D_0$, where D_0 is the market value of debt at date $t = 0$. Hence, the initial *shareholder value* equals

$$SV_0 := E_0 - (I + M_0 - D_0). \tag{B2}$$

Debt matures at date T (as in Section 1.2) and repays $\min\{S_T + M_T, B\}$ at maturity. It also pays the coupon stream $C = \{C_t, t \in [0, T)\}$. Therefore, the initial value of debt equals the expectation at date $t = 0$ of the discounted coupon stream, plus the present value of the final payout:

$$D_0 = \mathbb{E}\left[\int_0^T e^{-rt} C_t dt + e^{-rT} \min\{S_t + M_t, B\} \Big| S_0\right], \tag{B3}$$

As shareholders are left with $\max\{V_T + M_T - B, 0\}$ at date T and in the meantime they enjoy the dividend stream $L = \{L_t, t \in [0, T)\}$, the initial value of equity is

$$E_0 = \mathbb{E}\left[\int_0^T e^{-rt} dL_t + e^{-rT} \max\{S_t + M_t - B, 0\} \Big| S_0\right]. \tag{B4}$$

Using Expressions (B3) and (B4) we can determine initial shareholder value as

$$SV_0 = \mathbb{E}\left[\int_0^T e^{-rt}(C_t dt + dL_t) + e^{-rT}(S_t + M_t) \Big| S_0\right] - I - m_0.$$

From Equation (B1) we have that $C_t dt + dL_t = rM_t dt - dM_t$. Furthermore, it follows immediately from Itô's formula that $d[e^{-rt}M_t] = e^{-rt}(dM_t - rM_t dt)$; hence

$$SV_0 = \mathbb{E}\left[-\int_0^T d[e^{-rt}M_t] + e^{-rT}(S_t + M_t) \Big| S_0\right] - I - m_0$$

$$= \mathbb{E}\left[m_0 - e^{-rT}M_t + e^{-rT}(S_t + M_t) \big| S_0\right] - I - m_0$$

$$= \mathbb{E}\left[e^{-rT}S_t \big| S_0\right] - I = S_0 - I.$$

In other words, the firm's financial policy regarding its liquidity management, the structure of its debt and the way it distributes dividends to its equity holders bears absolutely no weight on shareholder value. Moreover, notice that only S_0 matters; thus, the volatility σ (given S_0) is also irrelevant to shareholder value. This implies that any risk-management activity geared toward reducing σ is, from the shareholders' perspective, at most useless, if it is costless, or value destroying, otherwise.

Given the profundity of the Modigliani-Miller theorem, it should come as no surprise that it was followed by many many publications that, roughly speaking, tried to elucidate the impact (and necessity) of the required assumptions. One such article is Stiglitz (1969), where the author deals with issues raised against the original Modigliani-Miller result, among others: the existence of "risk classes" (stocks and bonds in the Merton, Black and Cox world) and the competitiveness of the secondary markets. Stiglitz shows that none of these are necessary conditions. He does, however, point out that the absence of (costly) bankruptcy is crucial for Modigliani-Miller to hold. This work provides a thorough overview of the Modigliani-Miller theorem. Further discussion on the effect that default risk has on corporate leverage can be found in Milne (1975), who uses a static framework where taxes are absent.

C Useful Mathematical Results

The purpose of this appendix is to provide the reader with reference material on mathematical topics that are used repeatedly throughout the book. Our intention is not to present an in-depth treaty on stochastic analysis, a purpose that is well fulfilled by Applebaum (2009), Karatzas and Shreve (1991), Oeksendal (2003) and Revuz and Yor (1999), for instance.

C.1 Filtrations, Martingales and Itô Processes

The basic building block of the theories of probability and stochastic processes is the random variable. For our purposes this will be defined as a mapping Y from an abstract space Ω (the space of elementary events) into the real numbers[1] that has the crucial property of being *measurable*. In order to make this precise, we require the notion of σ-*algebra*. Let $\mathcal{F}$ be a collection of subsets of Ω with the following properties:

- both $\emptyset$ and Ω belong to $\mathcal{F}$;

- if $A \in \mathcal{F}$ then its complement $A^c \in \mathcal{F}$;

- given a *countable* collection $\{A_n \in \mathcal{F}, n = \mathbb{N}\}$ its union

$$\bigcup_{n \in \mathbb{N}} A_n \in \mathcal{F} \quad (\sigma - \text{additivity}).$$

Such an $\mathcal{F}$ is called a σ-algebra, a particular example of which is the Borel σ-algebra $\mathcal{B}(\mathbb{R})$ generated by the open intervals. The pair $(\Omega, \mathcal{F})$ is called a *measurable space* and the mapping $Y : \Omega \to \mathbb{R}$ is then said to be $\mathcal{F}$-measurable (sometimes one simply says "measurable" if there is no possibility of confusion) if the inverse image $Y^{-1}(B)$ of any set $A \in \mathcal{B}(\mathbb{R})$, defined as

$$Y^{-1}(B) := \{\omega \in \Omega | Y(\omega) \in B\},$$

---

[1] The image space of a random variable can be, in general, an abstract measure space.

belongs to $\mathcal{F}$. A *stochastic process* is a collection of random variables $X = \{X_t, t \geq 0\}$ such that each X_t is $\mathcal{F}$-measurable.

A concept that will be related to the evolution of information as time elapses is that of a stochastic process being *adapted*. This boils down to measurability with respect to smaller σ-algebras than $\mathcal{F}$. More specifically, we call a collection $\mathbb{F} = \{\mathcal{F}_t, t \geq 0\}$ a *filtration* of $\mathcal{F}$ if for all $0 \leq s < t < \infty$ we have:

- $\mathcal{F}_s$ is a σ-algebra;

- $\mathcal{F}_s \subset \mathcal{F}_t \subset \mathcal{F}$.

We then say that the stochastic process X is $\mathbb{F}$-adapted if for all $t \geq 0$ it holds that X_t is $\mathcal{F}_t$-measurable. A special filtration associated to a process X is the one that X generates itself, denoted by $\mathbb{F}^X$ or $\sigma(X)$. It corresponds to the collection of σ-algebras $\{\mathcal{F}_t^X, t \geq 0\}$ such that $\mathcal{F}_s$ is the smallest σ-algebra with respect to which X_s is measurable. This is commonly referred to as the *natural filtration*. The reason we say that $\mathbb{F}^X$ embodies the evolution of information is that if $F \in \mathcal{F}_t^X$, then someone who can observe the process X can tell at date t whether the event F has taken place.

Next we introduce the concept of a *probability measure*. This is a mapping $\mathbb{Q} : \mathcal{F} \to [0,1]$ such that

- $\mathbb{Q}(\emptyset) = 0$ and $\mathbb{Q}(\Omega) = 1$;

- given a countable collection of *pairwise disjoint* sets $\{A_n \in \mathcal{F}, n = \mathbb{N}\}$ its probability

$$\mathbb{Q}\left(\bigcup_{n \in \mathbb{N}} A_n\right) = \sum_{n \in \mathbb{N}} \mathbb{Q}(A_n).$$

Intuitively, for any event $A \in \mathcal{F}$, the number $\mathbb{Q}(A)$ tells us "how likely" it is that A occurs, with $\mathbb{Q}(A) = 0$ meaning "not a chance" and $\mathbb{Q}(A) = 1$ meaning (almost) "sure thing". From this point on, the relations $Y_1 \geq Y_2$ and $Y_1 = Y_2$ between random variables are to be understood in the $\mathbb{Q}$-almost-surely sense: when we write $Y_1 \geq Y_2$ we mean that there exits a set $A \subset \mathcal{F}$ such that i) $\mathbb{Q}(A) = 1$ and ii) $Y_1(\omega) \geq Y_2(\omega)$ for all $\omega \in A$ (resp. for the relation $Y_1 = Y_2$).

A *filtered probability space* is a quadruple $(\Omega, \mathcal{F}, \mathbb{F}, \mathbb{Q})$, where $\mathcal{F}$ is a σ-algebra, $\mathbb{F}$ is a filtration of $\mathcal{F}$ and $\mathbb{Q}$ is a probability measure on $\mathcal{F}$. The *expectation* of a random variable Y is its integral against $\mathbb{Q}$, we write

$$\mathbb{E}_{\mathbb{Q}}[Y] = \int_{\Omega} Y(\omega) d\mathbb{Q}(w).$$

Unless there are grounds for confusion (i.e. different probability measures are being used) one usually writes $\mathbb{E}[Y]$. It is also customary to avoid writing the argument ω in the integral.

One can imagine many scenarios where observing a random variable R provides us with information about the evolution of some other variable I. For example, an increase in interest rates may have an effect on inflation. Observing the former does not provide us with 100% accurate information about the latter, but it does tell us something about what we should expect I to be. This is precisely what the *conditional expectation* of I given R, denoted by $\mathbb{E}[I|R]$, does. Since observing R and observing $\mathcal{F}^R$ are informationally equivalent, we may also write $\mathbb{E}[I|\mathcal{F}^R]$, which is the more standard notation since it allows us to condition on σ-algebras without having to specify the random variables that generated them. Formally, the conditional expectation of a random variable Y given a sub-σ-algebra $\mathcal{G} \subset \mathcal{F}$ is a random variable[2] $\mathbb{E}[Y|\mathcal{G}]$ that is $\mathcal{G}$-measurable and satisfies

$$\int_G \mathbb{E}[Y|\mathcal{G}]d\mathbb{Q} = \int_G Y \, d\mathbb{Q} \quad \text{for all } G \in \mathcal{G}.$$

Three crucial properties of the conditional expectation are

- If the random variables Y and $\widetilde{Y}$ are independent, then
  $\mathbb{E}[\widetilde{Y}|\mathcal{F}^Y] = \mathbb{E}[\widetilde{Y}]$;

- for two random variables Y and $\widetilde{Y}$ such that Y is $\mathcal{G}$-measurable
  for some sub-σ-algebra of $\mathcal{F}$, we have that
  $\mathbb{E}[Y\widetilde{Y}|\mathcal{G}] = Y\,\mathbb{E}[\widetilde{Y}|\mathcal{G}]$ and

- given two sub-σ-algebras $\mathcal{G}_1 \subset \mathcal{G}_2$ it holds that
  $\mathbb{E}\big[\mathbb{E}[Y|\mathcal{G}_2]\big|\mathcal{G}_1\big] = \mathbb{E}[Y|\mathcal{G}_1]$ (tower property).

We can generalize the question of how much does knowing a random variable R tell us about the expected value of I to an intertemporal setting. In other words, given stochastic processes $R = \{R_t, t \geq 0\}$ and $I = \{I_t, t \geq 0\}$, and two dates $s < t$, what does observing R_s tell us about the expected value of I_t? This is precisely $\mathbb{E}[I_t|R_s] = \mathbb{E}[I_t|\mathcal{F}_s^R]$. This brings us to one of the most important concepts in the application of stochastic analysis to finance: *martingales*.

Let us consider the filtered probability space $(\Omega, \mathcal{F}, \mathbb{F}, \mathbb{Q})$ and an $\mathbb{F}$-adapted stochastic process X that satisfies $\mathbb{E}[|X_t|] < \infty$ for all $t \geq 0$. We then say that

---

[2]A conditional expectation is almost surely unique. This means that any two random variables that are conditional expectations of Y given $\mathcal{F}$ coincide for all $\omega \in F$ for some set $F \in \mathcal{F}$ such that $\mathbb{Q}(F) = 1$.

1. X is a *supermartingale* if for any $0 \le s < t$ it holds that
   $\mathbb{E}[X_t|\mathcal{F}_s] \le X_s$.

2. X is a *submartingale* if for any $0 \le s < t$ it holds that
   $\mathbb{E}[X_t|\mathcal{F}_s] \ge X_s$.

3. X is a *martingale* if for any $0 \le s < t$ it holds that
   $\mathbb{E}[X_t|\mathcal{F}_s] = X_s$.

A martingale embodies the idea of a "fair game," in the sense that knowledge at date $s < t$ does not provide us with additional information on the expected value of X_t. If X represented the price of a financial product, then X being a martingale means that information at date s does not provide us with privileged trading information; thus, absence of arbitrage opportunities is intrinsically tied to (discounted) price processes being martingales.

Two very relevant stochastic processes are Wiener processes (or Brownian motions) and compensated Poisson processes, which are martingales with respect to their own filtrations. The importance of these processes for us is that we repeatedly use integrals with respect to Wiener and Poisson processes to represent prices of assets and evolutions of cashflows. This brings us to the crucial concept of the *Itô integral*.[3] Let us consider $(\Omega, \mathcal{F}, \mathbb{F}, \mathbb{Q})$, where $\mathbb{F}$ is the filtration generated by a Brownian motion $Z = \{Z_t, t \ge 0\}$. Consider a $\mathbb{F}$-adapted process $H = \{H_t, t \ge 0\}$ that satisfies

$$\mathbb{E}\left[\int_0^t H_s^2 ds\right] < \infty, \quad \text{for all } t \ge 0.$$

We may then compute the Itô integral of H

$$X_t = \int_0^t H_s dZ_s,$$

which is a **continuous** martingale that satisfies $\mathbb{E}[X_t] = 0$. We highlight that the continuity property does not depend on H being itself continuous. The question of whether all continuous martingales can be expressed as an Itô integral is addressed in Section C.3.

Not all the stochastic processes that we are interested in are martingales. For example, the net-earnings process given in Expression (2.1.1) in Chapter 2 is not one:

$$Y_t = \int_0^t \lambda \, dt + \int_0^t \sigma \, dZ_s.$$

---

[3]The formal construction of the stochastic integral and the derivation of its properties is a delicate mathematical exercise. We refer the reader to Chapter 3 of Karatzas and Shreve (1991) for a fine exposition on the matter.

Clearly the constant function σ is square-integrable; thus, the Itô integral is well defined. However, if for $s < t$ we compute

$$\mathbb{E}[Y_t|\mathcal{F}_s] = \lambda t + \int_0^s \sigma dZ_l > Y_s,$$

i.e. Y is a submartingale (which is reasonable given that it would be very hard to find investors for a firm whose net earnings would not grow in expectation). While Y is not a martingale, it does belong to the important class of *Itô processes*. Given the natural filtration $\mathbb{F}$ of the Wiener process W, we say that an adapted process $H = \{H_t, t \geq 0\}$ is an Itô process (or an Itô diffusion) if there exists a Lebesgue-integrable function μ, an adapted, square-integrable process $h = \{h_t, t \geq 0\}$ and $h_0 \in \mathbb{R}$ such that

$$H_t = h_0 + \int_0^t \mu_s ds + \int_0^t h_s dZ_s. \tag{D.1.1}$$

The more common shorthand to write Equation (D.1.1) is the stochastic differential equation

$$dH_t = \mu_t dt + h_t dZ_t, \quad H_0 = h_0. \tag{D.1.2}$$

C.2 The Itô Formula

We are all well acquainted with the classical "chain rule" of differential calculus: given two differentiable functions $f : \mathbb{R} \to \mathbb{R}$ and $g : \mathbb{R} \to \mathbb{R}$, their composition $F := f \circ g$ is also a differentiable function whose derivative is

$$F'(x) = \frac{d}{dx}(f \circ g(x)) = f'(g(x))g'(x). \tag{D.2.1}$$

Using the Fundamental Theorem of Calculus, we may write Equation (D.2.1) in integral form as

$$F(x) = F(a) + \int_a^x f'(g(y))g'(y)dy$$

for any $x \leq a \in \mathbb{R}$. Clearly, we do not actually need both f and g to have the same domains. For instance, we could require $g : [0, \infty) \to \mathbb{R}$ (to think about "time"), which would then imply $F : [0, \infty) \to \mathbb{R}$. If we think of g_t as the position of a particle at date t and $f(x)$ the temperature at position x, then $F_t = f(g_t)$ tells us what the particle's temperature is as time evolves and F' is the rate of change of this temperature. In particular,

$$F_t = F_0 + \int_0^t f'(g_s)g_s'ds \tag{D.2.2}$$

provides us with a picture of how the particle's temperature evolves as time goes by. A crucial assumption in writing Equation (D.2.2) is that the mapping $t \mapsto g_t$ is differentiable, but what can we do if that is not the case. In particular, what if g were an Itô process

$$g_t = g_0 + \int_0^t \mu_s ds \int_0^t h_s dZ_s?$$

Under what conditions would $f \circ g$ be itself an Itô process? The answer to this question is provided by the celebrated Itô formula (also called *Itô's Lemma*):

Theorem C.2.1 (Itô's Formula). *Let* $X = \{X_t, t \geq 0\}$ *be an Itô process that satisfies the stochastic differential equation*

$$dX_t = \mu_t dt + h_t dZ_t, \quad X_0 = x_0$$

and assume that $f : \mathbb{R} \to \mathbb{R}$ *is a twice continuously differentiable function. Then* $f(X)$ *is again an Itô process that satisfies the stochastic differential equation*

$$dF_t = df(X_t) = f'(X_t)dX_t + \frac{f''(X_t)}{2}h_t^2 dt, \quad F_0 = f(x_0). \tag{D.2.3}$$

We may write Equation D.2.3 in integral form as

$$F_t = F_0 + \int_0^t f'(X_s)dX_s + \int_0^t \frac{f''(X_s)}{2}h_s^2 ds,$$

from which we get a "stochastic equivalent" of Equation (D.2.2). In this sense, we may interpret Itô's formula as a stochastic chain rule. The term $h_s^2 ds$ deserves special attention; it corresponds to the so-called *quadratic variation* of the process X, formally denoted by

$$\langle X, X \rangle.$$

The mnemonic to compute the quadratic variation of an Itô process is to multiply dX_t times itself and use the "rule" $dt \cdot dZ_t = dt \cdot dt = 0$ and $dZ_t \cdot dZ_t = dt$. The strict definition of the quadratic variation of a square-integrable martingale M is that it is the **unique** process $\langle M, M \rangle$ such that

$$M^2 - \langle M, M \rangle$$

is again a martingale. This becomes useful if we want to derive a generalized Itô formula that is applicable to processes beyond Itô ones, in particular, to processes that have jump components in their dynamics. Before we proceed to this, we present a simple generalization of Expression (D.2.3) when $f : [0, \infty] \times \mathbb{R}$ is also a continuously differentiable function of time:

$$
\begin{aligned}
df(t, X_t) = &\frac{d}{dt} f(t, X_t) + \frac{d}{dx} f(t, X_t) dX_t \\
&+ \frac{1}{2} \frac{d^2}{dx^2} f(t, X_t) h_t^2 dt, \quad F_0 = f(0, x_0).
\end{aligned}
\tag{D.2.4}
$$

The Itô formula also admits a multidimensional extension. Namely, let $Z = (Z^1, \ldots, Z^n)$ be an n-dimensional Brownian motion. If $f : \mathbb{R}_+ \times \mathbb{R}^n$ is continuously differentiable in its first coordinate and twice differentiable in the following n and if $X = (X^1, \ldots, X^n)$ is an n-dimensional Itô process such that

$$
dX_t^i = \mu_i(X_t) dt + \sigma_i(X_t) dZ_t^i,
$$

then

$$
\begin{aligned}
df(t, X_t) = &\frac{\partial}{\partial t} f(t, X_t) + \sum_1^n \frac{\partial}{\partial x_i} f(t, X_t) dX_t^i \\
&+ \frac{1}{2} \sum_{i,j=1}^n \frac{\partial^2}{\partial x_i^2} f(t, X_t) dX_t^i dX_t^j.
\end{aligned}
$$

To compute $dX_t^i dX_t^j$ we extend the "rule" above: $dt \cdot dZ_t^i = dt \cdot dt = 0$ and $dZ_t^i \cdot dZ_t^j = \rho_{i,j} dt$, where $\rho_{i,j}$ is the correlation coefficient of Z^i and Z^j. In particular, if we consider apply Itô's (multidimensional) formula to $f(x, y) = x \cdot y$, we obtain the STOCHASTIC PRODUCT RULE

$$
d[X_t Y_t] = X_t dY_t + Y_t dX_t + dX_t dY_t.
$$

In order to present the generalized Itô formula that we need, we have to state precisely the kind of (possibly discontinuous) processes that we have in mind. The most general version of Itô's formula would require the introduction of *semimartingales*, which would be out of this book's scope. We look for an extension to Expression (D.2.4) when the stochastic process X satisfies the stochastic differential equation

$$
dX_t = \mu_t dt + h_t dZ_t + dL_t - dK_t + m_t dN_t, \quad X_0 = x_0,
$$

where $L = \{L_t, t \geq 0\}$ is a nondecreasing process, $K = \{K_t, t \geq 0\}$ is a non-increasing one and $N = \{N_t, t \geq 0\}$ is a Poisson process. Then we have that

$$f(t, X_t) = f(0, x_0) + \int_0^t \frac{d}{dt} f(s, X_s) ds + \int_0^t \frac{d}{dx} f(s, X_s) dX_s$$

$$+ \frac{1}{2} \int_0^t \frac{d^2}{dx^2} V(X_s) d\langle X, X \rangle_s \qquad \text{(D.2.5)}$$

$$+ \sum_{s \in \Gamma} e^{-\rho s} \left(\Delta f(s, X_s) - \frac{d}{dx} f(s, X_s) \Delta X_s \right),$$

where Γ is the set of discontinuities of X and

$$\Delta f(s, X_s) := f(s_+, X_{s_+}) - f(s, X_s) \quad \text{and} \quad \Delta X_s := X_{s_+} - X_s.$$

C.3 The Martingale Representation Theorem(s)

We saw in Section C.1 that an Itô integral is a continuous martingale. The classic Martingale Representation Theorem, a very deep result, provides us with the contrapose:

Theorem C.3.1 (MRT for diffusions). *Consider the filtered probability space $(\Omega, \mathcal{F}, \mathbb{F}, \mathbb{Q})$, where $\mathbb{F}$ is the natural filtration of a Brownian motion Z. If the stochastic process $H = \{H_t, t \geq 0\}$ is $\mathbb{F}$-adapted, then there exist $a \in \mathbb{R}$ and an $\mathbb{F}$-adapted process $h = \{h_t, t \geq 0\}$ such that*

$$H_t = a + \int_0^t h_s dZ_s. \qquad \text{(D.3.1)}$$

Given that the expectation of an Itô integral is zero, taking expectations on both sides of Equation (D.3.1) yields $\mathbb{E}[H_t] = a$.

As we mentioned in Section C.2 at times we will be interested in working with processes that include a Poisson jump term (see, for instance, Expression (7.3.1) for the output flow in Chapter 7). Clearly such processes cannot be written as an Itô integral plus a constant as in Theorem C.3.1, as this would preclude the jump behavior. On the other hand, we know that given a Poisson process $N = \{N_t, t \geq 0\}$ with intensity λ, the corresponding compensated process C defined for each $t \geq 0$ as $N_t - \lambda t$, is a Martingale. This begs the question of whether a martingale that is adapted to the natural filtration $\sigma(Z, N)$ of a Wiener process and a Poisson process can be written as the sum of its expectation, an Itô integral and one with respect to the compensated Poisson process. This is indeed the case:

Theorem C.3.2 (MRT for jump-diffusion processes). *Any square-integrable process Y that is a martingale with respect to the filtration $\mathbb{A}$ generated by a Wiener process $Z = \{Z_t, t \geq 0\}$ and a Poisson process $N = \{N_t, t \geq 0\}$ with intensity λ can be written as*

$$Y_t = y_0 - \int_0^t h_s \left[dN_s - \lambda_s ds \right] + \int_0^t g_s dZ_s, \qquad \text{(D.3.2)}$$

where $h = \{h_t, t \geq 0\}$ and $g = \{g_t, t \geq 0\}$ are unique, $\mathbb{A}$-adapted, square-integrable processes.

C.4 The Optimal Sampling Theorem

In order to state this important result, we must first introduce two concepts that play important roles in probability theory: *stopping times* and *uniform integrability*. Let us consider the filtered probability space $(\Omega, \mathcal{F}, \mathbb{F}, \mathbb{Q})$. We say that a random variable τ is an $\mathbb{F}$-stopping time if the event

$$\{\tau \leq t\} \in \mathcal{F}_t.$$

Put differently, knowing $\mathcal{F}_t$ is sufficient to know if $\{\tau \leq t\}$ has occurred. Throughout this book we work with stopping times τ corresponding to the first passage time of some stochastic process M to a certain level m. For instance, if $M_0 > m$, we define

$$\tau := \inf\{t \geq 0 | M_t \leq m\}.$$

Clearly τ is a $\sigma(M)$-stopping time, since at date t we know if the first time that level m has been crossed has occurred and, if so, when.

Uniform integrability is a property of families of functions that is usually used to guarantee certain convergence properties. For our purposes these families will correspond to stochastic processes. Given a probability space $(\Omega, \mathcal{F}, \mathbb{Q})$, we say that a family $\{X_i\}_{i \in \mathcal{I}}$ of random variables is uniformly integrable if it satisfies following conditions:

1. There exists $M \in \mathbb{R}_+$ such that $\mathbb{E}[|X_i|] \leq M$ for all $i \in \mathcal{I}$;

2. for all $\epsilon > 0$ there exists $\delta > 0$ such that if $\mathbb{Q}(F) < \delta$ for any $F \in \mathcal{F}$, then

$$\int_A |X_i| d\mathbb{Q} < \epsilon \quad \text{for all } i \in \mathcal{I}.$$

In particular, X could be a stochastic process on $(\Omega, \mathcal{F}, \mathbb{Q})$ and the index i could correspond to time. In this case we would say that X is a uniformly-integrable process.

We are now in a position to state the theorem:

Theorem C.4.1 (Optimal Sampling). *Consider the filtered probability space $(\Omega, \mathcal{F}, \mathbb{F}, \mathbb{Q})$ and let $\tau \leq \eta$ be two $\mathbb{F}$-stopping times, then*

1. *If X is a uniformly integrable, right-continuous submartingale, then both X_τ and X_η are integrable and*

$$\mathbb{E}[X_\eta | \mathcal{F}_\tau] \geq X_\tau.$$

2. *If X is a uniformly integrable, right-continuous supermartingale, then both X_τ and X_η are integrable and*

$$\mathbb{E}[X_\eta | \mathcal{F}_\tau] \leq X_\tau.$$

3. *If X is a uniformly integrable, right-continuous martingale, then both X_τ and X_η are integrable,*

$$\mathbb{E}[X_\eta | \mathcal{F}_\tau] = X_\tau$$

and $\mathbb{E}[X_\tau] = \mathbb{E}[X_0]$.

References

Ai, H and R. Li (2015), 'Investment and CEO compensation under limited commitment', *Journal of Financial Economics* **116**, 452–472.

Akyildirim, E., I. E. Güney, J-C. Rochet and H. M. Soner (2014), 'Optimal dividend policy with random interest rates', *Journal of Mathematical Economics* **51**, 93–101.

Albrecher, H. and S. Thonhauser (2008), 'Optimal dividend strategies for a risk process under force of interest', *Insurance: Mathematics and Economics* **43**, 134–149.

Anderson, R. W. and A. Carverhill (2012), 'Corporate liquidity and capital structure', *The Review of Financial Studies* **25**(3), 797–837.

Applebaum, D. (2009), *Levy Processes and Stochastic Calculus*, number 116 *in* 'Studies in Advanced Mathematics', 2 edn, Cambridge University Press, New York.

Asmussen, S. and M. Taksar (1997), 'Controlled diffusion models for optimal dividend pay-out', *Insurance: Mathematics and Economics* **20**, 1–15.

Auh, J. K. and S. Sundaresan (2015), Repo rollover risk and the bankruptcy code, Columbia Business School research paper no. 13-8, Columbia Business School.

Avanzi, B. (2009), 'Strategies for dividend distribution: A review', *North American Actuarial Journal* **13**(2), 217–251.

Azcue, P. and N. Muler (2005), 'Optimal reinsurance and dividend distribution policies in the Cramér-Lundberg model', *Mathematical Finance* **15**, 261–308.

Barth, A., S. Moreno-Bromberg and O. Reichmann (2016), 'A non-stationary model of dividend distribution in a stochastic interest-rate setting', *Computational Economics* **47**(3), 447–472.

Bass, R. F. and P. Hsu (1990), 'The semimartingale structure of reflecting Brownian motion', *Proceedings of the American Mathematical Society* **108**(4), 1007–1010.

Bellet, L. R. (2006), Ergodic properties of markov processes, *in* S.Attal, A.Joye and C.-A.Pillet, eds, 'Open Quantum Systems II: The Markovian Approach', Springer-Verlag, Berlin, pp. 1–39.

Biais, B., T. Mariotti, G. Plantin and J.-C. Rochet (2007), 'Dynamic security design: Convergence to continuous time and asset pricing implications', *Review of Economic Studies* **74**(2), 345–390.

Biais, B., T. Mariotti, J.-C. Rochet and S. Villeneuve (2010), 'Large risks, limited liability, and dynamic moral hazard', *Econometrica* **78**(1), 73–118.

Bielecki, T. and R. Rutkowski (2004), *Credit Risk: Modeling, Valuation and Hedging*, Springer-Verlag Berlin Heidelberg, Germany.

Björk, T. (2009), *Arbitrage Theory in Continuous Time*, 3 edn, Oxford University Press, New York.

Black, F. (1975), Forecasting variance of stock prices for options trading and other purposes, Seminar on the analysis of security prices, University of Chicago.

Black, F. and J. C. Cox (1976), 'Valuing corporate securities: Some effects of bond indenture provisions', *The Journal of Finance* **31**(2), 351–367.

Black, F. and M. Scholes (1973), 'The pricing of options and corporate liabilities', *Journal of Political Economy* **81**(3), 637–654.

Bolton, P., H. Chen and N. Wang (2011), 'A unified theory of Tobin's *q*, corporate investment, financing, and risk management', *The Journal of Finance* **66**, 1545–1578.

Bolton, P., H. Chen and N. Wang (2014), Debt, taxes, and liquidity, NBER working paper 20009, Columbia Business School.

Bolton, P. and M. Dewatripont (2004), *Contract Theory*, MIT Press, Cambridge, Mass.

Brennan, M. J. and E. S. Schwartz (1978), 'Corporate income taxes, valuation, and the problem of optimal capital structure', *The Journal of Business* **50**(1), 103–114.

Brigo, D. and F. Mercurio (2006), *Interest Rate Models: Theory and Practice*, Springer Finance, Springer-Verlag, Berlin.

Brunnermeier, M. K. and Y. Sannikov (2014), 'A macroeconomic model with a financial sector', *American Economic Review* **104**, 379–421.

Cadenillas, A., Jaksa Cvitanić and F. Zapatero (2007), 'Optimal risk-sharing with effort and project choice', *Journal of Economic Theory* **133**, 403–440.

Carmona, R. and M. R. Tehranchi (2006), *Interest Rate Models: An Infinite Dimensional Stochastic Analysis Perspective*, Springer Finance, Springer-Verlag, Berlin.

Cheng, I.-H. and K. Milbradt (2012), 'The hazards of debt: Rollover freezes, incentives, and bailouts', *The Review of Financial Studies* **4**(25), 1070–1121.

Cvitanić, J. and J. Zhang (2013), *Contract Theory in Continuous-Time Models*, Springer Finance, Springer-Verlag Berlin Heidelberg, Germany.

Danisewicz, P., D. McGowan, E. Onali and K. Schaeck (2015), Monitoring matters: Debt seniority, market discipline and bank conduct, Working paper, Bank of England.

De Finetti, B. (1957), 'Su un impostazione alternativa dell teoria collettiva del rischio', *Transactions of the XVth International Congress of Actuaries* **2**, 433–443.

Décamps, J-P. and B. Djembissi (2007), 'Switching to a poor business activity: Optimal capital structure, agency costs and covenant rules', *Annals of Finance* **3**(3), 389–409.

Décamps, J-P. and S. Villeneuve (2006), 'Optimal dividend policy and growth option', *Finance and Stochastics* **1**(1), 3–27.

Décamps, J-P., T. Mariotti, J-C. Rochet and S. Villeneuve (2011), 'Free cash flow, issuance costs and stock prices', *The Journal of Finance* **66**(5), 1501–1544.

DeMarzo, P., D. Livdan and A. Tchistyi (2013), Risking other people's money: Gambling, limited liability and optimal incentives, mimeo, Stanford GSB.

DeMarzo, P. M. and M. J. Fishman (2007), 'Agency and optimal investment dynamics', *The Review of Financial Studies* **20**(1), 151–188.

DeMarzo, P. M. and Y. Sannikov (2006), 'Optimal security design and dynamic capital structure in a continuous-time agency model', *The Journal of Finance* **61**(6), 2681–2724.

DeMarzo, P. and Z. He (2016), Leverage dynamics without commitment, NBER working paper 22799.

Dixit, A. K. and R. S. Pindyck (1994), *Investment under Uncertainty*, Princeton University Press, Princeton, N.J.

Duffie, D. (2002), *Dynamic Asset Pricing Theory*, 3 edn, Princeton University Press, Princeton, N.J.

Duffie, D. and D. Lando (2001), 'Term structures of credit spreads with incomplete accounting information', *Econometrica* **69**(3), 633–664.

Duffie, D. and J. Singleton (2003), *Credit Risk: Pricing, Measurement and Management*, Princeton University Press, Princeton, N.J.

Dumas, B. (1991), 'Super contact and related optimality conditions', *Journal of Economic Dynamics and Control* **15**(4), 675–685.

Eisenberg, J. and H. Schmidli (2011), 'Optimal control of capital injections by reinsurance with a constant rate of interest', *Journal of Applied Probability* **48**, 733–748.

Ekeland, I. and E. Taflin (2005), 'A theory of bond portfolios', *The Annals of Applied Probability* **15**(2), 1260–1305.

Fleming, W. H. and H. M. Soner (2006), *Controlled Markov Processes and Viscosity Solutions*, Vol. 25 of *Stochastic Modelling and Applied Probability*, 2 edn, Springer-Verlag, New York.

Föllmer, H. and A. Schied (2004), *Stochastic Finance: An Introduction in Discrete Time*, De Gruyter, Berlin.

Franks, J.R. and S.V. Sanzhar (2006), Evidence on debt overhang from distressed equity issues, Working paper, London Business School.

Gerber, H. U. and E. S. W. Shiu (2004), 'Optimal dividends: Analysis with Brownian motion', *North-American Actuarial Journal* **8**, 1–20.

Goldstein, R., N. Ju and H. E. Leland (2001), 'An EBIT-based model of dynamic capital structure', *Journal of Business* **74**(4), 5–23.

Grasselli, M.R and T.R. Hurd (2010), Credit risk modeling, Lecture notes, Department of Mathematics and Statistics, McMaster University.

Gryglewicz, S. (2011), 'A theory of corporate financial decisions with liquidity concerns', *Journal of Financial Economics* **99**, 365 – 384.

Harrington, S.E., G. Niehaus and Y. Tong (2013), Insurance price volatility and underwriting cycles, *in* G.Dionne, ed., 'Handbook of Insurance', 2 edn, Springer, New York, pp. 647–667.

Harrison, M. and M. Taksar (1983), 'Instantaneous control of Brownian motion', *Mathematics of Operations Research* **8**(3), 439–453.

Harrison, M.J. (1985), *Brownian Motion and Stochastic Flow Systems*, John Wiley & Sons, New York.

Hayashi, F. (1982), 'Tobin's marginal q and average q: A neoclassical interpretation', *Econometrica* **50**(1), 213–224.

He, Z. (2009), 'Optimal executive compensation when firm size follows Geometric Brownian Motion', *The Review of Financial Studies* **22**(2), 859–892.

He, Z. (2011), 'A model of dynamic compensation and capital structure', *Journal of Financial Economics* **100**, 351–366.

He, Z. and A. Krishnamurthy (2012), 'A model of capital and crises', *Review of Economic Studies* **79**(2), 735–777.

He, Z. and A. Krishnamurthy (2013), 'Intermediary asset pricing', *American Economic Review* **103**(2), 732–770.

He, Z. and K. Milbradt (2016), Dynamic debt maturity, NBER Working Paper 21919.

Hennessy, C. A. and T. M. Whited (2005), 'Debt dynamics', *The Journal of Finance* **60**(3), 1129–1165.

Hoejgaard, B. and M. Taksar (1998), 'Controlling risk exposure and dividends pay-out schemes: Insurance company example', *Mathematical Finance* **9**, 153–182.

Hoejgaard, B. and M. Taksar (2004), 'Optimal dynamic portfolio selection for a corporation with controllable risk and dividend distribution policy', *Quantitative Finance* **4**(3), 315–327.

Horst, Ulrich (2008), Ergodicity and nonergodicity in economics, *in* S. N.Durlauf and L. E.Blume, eds, 'The New Palgrave Dictionary of Economics', Palgrave Macmillan, Basingstoke.

Hugonnier, J. and E. Morellec (2015*a*), Bank capital, liquid reserves, and insolvency risk, Working Paper 14-70, Swiss Finance Institute.

Hugonnier, J. N. and E. Morellec (2015*b*), Bank capital, liquid reserves and insolvency risk, Working Paper 14-70, Swiss Finance Institute.

Hugonnier, J., S. Malamud and E. Morellec (2015), 'Capital supply uncertainty, cash holdings and investment', *The Review of Financial Studies* **28**(2), 391–445.

Isohätälä, J., N. Klimenko and A. Milne (2016), Post-crisis macrofinancial modeling: Continuous time approaches, *in* E.Haven, P.Molyneux, J. O. S.Wilson, S.Fedotov and M.Duygun, eds, 'The Handbook of Post Crisis Financial Modeling', Palgrave Macmillan, London, pp. 235–282.

Jeanblanc-Picqué, M. and A. N. Shiryaev (1995), 'Optimization of the flow of dividends', *Uspekhi Mat. Nauk* **50**(2(203)), 25–46.

Jiang, Z. and M. Pistorius (2012), 'Optimal dividend distribution under Markov regime switching', *Finance and Stochastics* **16**(3), 449–476.

Karatzas, I. and S.E. Shreve (1991), *Brownian Motion and Stochastic Calculus*, Graduate Texts in Mathematics, Springer-Verlag, Berlin.

Kiyotaki, N. and J. Moore (1997), 'Credit cycles', *Journal of Political Economy* **105**(2), 211–248.

Klimenko, N. and S. Moreno-Bromberg (2016), 'The shadow cost of short–term debt and corporate policies', *Journal of Economic Dynamics and Control* **65**, 1–29.

Klimenko, N., S. Pfeil and J.-C. Rochet (2017), 'A simple macroeconomic model with extreme financial frictions', *Journal of Mathematical Economics* **68**, 92–102.

Kraus, A. and R. H. Litzenberger (1973), 'A state-preference model of optimal financial leverage', *The Journal of Finance* **28**(4), 911–922.

Kruk, L., J. Lehoczky, K. Ramanan and S. E. Shreve (2007), 'An explicit formula for the Skorokhod map on $[0, a]$', *The Annals of Probability* **35**(5), 1740–1768.

Leland, H. E. (1994), 'Corporate debt value, bond covenants and optimal capital structure', *The Journal of Finance* **49**(4), 1213–1252.

Leland, H. E. (1998), 'Agency costs, risk management and capital structure', *The Journal of Finance* **53**(4), 1213–1243.

Leland, H.E. and K.B. Toft (1996), 'Optimal capital structure, endogenous bankruptcy, and the term structure of credit spreads', *The Journal of Finance* **51**, 987–1019.

Lokka, A. and M. Zervos (2008), 'Optimal dividend and issuance of equity policies in the presence of proportional costs', *Insurance: Mathematics and Economics* **42**(3), 954–961.

Meh, C. A. and K. Moran (2010), 'The role of bank capital in the propagation of shocks', *Journal of Economic Dynamics and Control* **34**, 555–576.

Merton, R. C. (1969), 'Lifetime portfolio selection under uncertainty: The continuous-time case', *The Review of Economics and Statistics* **51**(3), 247–257.

Merton, R. C. (1973), 'Theory of rational option pricing', *The Bell Journal of Economics and Management Science* **4**(1), 141–183.

Merton, R. C. (1974), 'On the pricing of corporate debt: The risk structure of interest rates', *The Journal of Finance* **29**(2), 449–470.

Milne, A. and D. Robertson (1996), 'Firm behavior under the threat of liquidation', *Journal of Economic Dynamics and Control* **20**, 1427–1449.

Milne, A. and E. Whalley (2001), Bank capital and incentives for risk-taking, Research paper, Cass Business School.

Milne, F. (1975), 'Choice over asset economies: Default risk and corporate leverage', *Journal of Financial Economics* **2**(2), 165–185.

Moreno-Bromberg, S. and G. Roger (2016), Leverage and risk taking, Working Paper 132, Swiss Finance Institute.

Musiela, M. and M. Rutkowski (2005), *Martingale Methods in Financial Modelling*, number 36 *in* 'Stochastic Modelling and Applied Probability', 2 edn, Springer-Verlag Berlin Heidelberg, Germany.

Oeksendal, B. (2003), *Stochastic Differential Equations*, Universitex, 6 edn, Springer-Verlag, Berlin.

Paulsen, J. (2008), 'Optimal dividend payments and reinvestments of diffusion processes with both fixed and proportional costs', *SIAM Journal of Control and Optimization.* **247**(5), 2201–2226.

Paulsen, J. and H. K. Gjessing (1997), 'Optimal choice of dividend barriers for a risk process with stochastic return on investments', *Insurance: Mathematics and Economics* **20**, 215–223.

Pötzelberger, K. and L. Wang (1997), 'Boundary crossing probability for Brownian motion and general boundaries', *Journal of Applied Probability* **34**(1), 54–65. p. 55.

Press, W. H., S. A. Teukolsky, W. T. Vetterling and B. P. Flannery (2007), *Numerical Recipes: The Art of Scientific Computing*, 3 edn, Cambridge University Press, New York.

Radner, R. and L. Shepp (1996), 'Risk vs. profit potential: A model for corporate strategy', *Journal of Economic Dynamics and Control* **20**(8), 1371–1393.

Revuz, D. and M. Yor (1999), *Continuous Martingales and Brownian Motion.*, Springer-Verlag, Berlin.

Rochet, J-C. and S. Villeneuve (2005), 'Corporate portfolio management', *Annals of Finance* **1**(3), 225–243.

Rochet, J-C. and S. Villeneuve (2011), 'Liquidity management and corporate demand for hedging and insurance', *Journal of Financial Intermediation* **1**(20), 303–323.

Ross, S.A., R.W. Westerfield and B.D. Jordan (2008), *Fundamentals of Corporate Finance*, McGraw-Hill/Irwin, New York.

Sannikov, Y. (2008), 'A continuous-time version of the principal: Agent problem', *The Review of Economic Studies* **75**(3), 957–984.

Scheer, N. and H. Schmidli (2011), 'Optimal dividend strategies in a Crámer-Lundberg model with capital injections and administration costs', *European Actuarial Journal* **1**, 57–92.

Schmidli, H. (2008), *Stochastic Control in Insurance*, Springer, New York.

Skorokhod, A. V. (1961), 'Stochastic equations for diffusion processes in a bounded region', *Theory of Probability and Its Applications* **6**(3), 264–274.

Stiglitz, J. E. (1969), 'A re-examination of the Modigliani-Miller Theorem', *The American Economic Review* **59**(5), 784–793.

Stokey, N. L. (2003), *The Economics of Inaction: Stochastic Control Models with Fixed Costs*, Princeton University Press, Princeton, N.J.

Suárez, J. and O. Sussman (1997), 'Endogenous cycles in a Stiglitz-Weiss economy', *Journal of Economic Theory* **6**, 47–71.

Sundaresan, S. (2013), 'A review of Merton's model of the firm's capital structure with its wide applications', *Annual Review of Financial Economics* **5**, 5.1–5.21.

Sundaresan, S. M. and Z. Wang (2015), Bank liability structure, Research Paper 14-41, Columbia Business School.

Taksar, M. (2000), 'Optimal risk and dividend distribution control models for an insurance company', *Mathematical Methods of Operations Research* **51**, 1–42.

Tobin, J. (1969), 'A general equilibrium approach to monetary theory', *Journal of Money, Credit and Banking* **1**(1), 15–29.

Winter, R. A. (1994), 'The dynamics of competitive insurance markets', *Journal of Financial Intermediation* **3**, 379 – 415.

Index